SOC. MARIT. Y. COM. R.W. JAMES & Cº

VALPARAISO

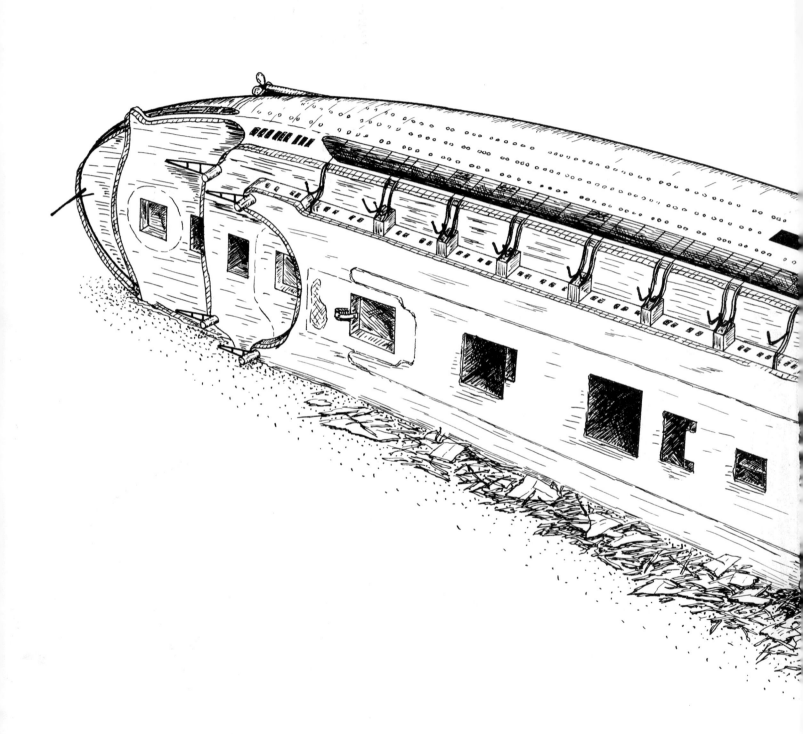

LOST VOYAGES

TWO CENTURIES *of* SHIPWRECKS
in the APPROACHES *to* NEW YORK

by BRADLEY SHEARD

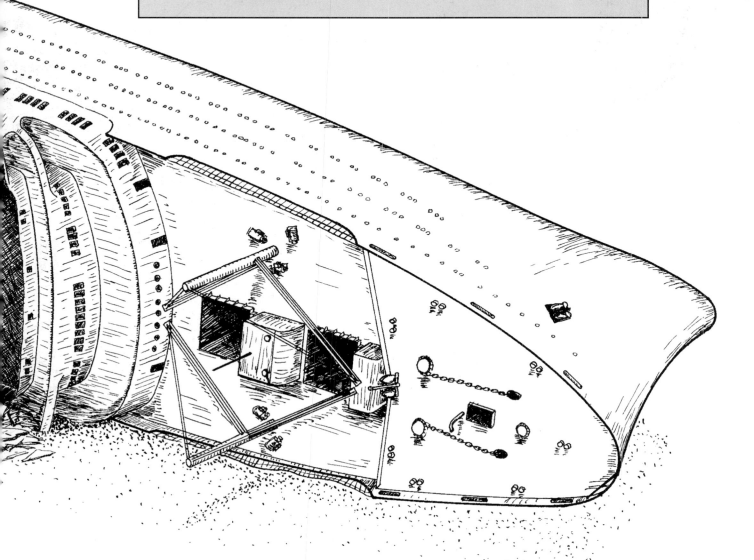

AQUA QUEST PUBLICATIONS, INC. ✠ NEW YORK

AUTHOR'S NOTE

This book is intended to tell a story—a story about the evolution of oceangoing ships, about the tragedy of shipwreck, and about the maritime history of the region encompassing the approaches to New York Harbor. The particular shipwrecks that I have used to illustrate this story were chosen purely for their appropriateness to the narration. Many important shipwrecks are only mentioned in passing, or left out entirely, while other more obscure wrecks may be covered in some detail. This work in no way claims to chronicle every shipwreck in the region—such a task would be virtually impossible due to the sheer number of wrecks that have occurred in these waters over the past two centuries.

Library of Congress Cataloging-in-Publication Data

Sheard, Bradley, 1958-
    Lost voyages : two centuries of shipwrecks in the approaches to New York / by Bradley Sheard
        p.   cm.
    Includes bibliographical references and index.
    ISBN 1-881652-17-3 (alk. paper)
    1. Shipwrecks—New York Region. I. Title.
G525.S514   1997
910'.9163'4—DC21   97-32170
                                                     CIP
                                                     r97

Cover: *The ribs of the USRCS* Mohawk, *a revenue cutter sunk in a collision in October 1917, rise eerily from the sand. The wreck is located 12 miles southeast of New York Harbor. In the foreground is the gun mount.*

Back cover: *The German steamship* Gluckauf *wrecked near the Blue Point Station on March 24, 1893. The first steamship expressly built to carry bulk oil, the* Gluckauf *was left to decay on the beach for decades before she was partially salvaged at the turn of the century. Courtesy of the Long Island Maritime Museum, West Sayville, NY.*

All photographs and drawings are by the author unless otherwise noted.
Cover design by Dan Smith.
Interior design and layout by Aqua Quest Publications.

Printed in Hong Kong
10 9 8 7 6 5 4 3 2 1

Acknowledgements

Diving the many historical shipwrecks lying along the East Coast has been a passion of mine for more than two decades. It is a passion that is largely possible due to the excellent services of a host of dive charter boats. I would like to express my appreciation to the following individuals, all of whom I consider personal friends: Captain Art Kirchner of the *Margie II*, Captains John Lachenmeyer and Frank Persico of the *Sea Hawk*, the late Captain George Hoffman of the *Sea Lion*, Captains John Chatterton, Dan Crowell and the late Bill Nagel of the *Seeker*, Captain Phil Galletta of the *Southern Cross*, and Captains Steve Bielenda, Janet Bieser, Hank Garvin and Don Schnell of the R/V *Wahoo*.

Collecting research material on shipwrecks is often difficult, time consuming and frustrating, and many people have helped me in this endeavor over the years. I would like to extend my gracious thanks to all, with a special thanks to Henry Keatts, who has provided me with enormous support for many years. I would also like to thank the helpful staff of the following organizations:

The East Hampton Library
The Long Island Maritime Museum
The Mariners' Museum, Newport News, Virginia
The Naval Historical Center, Washington, D.C.
The Peabody Museum, Salem, Massachusetts
The Steamship Historical Society of America
The United States Coast Guard
The United States National Archives

But most of all, I would like to thank the *Atlantic Wreck Divers*, who have been my close friends and companions throughout all of my diving adventures.

DEDICATION
To my parents, Bart and Charlotte Sheard, who gave
me a good upbringing, a good education and always
made time for *Look Out For Pirates!*

CONTENTS

Preface

Ghosts from the Past

The port of New York has long been synonymous with maritime history. For as long as men have inhabited the region, they have lived in harmony with the sea. Even before European explorers reached North America, the native inhabitants took to the ocean in pursuit of whales and fish for sustenance. It was the arrival of European settlers and their stout ships, however, that brought the true beginnings of seafaring, as we know it, to New York.

The approaches to New York have witnessed the arrival of Henry Hudson, the settlement of New Amsterdam, as New York City was known to the first Dutch settlers, and the battles of the Revolutionary War that brought the United States into being. New York went on to become the busiest shipping port on the globe, as well as the entry point from the Old into the New World. It was this immigrant traffic to America, spurred by the hopes and aspirations of millions, that fueled the great passenger-steamship rivalries of the late nineteenth and early twentieth centuries, with the port of New York as its focus. With all of this shipping traffic over the course of centuries, it was inevitable that there would be accidents, and that ships would be lost.

Estimates of the number of shipwrecks in the region run from the hundreds into the thousands. The Long Island and New Jersey coastlines form the two sides of a "funnel" directing traffic into New York's great harbor, and have witnessed more shipwrecks than anywhere else along the East Coast of the United States, with the possible exception of Cape Hatteras, along the Carolina Outer Banks. The shipping traffic within this funnel becomes denser and denser as it approaches New York Harbor. It should be no surprise that countless collisions between ships have occurred here. Darkness and fog both reduce visibility, increasing the inherent danger of collision when a multitude of ships operate at close quarters. But collisions have also occurred between ships in broad daylight with no apparent cause other than negligence, ignorance and human error. Indeed, as advancing technology

provided more and more sophisticated tools for navigation and communication, shipwrecks continued to occur with surprising regularity.

The low-lying, sandy barrier islands along the Long Island and New Jersey coastlines—the two sides of New York's "funnel"—have acted as an incredibly efficient ship trap over the years. During the days of sailing ships, hundreds of wooden vessels came crashing ashore, some helpless at the hands of a driving winter storm, others drifting aimlessly in an impenetrable fog or lost due to errors in the still imprecise art of navigation. Often stranded just off the beach, ships were pounded by mountainous breakers as their crews froze to death high in the rigging, while trying to escape death in the cruel seas below. This classic image of a full-rigged ship aground on the beach didn't pass entirely with the eclipse of the sailing ship, however, for numerous steamers have come ashore over the years as well. In fact, as the century turned and the sailing ship was increasingly replaced by the revolutionary steamship, ship groundings actually increased.

Man's cruel and endless wars have accounted for many lost ships and men off our coast. During the Revolution, wooden warships succumbed to enemy action, errors of navigation, and the untamable forces of nature. Two World Wars brought prowling German U-boats to our coast where they sank ships, planted mines and even landed a group of would-be saboteurs on the beach. U-boats were sunk as well, although the screams of their dying crews went unheard as they went to the bottom in their "iron coffins."[1] During the years of Prohibition a squadron of depot ships was established off Long Island to quench New York's thirst for liquor. This line of supply ships came to be known as "rum row," and its presence resulted in an undeclared war pitting the U.S. Coast Guard against "bootleggers" in battles of speed, stealth and gunfire; many ships and lives were lost by both sides.

While all of these events in history have passed, they have left behind traces of what once was. Just off the Long Island and New Jersey beaches, beneath the restless waves, lie the sunken relics of our past. A shipwreck is a time capsule from a different age—a tiny microcosm plucked suddenly from the world and preserved beneath the sea. In essence, a shipwreck is a ghost from the past—a ghost that can often communicate more about history than volumes of books can, for these shipwrecks *are history*.

Each of these wrecks has a unique story to tell, for each went down under its own peculiar set of circumstances. In many cases, a ship was not the only casualty of such an event. It is important to remember that these ships carried people—people with hopes, dreams and aspirations, people who had spent lifetimes building a niche in the world for themselves and their families. Many of the persons on board such a vessel, men, women and children alike, perished unmercifully at the hands of nature, while during wartime, they often perished cruelly at the hands of their fellow human beings. Like any life threatening crisis, a shipwreck can bring out the best or the worst in people, producing both heroes and cowards, as panic-stricken men and women display some of the highest moral spirits of humanity, as well as some of the lowest.

While the tale of each shipwreck is an individual one, often distinctive in its own right, none are isolated events in history. Shipwrecks are invariably a reflection of the world from which they came, always affected by, and often affecting the course of world events. In some cases, such as that of the *Titanic* or the *Lusitania*, a shipwreck literally changed the course of history. Like a yarn in the continuous fabric of history, each shipwreck is part of a much broader picture. It is often fascinating to step back from the individual stories and take in this broader view of events, examining how each individual story fits in.

Many of the ships have inter-relationships amongst themselves as well: when the Cunard line steamship *Oregon* became the victim of a mysterious nighttime collision in 1886, one of the theories advanced to explain her sinking was that she had struck the masts of the tramp steamer *Hylton Castle*, which had foundered in the same vicinity only three months earlier. The tiny Revenue Service cutter *Mohawk* assisted in freeing many wrecks grounded on Long Island's south shore beaches during her career: she was present at the scene of the wrecked steamer *Drumelzier* in December 1904, as well as that of the *Peter Rickmers* in May 1908. Nine years later it was the *Mohawk* who was the victim when she was run down in the fog by a merchant vessel—a ship she was trying to protect from German submarines during World War I.

With the tremendous volume and variety of ship traffic entering and leaving New York Harbor over the past two centuries, a broad spectrum of shipwrecks lie along the Long Island and New Jersey coastlines. Wooden warships and sailing merchant ships, paddle- and screw-powered steamships and passenger liners, warships of the dreadnought era, sunken submarines and torpedoed tankers and freighters can all be found in these waters. There are examples of every major ship type, illustrating the evolution of the ship over the past two centuries. A study of shipping evolution is even more alluring when one can see and explore these ships firsthand. To see the huge engine of a nineteenth century steamship towering above the ocean bottom, to gaze upon a half-buried china plate on the wreck of a nineteenth century passenger steamer, to swim through the rooms and corridors of a World War I warship, or to touch an eighteenth century cannon from an English warship sunk during the American Revolution is to see and touch history itself. All of these wonders can be found beneath our seas.

Bradley Sheard
March 1997
Sayville, New York

1

Oak Timbers and Iron Shot: The Wooden Warship

By the beginning of the eighteenth century the traditional wooden warship had become a highly evolved fighting machine. Stoutly built of wood (usually oak), she was driven by the action of the wind upon canvas sails supported by wooden masts and hemp rigging. Wooden ship construction had become a well-developed art and would change little before the introduction of first iron, and then steel as a construction material toward the middle of the nineteenth century. Heavy wooden frames were joined to a massive keel running the length of the vessel's hull—much as the ribs of the human skeleton are attached to its backbone. Each frame was sawn into the required shape from huge timbers, giving the hull its form. Ships were seldom built to a set of plans as we would recognize them, but rather to a builder's model. A scale model of the ship's hull was carved of wood, carefully shaped by the keen eye and fine touch of the builder. Once the hull shape was satisfactory, a set of "lines" was lifted off the model that completely described the hull shape. These lines were laid out full scale in the shipyard's loft, yielding a set of patterns used to cut each of the ship's frames to shape.

Once the ship's skeleton was complete, heavy planking was fastened both inside and out, attached to the frames with wooden treenails (effectively large wooden dowels), as well as iron or copper spikes. Planking up a ship's hull was an art in itself, for each plank had to be individually shaped and then steam-bent into place before being fastened. To make the hull watertight, the seams between planks were caulked with oakum and pine pitch. Sometimes the vessel's bottom was clad with copper or lead sheet below the waterline to prevent it from being devoured by ship worms. Masts were stepped onto the keelson, passed up through the decks and were supported aloft by a network of stays that made up the ship's standing rigging. The standing rigging was tarred to prevent rot, while lines used to operate the ship's sails and spars were left untarred so that they would run freely through blocks—this was the ship's running rigging.

Wooden warships were armed with cannon, most commonly cast of iron but also of brass and bronze. The heavy guns often weighed several tons and utilized charges of black powder to fire cast iron shot; sometimes they were loaded with scrap iron or "grapeshot" and used as a sort of shotgun to destroy the opposing ship's rigging. Cannon were rated by the weight of shot they fired, thus a "32-pounder" fired an iron ball weighing 32 pounds. Mounted on wooden carriages, the massive guns were moved about by block and tackle and fired through square gun ports in the side of the ship's hull. In battle, cannon were fired at the enemy in broadsides—devastating, coordinated firings of all the guns on one side of a ship.

The ships themselves were classed by "rates," referring to the number of guns the ship could carry: a 38-gun frigate or a 74-gun ship-of-the-line. These ratings are deceiving, however, for most ships carried more guns than their ratings indicated. The ship-of-the-line USS *Ohio*, for instance, was classed as a 74-gun ship, yet her normal armament varied from 86 to 102 cannon. When referring to a warship, the ship's name is usually followed by her rate—i.e., *Constitution* (44).

Gun battles between wooden warships were brutal and bloody affairs, yet were conducted under almost gentlemanly rules. Devastating broadsides, in which a full ton of iron shot might be exchanged between ships in a single blast, were often fired at point blank range. Stout oak planking was reduced to splinters while masts and rigging were shot away, reducing the ship's ability to maneuver and leaving her vulnerable. Sailors were maimed and killed by impacting shot and the flying splinters of shattered hulls and rigging. (Gun decks were often painted bright red so that the gun crews would not be distracted by the sight of blood.) Sharpshooters armed with rifles were stationed high in the rigging to pick off their opponent's gun crews. When a ship was disabled, however, and her crew had had enough, she was expected to "strike her colors" and surrender, becoming a prize of war to the victor.

A NATION IS BORN

On July 4, 1776, when the thirteen American colonies declared their independence from Great Britain, it was a declaration made in defiance of one of the world's greatest maritime powers. Great Britain had firmly established herself as a major naval, and thus a global, power during the three Dutch wars of the mid-17th century. Her naval supremacy would become unquestionable over a century later when, in 1805, Admiral Horatio Nelson defeated the combined French and Spanish fleets at the battle of Trafalgar. Great Britain would retain this mastery of the seas virtually unchallenged for a century. The strength of the Royal Navy had its roots in Britain's geographic status as an island nation and the enormous colonial empire she had established. It required a navy inferior to none to protect this empire and the seaborne commerce which supplied Britain with raw materials and carried her manufactured goods to other nations for trade. It was this supreme world power that the thirteen fledgling colonies challenged for their freedom.

The famous Declaration of Independence was not the start of the Revolutionary War. The first armed confrontation between the colonists and British soldiers occurred more than one year earlier, at Lexington and Concord, in the colony of Massachusetts. A relatively minor skirmish between armed colonists and British soldiers, this first exchange of gunfire brought a long developing confrontation to the brink of war. The British troops were forced to withdraw to Boston where the Battle of Bunker Hill followed. King George III reacted to the developing hostilities by declaring the colonies in rebellion. In December 1775, the British Parliament authorized a naval blockade of the entire Eastern Seaboard.

A week after the Declaration of Independence was approved by the Second Continental Congress, the British landed troops on Staten Island. General George Washington, appointed Commander in Chief of the Continental Army by the Second Continental Congress, placed a third of his troops on Long Island to face the powerful British force. The British troops, commanded by General Sir William Howe, crossed the Narrows (now the site of the Verrazano Narrows Bridge) from Staten Island to DeNyse's Point in Brooklyn on August 22nd, meeting no resistance. Meanwhile, ships of the British fleet moved into Gravesend Bay to cover the landing—the invasion of Long Island had begun.

The patriot forces had dug themselves in behind the Brooklyn Heights. For several days minor clashes and skirmishes occurred as General Howe felt out the patriot defenses. On the night of August 26th, Howe led a force of 10,000 men in driving rain through Jamaica Pass in an attempt to encircle the patriot fortifications and attack them from behind. He found only five officers standing guard at the Pass and they were quickly captured, allowing the British forces to move around behind the Americans. On the morning of August 27th the American troops found themselves facing the British on two fronts. Thirty-thousand well-trained British troops opposed a smaller number of Americans, who had little training and no heavy artillery. The Americans were also hampered by the driving rain, which fouled their arms and ammunition. On August 29th, after two days and nights of fighting in continuous rain that saw thousands of patriot forces killed, General Washington was forced to retreat across the East River to Manhattan. Howe followed in pursuit on September 15th. After a bitter fight Washington was once again forced to retreat farther up Manhattan Island. In October, a contingent of British troops marched north along the East River in order to attack the Continental forces from the rear, forcing Washington to withdraw his troops to White Plains. Howe then turned and attacked Fort Washington, located in northwest Manhattan, where 3,000 patriot troops still remained; their surrender came on November 16th. The British had gained control of the port of New York and all of Long Island, giving them an important staging point to land troops, base their naval forces, and move inland in an attempt to split New England from the remainder of the colonies.

By the spring of 1777, General Washington's forces were fighting Major General Charles Cornwallis's redcoats to the south, in Delaware and New Jersey. Meanwhile, a new British force under Major General John Burgoyne began a march south from Canada toward Albany. On July 6th, General Burgoyne's 7,700 troops easily captured Fort Ticonderoga at the south-

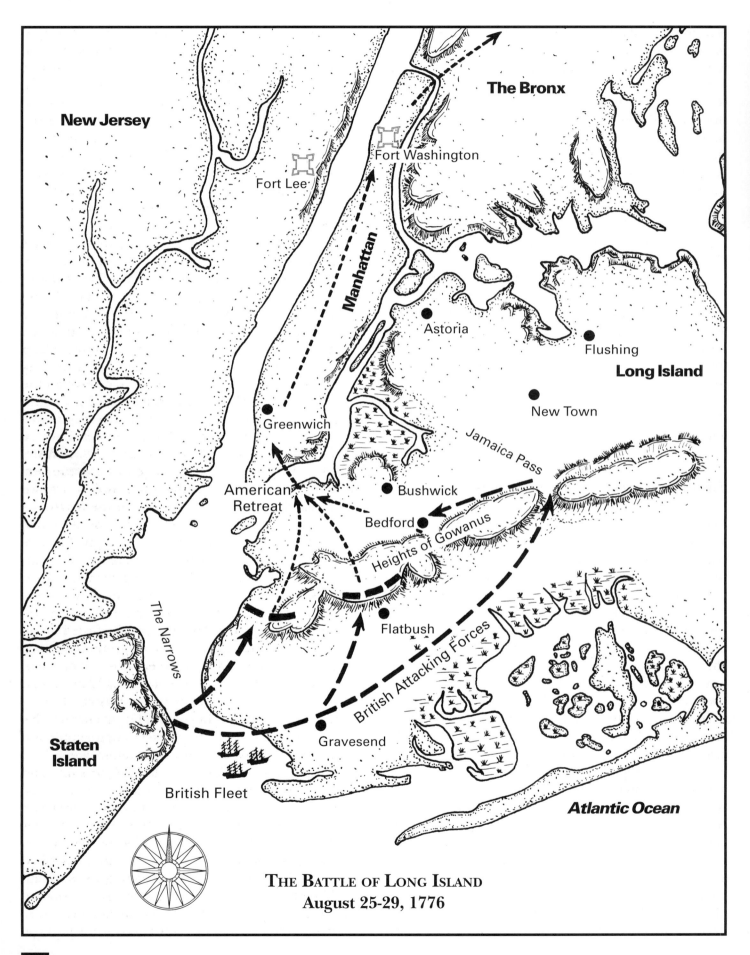

New Jersey

The Bronx

Fort Washington

Fort Lee

Manhattan

Astoria

Flushing

Long Island

Greenwich

New Town

Jamaica Pass

American
Retreat

Bushwick

Bedford

Heights of Gowanus

Flatbush

British Attacking Forces

The Narrows

**Staten
Island**

Gravesend

British Fleet

Atlantic Ocean

THE BATTLE OF LONG ISLAND
August 25-29, 1776

ern end of Lake Champlain, then continued their march south toward Albany. But the American army was steadily growing and a force of 6,000 troops had entrenched themselves just north of Albany. On September 19th the British troops tried to break through the American lines, but were stopped in the First Battle of Freeman's Farm. On October 7th, General Burgoyne again attacked the American forces in the Second Battle of Freeman's Farm, and was once again forced to retreat. The redcoats soon found themselves surrounded by some 17,000 American troops, and on October 17, 1777, General Burgoyne and his 5,000 remaining soldiers surrendered to Major General Horatio Gates. This was an important turning point in the war, for the victory induced France to enter the conflict on the American side. The French provided well-armed troops, a steady supply of much needed arms and munitions, and the powerful French naval fleet. Following France's entry into the war, Spain, too, declared war on Great Britain in June 1779, hoping to capitalize on the British preoccupation with her rebellious colonies. Holland entered the war against Britain the following year, forcing the British to fight a war on many fronts.

THE BRITISH FLEET AND THE LOSS OF THE *HUSSAR*

In early July 1780, a French fleet consisting of 13 frigates and 7 ships-of-the-line put into the harbor at Newport, Rhode Island. They landed sorely needed reinforcements for the patriot army in the form of 6,000 well-equipped troops, along with artillery. The proximity of the French warships posed a threat to the British fleet stationed in New York, making Lieutenant-General Sir Henry Clinton, the British commander in charge of the port, uneasy. General Clinton had other worries as well. The troops under his command hadn't been paid in a long time—so long that desertions were becoming a problem. German mercenaries, called Hessians, made up a significant portion of the British army and were particularly prone to desertion. General Clinton's repeated inquiries to London about the payroll were finally answered when the new, 28-gun British frigate HMS *Hussar* sailed up the Narrows into New York Harbor on September 13, 1780, setting anchor off the southern tip of Manhattan Island.

To observers ashore the *Hussar* had an unusual air about her. A large contingent of red-coated marines could be seen continuously walking the decks of the black-hulled frigate, but never came ashore. As first days and then weeks passed, the *Hussar*'s marines stead-fastly refused to leave their assigned vessel. Under normal circumstances, the soldiers would be fighting for a chance at shore leave after their long Atlantic crossing. The reason for their refusal to leave the ship soon became common knowledge ashore—the long-awaited British payroll was nestled securely in the *Hussar*'s hold. The pay ship's presence in the harbor only added to General Clinton's worries, however, and he became even more uneasy about the closeness of the French fleet. In command of a superior naval force, General Clinton decided to take the offensive and mount an attack against the French Navy.

Packing all the troops he could spare aboard his navy's warships, Clinton sent the assembled force up Long Island Sound to do battle with the French. Since this left New York only lightly defended and Clinton did not want the payroll to fall into enemy hands, the Captain of the British pay ship was ordered to weigh anchor and proceed secretly to a new anchorage along the Connecticut coast. The quickest route into Long Island Sound was up the East River and through the treacherous straight known as Hell's Gate. Strewn with rocky outcroppings, the narrow channel represents one of only two tidal interchanges between Long Island Sound and the Atlantic Ocean, creating a tremendous flow of water and dangerous currents. Restricting the tidal interchange even further are two small islands located in the middle of the narrows—Randall and Ward's Islands. The tremendous volume of water that must make its way through this constricted passage with the ebb and flow of the tides boils into a treacherous riptide, making navigation extremely hazardous. The only alternative, however, was sailing out the entrance to New York Harbor and proceeding east along Long Island's shoal-infested southern shore, with its inherent risk of grounding, until reaching Montauk Point at the eastern end of the island. There the *Hussar* would enter Long Island Sound within sight of Newport, Rhode Island, where the very French fleet she was trying to avoid lay at anchor. This was too great a risk for the *Hussar*'s commander and he opted for the passage through Hell's Gate.

The morning of November 3, 1780, was fine and clear, but to a sailing ship the winds were the most important aspect of the weather, and they were favorable for a passage up-river. The *Hussar*'s commander wisely took aboard a local river pilot for the dangerous voyage through Hell's Gate. The pilot, described as a "tall, intelligent Negro, belonging to the Hunt family of the Bronx,"[1] listened dutifully as the proposed voyage was explained to him. When his employers were finished, he advised them against making the passage.

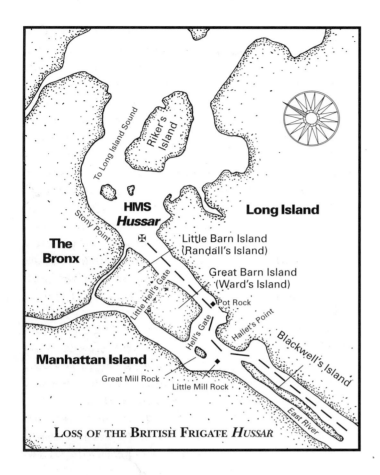

LOSS OF THE BRITISH FRIGATE *HUSSAR*

But the *Hussar*'s commander had set his mind on the East River route into Long Island Sound, and ordered the pilot to proceed. His advice rebuffed, the pilot had no choice but to attempt taking the warship through the narrow, rock-strewn tidal passage from New York Harbor into Long Island Sound.

The ship's anchor was hauled aboard and the *Hussar* headed up the East River. The pilot had to carefully balance the amount of sail carried aloft—just enough to maintain steerage way without proceeding at an excessive speed. A sailor was stationed at the ship's bow to continuously sound the depths with a lead line (a weighted line used to measure the water's depth). As they approached the narrow neck between the Long Island shore and the Bronx peninsula, the current strengthened. Swinging the ship's wheel first to port and then quickly to starboard, the pilot threaded his way past Great and Little Mill Rock, leaving these dangerous obstacles safely astern. To starboard passed Hallet's Point, on the Long Island shore. As the *Hussar* neared the end of the perilous voyage, only one obstruction remained—Pot Rock. This dangerous submerged reef extended some 130 feet into the already narrow channel, and was hidden eight feet below the water's turbulent surface. Approaching this final impediment, within sight of the unobstructed waters of

Long Island Sound, the breeze suddenly dropped, robbing the wind-powered vessel of its vital propulsion. Cursing and madly swinging the *Hussar*'s wheel in vain, the pilot was helpless as the ship lost steerage way and began drifting out of control in the current.

The *Hussar* swung broadside to the quick current, smashing into the submerged rock with a sickening shudder. The damage done, the breeze began blowing once again, restoring the ship's steerageway and she headed away from the danger. Officers were sent below to survey the damage—they found a deluge of water pouring in through broken planking. The ship quickly took on a list as she began to settle. Although the *Hussar*'s captain made a valiant attempt to head her toward the Bronx shoreline, hoping to beach the ship, she sank before reaching the other side of the narrows. The crew managed to escape in the ship's boats before she went down. The poor American pilot, charged with the safe conduct of an enemy's warship through the dangerous strait, undoubtedly feared for his own safety more than the British soldiers did as they all watched the vessel disappear.

As she settled on the bottom, the tops of the *Hussar*'s masts remained above water. Despite her well-marked location, however, no salvage was attempted by the British for the remainder of the war—surprising considering her valuable cargo. The first recorded salvage attempt that brought anything to the surface occurred in 1819, when several cannon and some copper hull sheathing were reportedly recovered. Since that time, there have been numerous reported attempts to salvage her treasure, but none have met with success. Her treasure still lies at the bottom of Hell's Gate.

As for the British expedition bent on attacking the French fleet in Newport, General Washington managed to foil the attack. Knowing that if he chose to chase the British to Newport he would arrive too late to be of much assistance, Washington correctly calculated that he held a better chance of success against the now depleted forces defending New York. As the American forces massed for an attack, General Clinton was forced to recall the British fleet for fear of losing the great port of New York, leaving the French fleet unmolested in Newport.

LOST IN A SNOWSTORM: HMS *CULLODEN*

The *Hussar* was not the only British ship to arrive in New York on September 13, 1780; she arrived in company with thirteen other warships: *Sandwich, Terrible, Russel, Centaur, Triumph, Culloden, Alcide, Torbay,*

Shrewsbury, Yarmouth, La Fortune, Boreas and *Greyhound*. Ten of these ships were large line-of-battle ships, mounting 64 guns or more, referred to as "ships-of-the-line." A ship-of-the-line was a vessel big enough and powerful enough to take a place in the line of battle, the basic naval fleet tactic of the period. Each fleet's ships formed and maneuvered in single file, exploiting the powerful broadside gun power packed on each vessel. This substantial fleet had arrived from the West Indies, under the command of Admiral George Brydges Rodney, to reinforce the smaller British naval force stationed in Gardiner's Bay under the command of Admiral Marriot Arbuthnot.

When General Clinton had proposed his plan of storming Newport to Admiral Arbuthnot, the British Admiral had protested that the fleet he commanded was not large enough to accomplish the task. Arbuthnot then sent a request for reinforcements to his senior officer, Admiral Rodney, stationed in the West Indies. Little did he expect that Rodney himself would arrive with the requested reinforcements, however, effectively relieving him of command of the North American Station, which he had held since March 1779. Arbuthnot was extremely unhappy with the resulting situation and refused to even meet with his senior officer in New York, instead remaining at Gardiner's Bay. Rodney in turn became furious with Arbuthnot for his insubordination in these and other matters. It was Rodney's fleet that embarked upon the planned raid on Newport, only to be recalled when an attack on New York by General Washington's troops appeared imminent.

In October, Admiral Rodney sent four of the newly arrived 74's, *Russel, Centaur, Shrewsbury* and *Culloden*, to the anchorage in Gardiner's Bay. There they were to assist Arbuthnot in patrolling the area between Nantucket Shoals and Montauk Point. He also sent instructions to Rear-Admiral Graves, also stationed with the fleet in Gardiner's Bay, that if the French fleet was to leave Newport and attempt to break through the British blockade of the coast, he was to pursue. In November, Rodney ordered Arbuthnot to send the ships *Centaur* and *Culloden* back to him in New York immediately, as he would soon be leaving to return to the West Indies. With Rodney's consent, Arbuthnot kept *Culloden* and sent the *Russel* and *Centaur* instead. On November 19th, much to Arbuthnot's delight, Rodney left for the West Indies and Arbuthnot once again regained his command. He immediately traveled to New York and replaced Rodney's appointed officers with counterparts of his own choosing.

Gardiner's Bay provided an excellent anchorage and base of operations for the British fleet. Its calm, protected waters, nestled between Long Island's two eastern forks provided a base of operations virtually within sight of the French fleet's location in nearby Newport. Eastern Long Island was an important agricultural district, and the British soldiers and sailors helped themselves to vegetables, fruits and livestock, although they were ordered to pay for anything they took. Admiral Arbuthnot and Admiral Graves became quite friendly with the Gardiner family, and they took turns entertaining each other at dinner gatherings. Over the course of the winter of 1780-1781, more than one-hundred officers took up residence in the manor house on Gardiner's Island. This many British sailors quartered ashore was bound to cause mischief, and thievery and drunkenness were reportedly a problem.

On January 20, 1781, word reached Admiral Graves, temporarily in charge of the Gardiner's Bay fleet while Arbuthnot was in New York, that three French warships were preparing to leave Newport in an attempt to run the blockade. Graves dispatched the *Culloden*, *Bedford* and *America* to chase down and capture the French warships. That afternoon the *Bedford* set sail from Gardiner's Bay; the *Culloden* and *America* joined her in Block Island Sound the following morning, and the trio set out in pursuit of the French warships.

On the afternoon of January 23rd, the wind rose to gale force and was accompanied by wet sleet and driving snow. Huge seas pounded the wooden vessels; the wind howled through the rigging and embraced those on watch with a bone-chilling cold. The thick snow and sleet descended in an opaque veil, nearly blinding the frozen lookouts. Navigation became a matter of faith—the *Culloden* found herself blindly following the *Bedford* a few hundred feet ahead. Night fell, and still the storm battered the ships. The *Culloden* continued in the *Bedford*'s wake, her lanterns just visible through the white curtain of snow. At 10:00 P.M. the pilot assured the *Culloden*'s commander, Captain Balfour, that there was no immediate danger. Balfour went below to his quarters, leaving instructions to summon him if the situation changed. The hand lead was thrown every half-hour, groping for the bottom, but none was found.

Just past midnight the *Bedford* was seen to come about, and the officer on watch aboard the *Culloden* immediately informed the Captain. Balfour decided that since neither they nor the *Bedford* knew their exact whereabouts, they would not follow, and the *Culloden* continued on her course. Minutes later the main topsail blew out in the gale force winds, while the *Bedford*'s lights disappeared from sight—the

Culloden had lost her guide through the hostile night.

The midnight watch passed uneventfully for Third Lieutenant John Cannon. Still, the cold and tired sailor must have been glad when Lieutenant Ralph Grey came on deck at 4:00 A.M. to relieve him. Only minutes later a crewman shouted out that there were breakers on the lee bow—land was in sight and the *Culloden* was headed directly for shore! Captain Balfour was immediately summoned; when he appeared on deck and saw the breakers close at hand he ordered the anchors cut free at once. If the anchors could be made to grab the bottom, the ship might be stopped before she ran headlong into the beach. But before Captain Balfour's order could be carried out, the oak timbers of the British warship hit bottom with a sudden jolt, and the crew of the *Culloden* found their stout ship aground in the midst of a raging winter gale.

In the late dawn of midwinter, the crew of the *Culloden* could barely make out the shoreline. The sailors were still ignorant of their exact position; the pilot ventured the opinion that they were aground on Block Island. When daybreak came hours later, they found themselves stranded off Will's Point (now known as Culloden Point). Sometime after striking bottom the ship's rudder had broken in two and was lost. At 8:00 A.M. the crew backed the *Culloden*'s headsails in order to swing her bow toward the west, away from shore. As she slowly swung about, the *Culloden*'s sails were allowed to fill with wind as the crew attempted to get

her off the bar, but her bow grounded once again.

As the morning wore on the *Culloden*, her bottom gripped tightly by sand, lay at the mercy of the wind and sea while the weather began to worsen. At 10:00 A.M. the gale increased and the ship began to strain; the carpenters were ordered to cut away the top masts to relieve the stress on the rigging. The hull began to leak badly and the crew was forced to man the pumps continuously; sand and gravel spewed overboard along with water, telling of much lost caulking in the hull. Throughout the day the storm pounded the *Culloden*. Her crew was helpless, unable to extricate themselves, or their ship, from the pounding seas.

Finally on the afternoon of January 24th the storm broke. Captain Balfour ordered boats lowered to survey the damage. The men found the ship firmly embedded in the sandy bottom. Taking soundings around the hull, they found 15 feet of water at the ship's bow and only 13 at the stern. Balfour ordered the anchor taken out in the boats and set in deep water—his only remaining hope was to try to "kedge" his ship off the bar. The anchor set, the crew labored at the capstan, straining against tons of sand to pull the ship free of her bonds. But the heavy hull would not budge. An hour later the carpenter reported that some of the hull planking had given way, and the hull was rapidly filling with sea water. The *Culloden* was doomed.

Captain Balfour set the crew to work salvaging everything possible from the grounded ship. Gun pow-

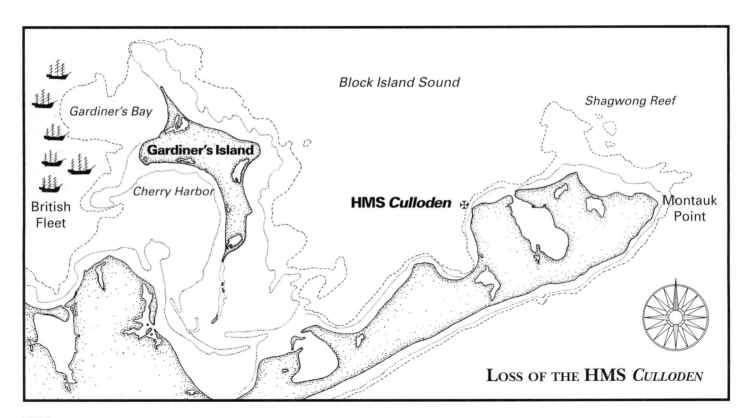

LOSS OF THE **HMS** *CULLODEN*

der, blocks, sails, stores and provisions were all loaded into the *Culloden*'s boats and brought ashore. Tents were set up for the crew, while one of the ship's boats was sent to Gardiner's Island to report the accident to Admiral Arbuthnot. It was discovered that the *Bedford* had very nearly met the same fate as the *Culloden*, dropping her anchor and cutting away her masts to prevent going ashore. (The *America* had disappeared altogether, only to show up two weeks later off the Virginia Capes.) The following day brought calmer weather, and the men set to the work of salvage once again. They took off anything of value in order to prevent it from falling into enemy hands. Much of the rigging and several masts, including the bowsprit, were removed and utilized to re-rig the dismasted *Bedford*. Forty-six cannon were recovered during several weeks of salvage operations, and when the work was finished, the *Culloden*'s hull was burned to the waterline so that nothing remaining could serve her enemies.

In the spring, after the British had left Long Island, Joseph Woodbridge of Groton, Connecticut, managed to salvage 16 of the *Culloden*'s cannon, which he offered to sell to General Washington and the Continental Army. Unfortunately, the army had no funds and could not afford the pieces. What became of these salvaged guns is not known.

On November 30, 1782, the British and Americans signed a preliminary peace treaty in Paris; almost one year later, on September 3, 1783, the two parties signed the final peace treaty ending the Revolutionary War. A new nation had been born.

A NEW NATION IN NEED OF A NAVY

During the war, patriot naval resistance consisted largely of privateering, since the colonies had no navy of its own. Privateers were essentially "legalized" pirates who often used small brigs and sloops outfitted with perhaps a dozen cannon. Operated by private individuals, they captured enemy merchant ships, confiscated their cargo and sold it at a profit. They were "legal" in the sense that they were granted a charter by a government, whose interests they served by preying on a rival nation's shipping. Privateers were generally lightly armed and relied on superior speed to outrun larger warships.

In late 1775, funds were approved by Congress for a formal Continental Navy, and several frigates and sloops of war were contracted for. Unfortunately for the colonists, this fledgling navy was doomed to failure against the mighty British fleet. Hastily organized

in the midst of war, the new navy had three main weaknesses: no trained officers, a lack of cannon and ordinance, and almost no money with which to establish, operate and build the new service. Many of those chosen to command the new warships were political appointees—relatives or friends of influential people, often without any qualifications for commanding a warship. Most of the vessels built were either quickly lost to the British in one-sided actions, or burned on the stocks by invading British forces or by retreating Colonial forces before they were completed. Late in 1776, five more frigates and three 74-gun ships-of-the-line were authorized by Congress. Three of the frigates and two of the line-of-battle ships were never completed due to lack of funds; of the two frigates actually built, one was quickly lost to the British while the other remained in American hands for the duration of the war. The only ship-of-the-line to be completed, *America*, was given to the French as a gift, a replacement for one of their own ships that had wrecked on a bar in Boston Harbor in September 1782.

Early in the war the powerful British fleet controlled the shipping lanes along the Eastern Seaboard. It was their naval strength that allowed the British to move troops and supplies along the coast at will. Only after the French had entered the war was this vital control of the sea significantly challenged. It was the French fleet that kept British warships from entering Chesapeake Bay in September 1781, effectively isolating the British forces under General Cornwallis and forcing their surrender at Yorktown the following month.

Despite such clear evidence for the establishment of a strong navy, the new nation would have none for fifteen years following the close of the war. The only armed ships she possessed consisted of a handful of cutters belonging to the United States Revenue Cutter Service, established in 1790 at the urging of Secretary of the Treasury Alexander Hamilton. The bill creating the service provided for the acquisition of ten cutters to "enforce the revenue laws and to prevent smuggling"[2] along the coast of the new nation. One-hundred-twenty-five years later in 1915, the Revenue Cutter Service would merge with the United States Life-Saving Service to form what we know today as the United States Coast Guard.

The Revenue Service's cutters were intended for coastal operations, however, and could provide little military muscle overseas. American merchant vessels had become increasingly important to world commerce, yet they traveled the oceans unprotected. This merchant fleet, unshielded by a powerful navy, was ripe for plunder. War between Revolutionary France and Great Britain erupted several years after the American Revolution and would last for more than two decades. French privateers began to prey on neutral American shipping in the Caribbean, and there was also the problem of the Barbary pirates. The four North African states known collectively as the Barbaries—Morocco, Algiers, Tunis and Tripoli—had existed for centuries as pirate nations, preying on shipping traffic in the Mediterranean. All the great sea powers of the world paid subsidies to the Barbary powers, and the Americans were forced to follow suit. Yet despite these payments of ransom, eleven American ships were captured by the Algerians during 1793. The nation was helpless to do anything about the situation—again the need for a navy became apparent.

President Washington requested funds from Congress to build six frigates. The funds were approved, but construction of the vessels was stopped when a treaty agreement was reached with Algiers. Three years later, construction was resumed when the problem with Revolutionary France came to a head. These six magnificent frigates, *United States*, *Constellation*, *Constitution*, *President*, *Congress* and *Chesapeake*, would form the backbone of the nation's new navy. Designed by Joshua Humphreys of Philadelphia, the vessels were conceived to be larger, faster and more heavily armed than comparable frigates in rival navies. Faster and more maneuverable than battleships in light airs, their extraordinary speed allowed them to outrun ships of superior strength. But first-rate ships were only half the answer; the rest of the equation was supplied by commanders such as Captain Thomas Truxton of the *Constellation* and Captain Edward Preble of the *Constitution*. These visionary commanders instituted tight discipline into the new navy. They also began a routine unheard of in the British Navy—the use of powder and shot for unlimited practice firing drills.

There remained one more necessary ingredient for success: confidence. At the close of the eighteenth century, two outstanding victories were won by Truxton's *Constellation*. In two battles, occurring one year apart, the *Constellation* defeated French warships of equal or superior strength. These victories gave the American Navy something to be proud of and a chance to believe in themselves. Now equipped with superior ships, manned by better trained seamen than rival navies and instilled with confidence, the American navy began to establish a respectable reputation among the world's seafaring powers. It was American warships that silenced the Barbary pirates in the early nineteenth century, before once again taking on the British Navy in the War of 1812.

After the turn of the century, the British Navy was having increasing difficulty meeting its personnel needs, forcing them to turn to impressment to fill their warships by stopping merchant vessels on the high seas to search for "deserters." The British did not recognize the practice of naturalization, where a citizen of one country could choose to become a citizen of another country. Thus former British subjects who had become American citizens were subject to impressment, and a lack of documented proof of American citizenship generally resulted in being declared a deserter. This practice worsened through the first decade of the nineteenth century. Finally in June 1812, American patience had run out and President James Madison declared war on Britain.

The United States entered the war with an assortment of nearly useless gunboats and sixteen warships: the original six frigates designed by Humphreys and an assortment of corvettes and sloops-of-war. Numerically, the American Navy was no match for its British counterpart. Yet one-on-one, in an equal match of force, the American Navy would prove themselves superior. Better trained and better disciplined men, combined with stout ships possessing sighted guns that allowed more accurate fire (a fact that the British were unaware of) and a will to fight born of ten years' frustration with the wrongs of impressment, brought spectacular single-ship victories to the Americans. Such famous battles as *Constitution*'s defeat of the British frigate *Guerriere* and later *Java*, as well as lesser known victories such as the USS *Essex*'s destruction of the British sloop-of war *Alert*, and the frigate *United States*' defeat of the HMS *Macedonia*, set off shock waves in London. In the United States, victory celebrations contrasted with the panic of the British. On January 2, 1813, Congress authorized funds to expand the U.S. Navy by building four ships-of-the-line. The resulting four vessels were named *Independence*, *Franklin*, *Washington* and *Columbus*, although none were completed before the end of the war.

Despite these stunning individual victories by the American Navy, the sheer size of the British fleet proved an overwhelming force. Early in 1813, a blockade utilizing ninety-seven British warships shut down merchant shipping along the entire American coast. This huge force, not the whole of the British Navy by any means, was *six times* the size of its opponent's entire navy. Outmatched, the American Navy was shut down, but once again privateers picked up the slack. These fast little raiders cruised the world's oceans and captured 1,344 British ships in less than three years of war. British commerce suffered (Continued on page 22)

U.S. NAVY'S OLDEST WARSHIP: USS *CONSTITUTION*

Her keel was laid down in 1794, making the USS *Constitution* (top, left) the oldest warship still in commission in the United States Navy. Stoutly built of live oak, red cedar, white oak, pitch pine and locust, she was designed to outfight any ship of similar size and outrun ships that were more heavily armed. Undoubtedly the most famous of any of the United States' wooden warships, the *Constitution* won spectacular victories against the British ships *Guerriere* and *Java* during the War of 1812. It was during the quick and decisive battle with the *Guerriere* that the *Constitution* was nicknamed "Old Ironsides" by British sailors, who watched their iron shot bounce harmlessly off the *Constitution's* stout oak planking. The *Constitution* was armed with 32-pound carronades on her upper deck (top, right) and 24-pound long guns on her gun deck (above, right). Combined, the fast warship could throw a broadside of more than one-quarter ton of iron shot at her opponents.

Nearly broken up for scrap in 1830, the ship was saved by public sentiment stirred by Oliver Wendell Holmes' poem "Old Ironsides" and rebuilt in 1833. During the Civil War she served as a training ship, for the ironclad USS *Monitor* had made her services nearly obsolete. The ship was rebuilt several more times in 1878, 1905, 1925, 1973 and 1996. She took part in the American bicentennial in 1976, leading a parade of tall ships into Boston Harbor, the *Constitution's* birthplace. Every year on July 4th the *Constitution* gets under way for a trip around Boston Harbor and fires her ancient guns in salute to the nation she has so proudly served for nearly two centuries.

HMS *CULLODEN*

The wreck of the HMS *Culloden* is located off aptly named Culloden Point, near Montauk at Long Island's eastern end. The ship was stripped and burned to the waterline by the British after she grounded there more than 200 years ago during the Revolutionary War. Today her remains are almost entirely buried in a sandy patch of bottom along a rock strewn shoreline in only 15 feet of water. The wreck is accessible from the beach and visiting divers may view worm-eaten timbers and an occasional cannon where they were abandoned by the British Navy. The wreck should not be disturbed, however, for she is one of New York State's few officially protected shipwreck sites. Unfortunately, she is sometimes vandalized by visiting scuba divers.

Like many old wooden shipwrecks, most of the *Culloden*'s remains are buried beneath the sand, with only a few hull timbers showing. Wooden ships, the *Culloden* included, were fastened together largely with wooden "treenails." Treenails were essentially large wooden dowel pins driven into holes bored through wooden timbers. These simple but strong fasteners, combined with copper and iron spikes, nails and drift pins, served to fasten together a ship's many individual wooden timbers into a stout hull. Treenails can still be seen in some of the *Culloden*'s wooden timbers (right, center).

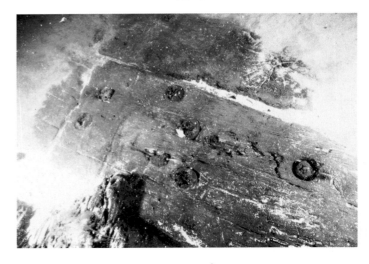

Although most of the *Culloden*'s cannon were removed by the British, one cannon (below, right) was recovered from the wreck site in 1973 by Carlton Davidson and donated to the East Hampton Town Marine Museum, where it can be seen today. At least five more of these huge iron cannon can still be seen on the *Culloden* wreck site. Each gun is buried muzzle down with only the breech end protruding from the sand. They are easily identifiable by the round cascabel (the ball-like protrusion) at the breech end of each gun (below, left).

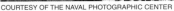
COURTESY OF THE NAVAL PHOTOGRAPHIC CENTER

The remains of the USS *Ohio* can be found lying on a silty bottom near Greenport on Long Island's North Fork. She lies in 15 feet of water and, like the *Culloden,* is largely buried. Unlike the *Culloden,* there are no cannon for visitors to find, for the ship was sold and dismantled for scrap before being blown-up and burned. Today, visiting divers will find only the overgrown ends of a few worm-eaten timbers protruding from the muddy bottom (top, right). Those with sharp eyes can sometimes find tiny copper nails, as well as an occasional spike or drift pin (below). Some of the drift pins are stamped "US." It is quite possible that these fastenings were made in the famous Paul Revere foundry. The *Ohio*'s magnificent figurehead (left) was sold when she was broken up and has survived undamaged. Today it can be seen in the town of Stonybrook near the village green along with one of the ship's anchors.

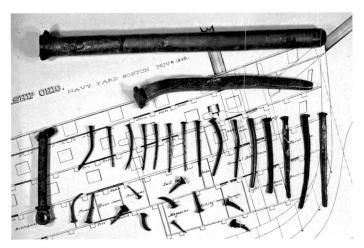

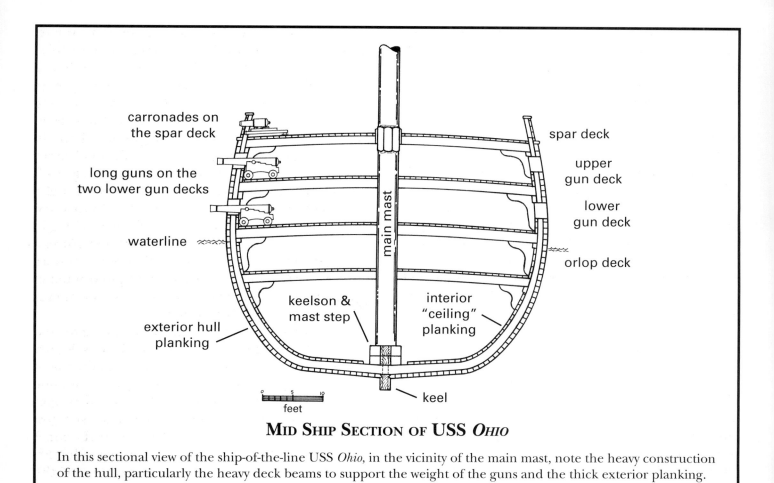

carronades on
the spar deck

spar deck

long guns on the
two lower gun decks

upper
gun deck

lower
gun deck

waterline

orlop deck

main mast

keelson &
mast step

interior
"ceiling"
planking

exterior hull
planking

keel

0   5   10
feet

MID SHIP SECTION OF USS *OHIO*

In this sectional view of the ship-of-the-line USS *Ohio*, in the vicinity of the main mast, note the heavy construction
of the hull, particularly the heavy deck beams to support the weight of the guns and the thick exterior planking.

heavily, finally causing merchants in London to take up petitions calling for an end to the war with America. This pressure, combined with the defeat of a hastily constructed British fleet on the Great Lakes, brought an end to the war in December 1814.

The ineffectiveness of the American Navy during the war bore an important lesson: to effectively maintain the nation's independence and respect in the world, she would need a strong navy. In April 1816, Congress passed "An Act for the Gradual Increase of the Navy of the United States," authorizing the building of "nine ships, to rate not less than 74 guns each,"[3] as well as continual funding of one-million dollars per year for the next eight years. The first ship to be launched, USS *Columbus*, missed by two days a second act of Congress passed in March 1819, decreeing that the 74-gun ships be named after states of the union. The remaining eight ships were named *Alabama* (renamed *New Hampshire* during the Civil War), *Delaware*, *New York*, *North Carolina*, *Ohio*, *Pennsylvania*, *Vermont* and *Virginia*. Economics dictated a policy of building the ships only partway, leaving them unfinished but ready to be fit out and commissioned if and when they

were needed. This inactive state of readiness was termed "in ordinary." Of the nine ships-of-the-line authorized by Congress, only seven were actually launched, and three of those were used as training vessels, as well as depot, or receiving, ships. Neither the *New York* nor the *Virginia* was ever launched. The *New York* was burned on the stocks at Norfolk on April 20, 1861, to prevent her capture by Confederate forces, and the *Virginia* remained on the stocks until 1884 when she was broken up.

Of those ships that actually saw service, the USS *Ohio* was the outstanding vessel. She was once called "perfection of a line of battleship"[4] by a British naval officer, and was considered one of the finest 74's in the world. Designed and built by Henry Eckford at the New York Navy Yard in Brooklyn, her keel was laid down in 1817. Her hull was built of yellow pine and "the best Jersey white oak,"[5] measuring 208 feet overall (not including her bowsprit) with a beam of nearly 54 feet. Her bow was gracefully decorated with a hand-carved bust of Hercules, carved in New York by Dodge & Sharpe and reportedly costing $1,500, while the ship herself cost $550,000. Taking three years to complete, she was launched on May 31, 1820, and then placed in ordinary, where she reportedly decayed badly. After seventeen years of waiting, the nation finally foresaw a need for her in 1837, and she was moved to the Boston Navy Yard. Here she was completed and then commissioned on October 11, 1838. She was noted as a particularly fast ship, repeatedly exceeding 12 knots, and it was often said that she handled like a frigate. Eckford built the *Ohio* deeper than the other 74's built at the time, and because of this she carried her guns higher than her sisters. One of the defects of the original four battleships was that they had insufficient freeboard to their lower gundecks, preventing effective use of the lower guns in all but the calmest seas; the *Ohio* overcame this defect largely due to the additional depth provided by Eckford. She was originally armed with 32-pounder cannon throughout, although later in her career she was rearmed with 42-pounders. The number of guns varied, ranging from 86 to 102 cannon, in spite of her 74-gun rating.

After commissioning, the *Ohio* became the flagship of Commodore Issac Hull. She left New York on December 6, 1838, and headed for the Mediterranean. On the passage to Gibraltar she demonstrated her superior speed by reaching the entrance to the Mediterranean in just 21 days—an *average* speed of 12 knots, which is outstanding for a sailing vessel. She spent two years protecting commerce and suppressing the slave trade before returning home in 1840, where she went into ordinary until she was recalled to duty in December 1846. Recommissioned to serve in the Mexican War, the *Ohio* departed for the Gulf of Mexico in January and arrived off Vera Cruz on March 22, 1847. Here she landed ten guns and a complement of marines. She remained in Mexican waters until departing for New York, where she arrived in May 1847. In June the *Ohio* once again went to sea, heading south to round the infamous Cape Horn and enter the Pacific Ocean. She served in the Pacific fleet for two years, protecting commerce and cruising off the coast of California during the early days of the gold rush. Returning to Boston in April 1849, she was decommissioned and put into service as a receiving ship. She remained occupied with this sedentary duty throughout the Civil War, while her sisters *Pennsylvania* and *New York* were burned on the stocks to prevent capture by Confederate forces, and the ironclads *Virginia* (ex *Merrimack*) and *Monitor* made naval history with their famous battle off Hampton Roads, Virginia. This epic battle, which produced no victor, demonstrated the obsolescence of the wooden warship—oak timbers and iron shot would do no longer.

The now obsolete *Ohio* remained on duty as a receiving ship in Boston Harbor until October 1875, when she was again retired and placed in ordinary. She would never again be called to active duty, however, and on September 27, 1883, she was sold to Israel L. Snow of Rockland, Maine, for the sum of $17,100. She was soon resold to a group of Long Islanders for $20,000, and towed out of Boston Harbor on October 28, 1883. The tow was struck by a gale off Cape Cod, undoubtedly giving her new owners a fright, while later in the voyage she was reportedly followed by a tremendous humpback whale. Finally arriving in Greenport on Long Island's northern fork on November 1st, the *Ohio* was put on exhibit for several months. Visitors were charged admission and given tours of one of the most powerful wooden warships that ever served in the United States Navy.

In the spring, workmen began dismantling the old warship. Anything salable was removed and sold; her hull was stripped of wood nearly down to the waterline. Many barns and houses on the east end of Long Island were reportedly built partly of wood bought from the *Ohio*. She was later dynamited at a spot just off Fanning Point, to the west of Greenport Harbor. A large crowd gathered early on the morning of July 26, 1884, to watch as Bob Corey, a member of the Greenport Fire Department, set off a charge that would blow the old *Ohio* to pieces. After lighting the fuse, the unfortunate Bob Corey ran some eighty paces to escape the explosion, only to be hit in the head by a flying iron bolt as the *Ohio*'s sides were blown out. Corey died a few hours later.

A bell cast of copper and brass salvaged from the *Ohio*'s fittings reportedly hung in the steeple of the Greenport Methodist Church for many years. Her figurehead of the mythological Hercules was bought for $10 by John Elliot Aldrich of Aquebogue, who later sold the piece for $15 to Miles Carpenter, owner of the Canoe Place Inn, located in Canoe Place next to the Shinnecock Canal. The figurehead remained there until 1954, when it was moved to the village green in Stonybrook, where it now resides along with one of the *Ohio*'s anchors. When the figurehead stood next to the Canoe Place Inn, a plaque below the mythological figure read:

> The maid who kisses his mighty cheek
> Will meet her fate within a week;
> The one who presses his forehead,
> In less than a year will wed.
> No maid, no matron ever taunted
> Him with refusing what he wanted.

2

THE SAILING MERCHANT SHIP:

FORGOTTEN FLEET OF FLYING DUTCHMEN

The development of the United States Navy, from the six fine frigates laid down in the 1790's to the disputes with the Barbary Pirates, through the War of 1812 and the building of the first proud line-of-battle ships, was driven by a single, unifying purpose: the protection of American merchant shipping. Following the War for Independence, having rid herself of the British Empire's drain on her economy, America's seaborne trade began a rapid expansion. Soon the new nation found itself in possession of the second largest merchant marine in the world. American raw materials and products were transported to ports across Europe and the Far East, while European manufactured goods were carried back to the former colonies. Cargoes of all sorts needed transport across the globe—sugar from the West Indies, cotton from the American south, and even human cargo, such as slaves from Africa. All these pursuits required ships, and America jumped at the chance to provide them.

The war with England had produced a large fleet of privateers, and at the close of the war their owners turned to the merchant trade. However, these ships were soon found to be ill-suited for their new duties. Fast, fine-lined vessels designed for merchant raiding, they had insufficient cargo capacity for efficient use in the merchant marine. A successful merchant ship needed a balanced marriage of the contradictory qualities of speed, cargo capacity and low operating costs. The privateers had sacrificed cargo capacity for speed and maneuverability, and after the war they were quickly replaced by slower, full-hulled trading vessels. The careful balance between speed, cargo capacity and economics would drive the continuously changing design of merchant sailing vessels throughout the nineteenth century.

Much of the work of the merchant marine involved long overseas voyages transporting cargoes to and from distant lands. Such ventures required a vessel capable of carrying sufficient freight to make the long voyage economically worthwhile to the ship's owners. A few extra knots on a passage were generally of little consequence, since a small increase in speed was unlikely to allow another complete voyage in a single season—large cargo capacity was much more valuable. The world's deep-sea trade routes had developed with the recognition of constant and reliable global wind patterns. These steady winds of constant direction, appropriately called trade winds, enabled sailing ships to make efficient offshore passages and were best utilized by the "ship-rig." The term "ship," in addition to its common generic usage, refers to a specific type of sailing vessel—a three-masted vessel rigged with square sails on all her masts. Such a "square-rigger" sailed best downwind, and not at all upwind, making her ideally suited to following the steady trade winds on long journeys across the worlds' oceans.

The European packet trade began to grow in importance after the War of 1812. These ships carried both passengers and freight on regular routes across the Atlantic between Europe and America. The competition between packet lines, combined with growing numbers of transatlantic passengers, began a demand for speed that would cause the packet ship to evolve as a distinct type. Fine-lined hulls carrying acres of canvas allowed fast passages, which finally allowed packet owners to establish regularly scheduled departures, an innovation begun by the Black Ball Line's *James Monroe* on January 5, 1818. Previously, the departure of a transatlantic vessel was often delayed by days or weeks while her owners searched for sufficient cargo to fill her holds, or to wait out bad weather. Passengers who booked on board the vessels were often summoned on short notice when the packet was finally ready to leave. The packet trade reached its peak during the 1840's; thereafter, steamships began to compete successfully for their business, giving rise to the great passenger steamers of the late nineteenth century.

The rising passion for speed reached its height with the famous clipper ships of the mid-nineteenth century. Long, graceful hulls flying mountains of canvas sail, these fast ships brought the romance of the great age of sail to its apogee. Although first employed in the China trade, it was the enormous demand for speedy passages to California during the gold rush years of 1849-57 that made these large, fast ships economically feasible. Putting a premium on speed at the expense of cargo capacity, the clippers incurred enormous operating costs and were doomed to extinction, disappearing around 1859 after a reign of less than fifteen years.

Certainly the most important type of sailing vessel found along the Eastern Seaboard throughout the nineteenth and into the early twentieth century was the schooner. Although not really an American invention, the schooner was the first type of vessel to be distinctly recognized as an American type. The British naval historian William James once observed: "None can compete with the Americans in the size, beauty, swiftness, or seaworthiness of their schooners."[1] The schooner's fore-and-aft rig enabled it to sail much closer to the wind (that is, more nearly into the direction from which the wind is blowing) than a square-rigged vessel, making it ideally suited to the coastal shipping trade. The light and variable winds generally found along the East Coast required vessels that could easily sail north or south efficiently regardless of the wind's direction. The additional challenge of coastal navigation among numerous narrow bays and inlets made the schooner a natural choice for the duty. Schooners were much more maneuverable than full-rigged ships in the close confines near shore, since their sails could be operated from the main deck—there was no need to send men aloft as was necessary in a square-rigged vessel. With reduced crew requirements and the lower initial investment of building the relatively simple schooner rig, as well as lower maintenance costs, the vessels proved very economical to operate. Following the Civil War, the three-masted schooner held a virtual monopoly on coastal shipping, particularly in the lumber trade. Later in the century, four-, five- and six-masted schooners were experimented with, and there was even one seven-master, the *Thomas Lawson*. The coastal (Continued on page 29)

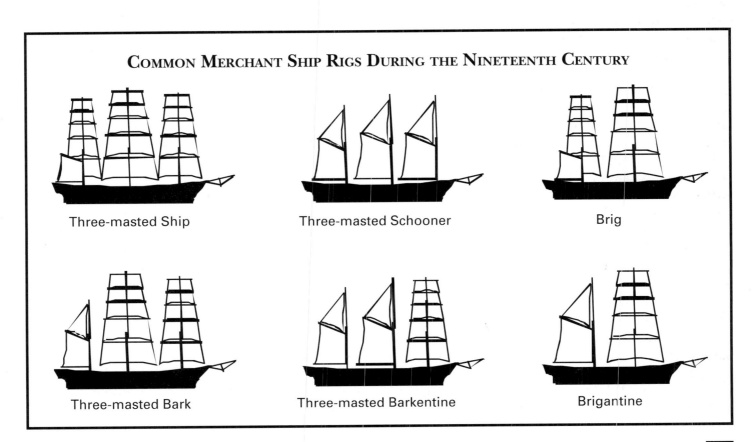

COMMON MERCHANT SHIP RIGS DURING THE NINETEENTH CENTURY

Three-masted Ship

Three-masted Schooner

Brig

Three-masted Bark

Three-masted Barkentine

Brigantine

CONSTRUCTION OF A WOODEN SHIP

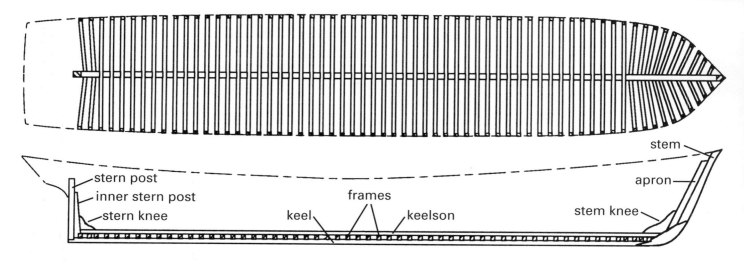

stem

stern post

inner stern post

apron

stern knee

frames

keel

keelson

stem knee

The ship's skeleton, built of huge wooden timbers, was constructed first. Frames were fastened to the ship's keel much like the ribs of the human skeleton are attached to the spine.

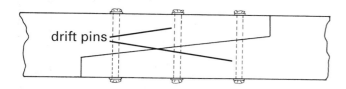

drift pins

Long timbers, such as the ship's keel, were spliced together from several pieces of timber using "scarf joints."

drift pin, or bolt, driven into pre-drilled holes

keelson

frame

exterior planking

keel

The vessel's frames were sandwiched between the keel and the keelson, and the entire assembly was through bolted using copper or iron "drift bolts."

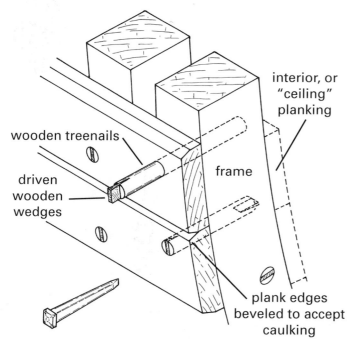

interior, or "ceiling" planking

wooden treenails

frame

driven wooden wedges

plank edges beveled to accept caulking

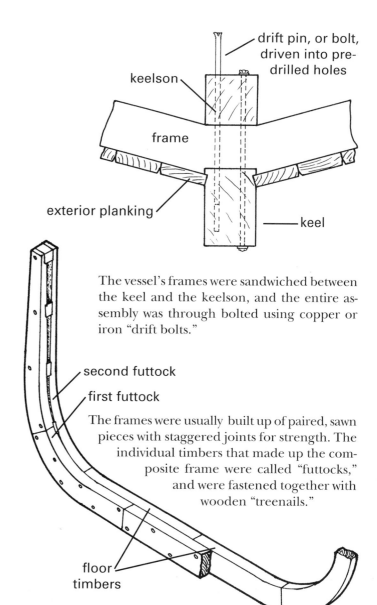

second futtock

first futtock

The frames were usually built up of paired, sawn pieces with staggered joints for strength. The individual timbers that made up the composite frame were called "futtocks," and were fastened together with wooden "treenails."

floor timbers

Once the ship's skeleton was completed, it was planked both inside and out. The planks were secured to the frames using treenails—wooden pins with wedges driven into the ends to hold them tightly in place. Copper, brass or iron spikes were also used at plank ends.

The ship's masts were "stepped" onto the keelson, and supported aloft by a series of "stays" that made up the ship's "standing rigging." A pair of "dead-eyes," woven together with a rope lanyard, was used to make the stays taut. The deadeyes served the same function as a modern turnbuckle, which eventually replaced deadeyes aboard sailing ships toward the end of the nineteenth century.

When completed, a well-built wooden ship was a strong and durable structure that could last for decades, and face some of the most punishing conditions Mother Nature had to offer.

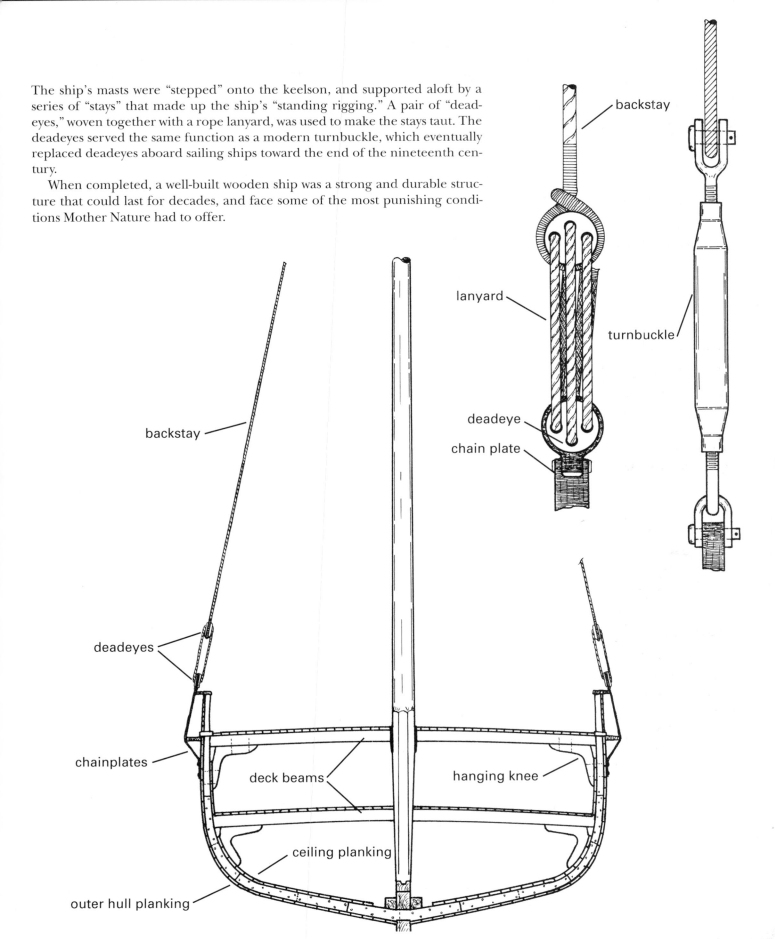

backstay

lanyard

deadeye

chain plate

turnbuckle

backstay

backstay

deadeyes

chainplates

deck beams

hanging knee

ceiling planking

outer hull planking

DETERIORATION OF A SHIPWRECK

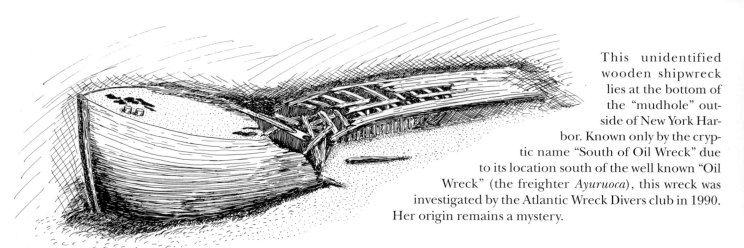

This unidentified wooden shipwreck lies at the bottom of the "mudhole" outside of New York Harbor. Known only by the cryptic name "South of Oil Wreck" due to its location south of the well known "Oil Wreck" (the freighter *Ayuruoca*), this wreck was investigated by the Atlantic Wreck Divers club in 1990. Her origin remains a mystery.

Thirteen miles south of Long Beach, Long Island lies an unidentified wreck known only by the name "Bald Eagle," a name which is also of unknown origin. The wreck's wooden ribs are covered by a large mound of square stone blocks that appear to be cobblestones, and were most likely the vessel's final cargo. One end of the site is littered with nuts and fruit pits, perhaps another clue to her identity, although these may be remnants of New York City's offshore garbage dumping during the early twentieth century.

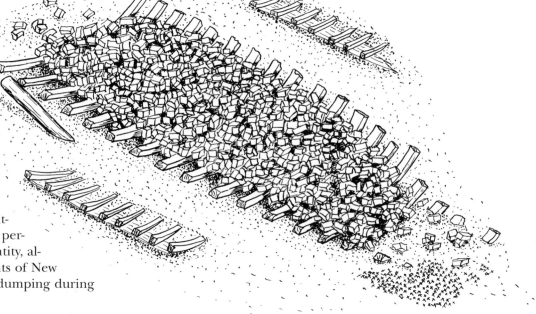

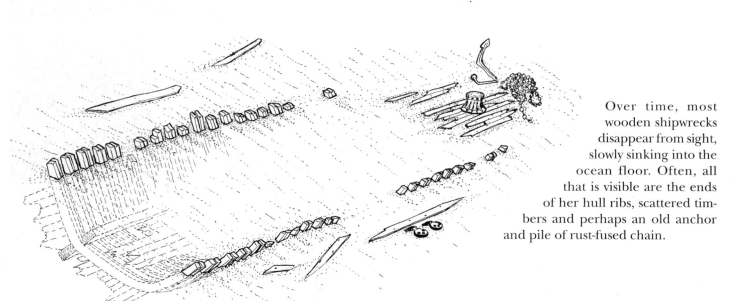

Over time, most wooden shipwrecks disappear from sight, slowly sinking into the ocean floor. Often, all that is visible are the ends of her hull ribs, scattered timbers and perhaps an old anchor and pile of rust-fused chain.

schooner's efficiency can be attested to by the fact that they could still be found carrying cargoes along the Eastern Seaboard well into the twentieth century, long after the steamship had become the dominant force in world shipping. In fact, World War I brought to the American coast the strange irony of German U-boats preying on defenseless wooden schooners!

DISAPPEARANCES AT SEA

All of these wooden merchant ships, stoutly built of white oak, mulberry, pine, sassafras, chestnut, cedar, hackmatack, birch and fir, rigged with from one to seven masts and a variety of sail configurations, had one thing in common: they were terrible insurance risks. One author goes so far as speculating that they were "probably the most dangerous vehicle ever regularly used by man."[2] Ships persistently met with disaster at sea, and in an age without radio or wireless communication, many simply disappeared without a

trace. Crews fortunate enough to be rescued by a passing vessel told tales that were undoubtedly similar to those who never returned.

In early November 1862, the steamship *Scotia* came upon a dismasted and wrecked vessel adrift in mid-Atlantic. Plucking her grateful crew from the wreck, they discovered her to be the 388-ton British bark *Mary Rogerson*. Her decks had been swept clean by a hurricane and the crew had cut away her masts to ease the strain on the vessel. One sailor had been washed overboard during the storm; those remaining clung helplessly to the slowly sinking hulk and prayed for rescue.

A similar story was told by the remaining crew of the British bark *Burnside* when they were picked up by the steamer *City of Dublin* in mid-ocean. Overtaken by a strong southwest gale in late December 1864, the ship's deck houses were washed away and the pumps were unable to keep pace with the rising water in the hold. It was her cargo of oak timbers that had kept the hapless vessel afloat. Only three survivors were picked up from the original crew of thirteen, and they

The full complement of standing and running rigging on a sailing ship appears to be a complicated maze to the casual observer, yet each individual line satisfied a specific need, and was the product of centuries of evolution.

Belaying pins served as a kind of quick-release cleat for fastening lines aboard a sailing ship. With a single pull, the belaying pin could be removed from its socket and the line it held quickly released.

Deadeyes, like these on the Charles W. Morgan, *served to tighten the stays supporting the masts of a sailing ship. The upper deadeye was attached to the lower end of the stay, while the lower deadeye was strapped to the side of the ship's hull with a chainplate. A lanyard was then rove between the two deadeyes; tightening the lanyard applied tension to the stay, much like a modern day turnbuckle.*

had nearly given up hope after spending six days clinging to the splinters of their vessel in the mountainous winter seas.

The sea can be a cruel foe, and often strikes in unpredictable ways. The schooner *Moses Knowlton* was headed for Trinidad, Brazil, with a mixed cargo when she was suddenly overtaken by a heavy gale. After surviving the gale she was utterly destroyed by a waterspout that followed. Captain A.H. Turpie later told how his vessel was tossed about like a toy: "The wind seemed suddenly to seize hold of the vessel and lift her up bodily and swash her down once or twice. Then she was driven around with her bows up; the water seemed to heave up under her and then the squall whirled her over on her broadside, and drove her round and round like a top."[3] The crew managed to escape in one of the boats; adrift without food or water 125 miles from Jamaica, the men held out little hope for survival. But two days later, the parched and dehydrated

men were rescued by the British bark *Elsie.*

High winds and enormous breaking swells were not the only hazards associated with storms at sea. In May 1895, the bark *Carrie E. Long,* carrying bulk petroleum, was struck by lightning and completely destroyed near the Bahama Islands. The captain, first mate and two seamen were killed in the accident, while ten of the crew managed to escape in the ship's boats.

Sailors have always been a superstitious lot, and their traditional beliefs and lore die hard. Captain Larsen, commander of the Norwegian bark *Columbia,* undoubtedly believed the story he told when he and his crew were brought into New York aboard the steamship *P. Caland* on September 9, 1879. He and his crew of eleven had been picked up southeast of the Grand Banks after being forced to abandon the *Columbia* in the ship's two boats. It seems that on September 4th, while sailing before a moderate wind on a relatively calm sea, a tremendous shock suddenly shook the bark from stem to stern. Running to the port side of the vessel and peering down into a bloodied ocean, Captain Larsen and his crew were confronted by a huge sea monster thrashing madly about beside the ship! Its tremendous tail and fins flailed about painfully, slapping the ocean into a frothy maelstrom of blood and foam. Checking below for damage, the crew found the *Columbia* filling rapidly through broken planking near the ship's bow. The frightened crew quickly abandoned ship and watched the *Columbia* sink before being rescued by the *P. Caland.*

While Captain Larsen's identification of his ship's destroyer is open to question, it was indeed sunk by a living marine creature. This was not uncommon; the story told by the crew of the Norwegian bark *Inga* is not only more believable, it likely provides the explanation for the *Columbia*'s demise as well. At 7:00 A.M. on April 30, 1883, while sailing on a smooth sea before a moderate breeze, the small bark *Inga* was battered by a sudden shock. Scurrying quickly to the vessel's side, Captain Corneilsen found a huge whale thrashing about beneath the ship's bow. A few moments later the whale sounded and was not seen again. Although the bark's cutwater had been knocked cleanly off the vessel, this appeared to be the only damage suffered by the bark. A piece of the whale's flesh was retrieved from the badly smashed stem and Captain Corneilsen plopped the souvenir into a bottle of spirits to preserve it. Three days later, however, when the integrity of the *Inga*'s wooden hull was tested by a severe storm, she sprang a bad leak precisely where the whale had rammed her. Although they struggled against the rising water with the ship's pumps, the crew was unable to stem the inrushing sea. When the steamship *Leerdam* hove into sight, Captain Corneilsen made the decision to abandon his vessel for the safety of the steamship, and the *Inga* was left to the mercy of the sea. Captain Corneilsen's souvenir of whale blubber was lost along with his ship.

Sinking vessels like the *Inga* and the *Burnside* were often abandoned at sea—but they didn't always sink immediately. Made of wood, they would often fill with water but refuse to sink, becoming waterlogged hulks floating aimlessly on the open ocean. Vessels carrying a buoyant cargo of timber were particularly notorious for staying afloat for a long time. Half-submerged and nearly impossible to see, these floating hulks presented a new danger to unwary shipping, and many a vessel was sunk after colliding with one of these derelict "ghost ships." An article in *The New York Times* on December 17, 1882, complained of these dangers to shipping, speculating that: "Doubtless some of the vessels which left port in an apparently seaworthy condition but were never afterward heard from went down with all on board after coming into collision with waterlogged wrecks which had not been observed by the men on lookout." These floating derelicts were such a problem that the U.S. Navy Hydrographic Office published a chart plotting the tracks of all reported abandoned wrecks covering the period from 1887-1891. Over this five year period, 332 abandoned vessels, along with 625 unknown derelicts, were reported adrift in the North Atlantic—a total of 956 abandoned vessels inviting collision. Over this same period, a total of 38 collisions with floating wrecks were reported, several of which sank the colliding vessel. On May 12, 1888, the bark *Virgo* actually passed between the two masts of a barely floating wreck!

All of the above stories are known to us because there were a few who survived to tell their tale to the world—but just as often there were no survivors, and the fate of the crew was left to the imagination. There were several occasions, however, where the mishaps of ships and the sea left behind a few subtle clues despite the lack of survivors. The renowned fairy tale of finding a note in a bottle washed up on the seashore apparently has some truthful basis behind it. Such bottles were occasionally found, and while denounced as hoaxes by many, their tales can only be dismissed at the expense of the lost human souls who may have authored the notes. A dock worker, Mr. Andrew Dowley, found a bottle bobbing alongside the pier in Brooklyn one September evening in 1873. Inside he found a slip of paper bearing the message: "Lost at sea, sloop *Wild Cat*, with all hands, Captain Stratford,

Roache's store, Jersey City, New Jersey."[4] In February 1894, a small bottle was found on the beach containing the following note: "September, 1893.—Sinking mid-Atlantic. *Horn Head*. Collision iceberg.—Mate."[5] The *Horn Head* had left Hampton Roads, Virginia on August 20, 1893, and had never been heard from. Another vessel that had left port never to return was the White Star steamship *Naronic*, which left Liverpool in February 1893. Her loss had never been explained until a bottle was found containing this note: "Struck iceberg; sinking fast; mid-ocean; *Naronic*. YOUNG."[6]

One of the strangest shipwreck reports on record is the loss of the schooner *Robert J. Edwards*. Her news was reported to the world from notorious Sable Island off the coast of Nova Scotia by carrier pigeon! The exhausted bird collapsed after landing on board the schooner *Mabel Leighton* bearing the following note, attached to its leg: "Sable Island, 9:30 A.M., 21st, 1.94, E. 30 minutes, 113 and 119 together. American schooner *Robert J. Edwards* lost with all hands, south side, southwest hurricane. Jan. 12, R. J. Boutiler, to J. W. Johnstone, all well."[7] The over-fatigued pigeon met a fate similar to the *Edwards'* sailors, however, when it died on board the *Mabel Leighton* after its long flight.

For all of these fascinating tales of disaster, there were countless others whose stories we will never know; hundreds of vessels have left port on routine voyages never to be heard from again. Occasionally some wreckage from the vessel was found; in September 1873, a mainsail with the name "*Asviana*" on it, along with a medicine chest similarly marked, was picked up at sea. But more often than not the vast sea swallowed all evidence of whatever calamity befell the missing vessel. With hundreds or thousands of vessels a year lost throughout the world's oceans, overdue ships caused much anxiety in port. A *New York Times* article dated February 28, 1895, tells a typical story: "At the Maritime Exchange they are anxiously looking for news of thirteen vessels that are still overdue and unheard from." The article goes on to list the missing vessels: the British steamers *Warren* and *Kingdom*; schooners *Angie L. Green* of Jacksonville and *Emma J. Meyer* of Charleston; the ship *Emily G. Reed* of Manila; schooners *Governor Ames* of Salem, *George E. Dudley* of New Haven, *Rebecca J. Moulton* of New Orleans, and the *John H. Cannon* of Jacksonville; the brig *Stockton* of Fink's Island; and the schooners *Joel F. Sheppard* of Norfolk, *Mavooshen* of Philadelphia, and the *Mary O'Neill* of Boston—all overdue and feared missing.

All these missing ships and others, lost without a trace over the course of centuries, are the thing legends are made of.

THE *FLYING DUTCHMAN*

Legends of ghost ships sailing the world's oceans and luring ships to their destruction have persisted for centuries among superstitious sailors. The most famous of these phantom vessels is the *Flying Dutchman*. The legend recounts how the ancient mariner Captain Vanderdecken, a Dutch seaman, is condemned to perpetually sail the seas until Judgment Day. The story has it that in life Vanderdecken recklessly swore to round the Cape of Good Hope despite a terrible storm, putting both his passengers and crew at risk. For his poor judgment he was condemned to his eternal fate. The legend claims that the Dutchman's ghostly ship still haunts the stormy seas near the Cape, and the spectral apparition of Vanderdecken's ship was greatly feared by superstitious sailors during the age of sail. Sighting her phantom form in the stormy night was considered a sure sign of imminent disaster.

Another of these ghoulish stories tells of an East Indiaman, deeply laden with bullion, also condemned to perpetually sail the seas. The Indiaman was preparing for a homeward passage from the Indies, but before departing the captain took on board a dark character known only as "Yellow Jack." So disagreeable was this individual, and so dastardly his reputation, that the ship was forbidden to enter any port that she called upon. Forced to cruise about the oceans endlessly, the ship's crew eventually went mad and murdered each other. It is said by some that she is still under way, cruising from port to port and manned by the ghosts of her dead sailors.

Still another legend depicts one Baron Falkenberg as the figure sailing the ghostly apparition of a ship. The story begins with the Baron's long-lost brother suddenly returning home and marrying the very maiden that Falkenberg had his eye on. After consuming ample champagne at the wedding feast, Falkenberg killed his sibling and then tried to seduce his brother's bride. His love refused, he plunged a dagger into her heart and fled to the seacoast, where he found a ship waiting offshore for him. A man standing on the beach spoke to him: "The Captain expects you, Baron—our ship lies out yonder."[8] The two figures stepped into a small boat and rowed out to the waiting ship, which left port and has not returned in over 600 years. They say that on wild winter nights she can still be seen sailing to and fro in the North Sea—on deck sits the Baron, playing dice with the devil for his soul.

Such sagas are dismissed by most as old sailor's yarns—nothing more than diabolical fairy tales told on cold winter nights by old, superstitious seamen. Yet there are those who believed them as gospel, and others still who claimed to have beheld the unearthly ships themselves. On March 18, 1754, the New York *Gazette* published a letter written by several men from Plum Island, located off Orient Point on Long Island's eastern end. The men had been fishing for menhaden in Gardiner's Bay when three ghostly ships appeared before them. Sails set, the ships came so close to the fishermen that they could make out sailors walking about on their decks. For fifteen minutes the three ships fought a fierce gun battle amongst themselves, firing silent, smoking broadsides at each other before slowly fading away.

The appearance of a second ghost ship in Gardiner's Bay was reported in the March 22, 1882 edition of the New York *Sun*. The writer had joined a menhaden fishing schooner the summer before, and had this tale to tell: Two nights out the schooner was anchored in a dead calm in Gardiner's Bay. Sleeping on deck, the writer was suddenly awakened by the first mate, visibly shaken. The mate claimed that seconds earlier a big schooner appeared out of the darkness with all sails set, heading straight for the anchored vessel. Just before the schooner struck, it dissolved into thin air.

While frightening, these appearances left their human witnesses unharmed—such was not always the case. On June 28, 1883, Captain Harding brought his vessel, the brig *Aristos*, into Boston with the following tale to tell: Twelve days earlier, while 140 miles southeast of Nova Scotia, Captain Harding reported that he had hailed an unidentified Dutch ship to stop, hoping to obtain desperately needed provisions. Assigning the first mate, two seamen and three passengers the duty of obtaining supplies, he dispatched them to the Dutchman in a small boat. The boat easily crossed the short distance between the two ships and her crew embarked on board the foreign vessel. Shortly thereafter, a fresh breeze sprang up and Captain Harding was astonished to see the stranger come about and sail away with his passengers and crew still aboard! The *Aristos*' Captain gave chase for the better part of a day, but could not keep up with the strange Dutch vessel, and she slowly disappeared over the horizon. Although the identity of the Dutch ship remained unknown, it should be obvious that it was none other than Captain Vanderdecken.

Nearly four years later, in the dead of winter, 1887, a mysterious ship appeared on at least two occasions off the New Jersey beaches. Grounding on the offshore bar late at night, wild cries could be heard coming from the strange vessel. In both *(Continued on page 37)*

A Mysterious Fleet of Flying Dutchmen

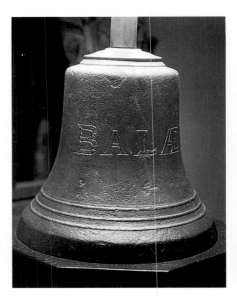

All along the Atlantic coast lie hundreds of forgotten ships from the age of sail. Most are nothing more than broken mounds of ballast stones and rotting wooden timbers. It is only rarely that one of these old wooden shipwrecks is positively identified, most often by the recovery of her ship's bell. Traditionally engraved with a ship's name and birth date, the bell is a highly sought-after prize among wreck divers and usually the key to her identity. Occasionally, however, the recovery of a ship's bell only serves to deepen the mystery surrounding these shipwrecks. Take the "Linda" wreck, whose identity has remained a challenging mystery for decades. When Tony Bliss found and recovered her bell in 1986 (above, left), he felt sure that the mystery had been solved. Unfortunately, the bronze bell bore no telltale inscription at all, leaving a deepening puzzle as to the ship's identity. In contrast, the discovery of the ship's bell on a large wooden shipwreck off the New Jersey coast by Captain George Hoffman many years ago created a different kind of enigma. The cast bronze bell (above, right) indeed bore the ship's name, BALÆNA, but no date. The mystery began when attempts were made to uncover her past. To date, researchers have been unable to find any record of a ship bearing this name sinking anywhere in the vicinity. Her hull appears stoutly built with a bluff, rounded bow, and at least two masts lie alongside her hull. Whatever her identity, she was apparently carrying a cargo of coal when she went down, for it is scattered all over the wreck site.

Members of this fleet of forgotten Flying Dutchmen abound all along the coast. Many are frequented by divers hunting for the delicious northern lobster, who make the scattered timbers of these wrecks their homes, and by sport fishermen seeking a fresh dinner or that longed-for trophy fish

Jeff Pagano (above) examines a timber on the "Harvey-H" off the New Jersey coast. Abandoned fishing nets are frequently found stretched across the wooden ribs of these old ships (left), like this one located south of Shinnecock Inlet, Long Island.

A Wooden Wreck Awaits Identification: "Linda"

The wreck of the "Linda" is but one of a vast fleet of unidentified wooden sailing ships littering the ocean bottom along the Long Island and New Jersey coastlines. "Linda" is merely a fictitious name assigned to the wreck site long ago, likely by the wreck's finder. While there are many such wrecks scattered along the coast, few are as intact and recognizeable as this one; most consist of a few timbers poking above the sandy bottom, scattered wooden planks and perhaps a rusted iron anchor. In contrast, the "Linda" sits upright on a sandy bottom in approximately 135 feet of water; the sides of her hull are still standing and much of her planking is in place. Bits of rigging and machinery are scattered about in the sand, while coal, apparently her final cargo, lies everywhere.

Kevin Brennan explores the upright sides of the "Linda's" hull.

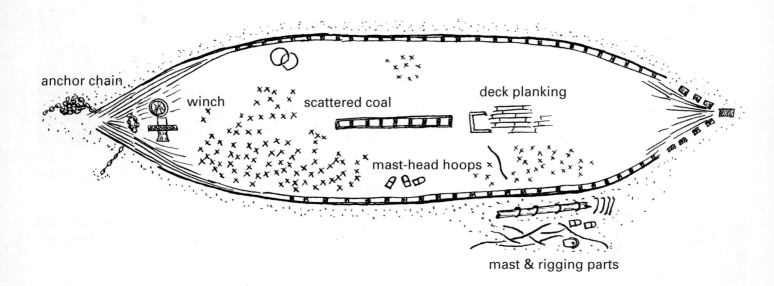

anchor chain · winch · scattered coal · deck planking · mast-head hoops · mast & rigging parts

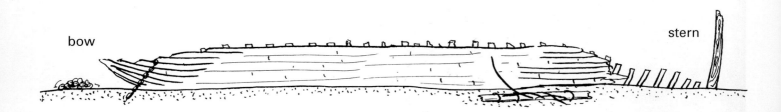

bow · stern

A pair of ocean pouts have taken up residence beneath a rusted pile of anchor chain near the ship's bow (top, left).

The gaps between the ship's ribs, and the interior and exterior hull planking provide perfect homes for creatures such as lobster (top, right).

The ship's anchor was once laboriously raised using a man-powered winch (above).

Blood stars form a decorative pattern on the interior, or ceiling planking, of the ship's hull (left).

Near the unidentified vessel's bow, another pair of ocean pouts (above, left) has found a cozy home inside a broken hawsepipe that once led the ship's anchor chain through her hull. Iron mast hoops (above, right), used to secure blocks and shrouds to wooden masts or to fasten two spars together, can be found scattered about the wreck site, particularly amidships. Although no sign of the spars that once supported the ship's sails are apparent, the ship appears to have been at least partly rigged, for numerous deadeyes have been recovered from the wreck. Further evidence is provided by a wooden block that once formed part of the running rigging, along with a piece of wire stay (below, right). Note that the wire rope has been "served and parcelled"—covered with tarred canvas for protection. An iron bollard, used for securing heavy lines, lies amidst a pile of coal (below, left). Nearby, a scupper made from lead sheeting lies astray among coal and scattered wooden debris (right).

instances the ship slowly worked herself off the bar and disappeared into the misty ocean before dawn, headed for New York, but never arrived. Following these two sightings, a writer for the *New York Times* speculated that the mysterious ship must be under the command of the infamous Captain Vanderdecken. The reporter theorized that the Dutch Captain had traded in his old and worn sailing vessel for a modern steamship, from which he was continuing his legendary haunting.

A FORGOTTEN FLEET OF SUNKEN GHOST SHIPS

While the legend of the *Flying Dutchman* has never been disproven, its existence outside of storybooks and the colorful imagination of the sailors of antiquity is doubtful. But on the sandy ocean flats south of Long Island, beneath the crowded shipping lanes leading into the great harbor of New York, lies a veritable graveyard for many a *Flying Dutchman*.

Today, a legion of sport divers spend their weekends exploring these ghost ships. Beneath the coastal ocean, modern electronic navigation equipment and decades of knowledge gleaned from fishermen have revealed the location of hundreds of sunken ships. Amateur divers poke and prod at their remains, but clues to the identity of these wrecks are often few and far between.

In life, a wooden sailing ship struggled for decades against the harsh elements, fighting an endless battle to remain afloat. Once that life ended, however, and she came to rest at the bottom of the sea, her surrender was complete. Each sunken ship becomes a new oasis on the ocean floor, creating a lush habitat for the sea's infinite variety of marine life. At the same time, however, the sea has promoted the mystery surrounding each of these wrecks by blending all evidence of former existence into obscurity. All that now remains of many of these stout ships are a few rotted timbers, a pile of ballast stones and perhaps a mast or two—scant clues with which to resurrect their forgotten stories.

Many of these ships are known today only by names such as "Linda," "59-Pounder," "Happy Days," and "Wolcott," cryptic names bestowed by their most recent discoverer. The enigma of many is so deeply rooted that the source of their popular names has also been largely forgotten. A very few have yielded their secrets to the persistent or the lucky over the years. A case in point is a broken schooner lying south of Montauk Point on Long Island's eastern end. Submerged under 150 feet of water and, like many, partly buried under the shifting sands of the ocean floor, her true identity was revealed when divers John Dudas and Evelyn Bartram recovered her ship's bell. The bell bore the inscription "TENNYSON—1864," revealing both her proper name and birth date. Another example is the large and intact wreck of the wooden sailing ship *Balæna*, whose identity was also revealed by the recovery of her ship's bell. But the life and death of this vessel remain a mystery, however, for the bell bore only her name, and no record of her sinking has ever been found.[9]

While the finding of a ship's bell is usually the surest form of identification for one of these mysterious wrecks, sometimes even this feat defies the efforts of explorers. Such is the case with a relatively small wooden vessel lying 18 miles off Fire Island, directly south of Patchogue. The wreck is the perfect picture of a small sailing ship. Sunk deeply into the soft ocean bottom, her bulwarks still stand stoutly in place from bow to stern, while her belly is filled with her final cargo of coal. Often visited by divers in search of lobster, she finally yielded her ship's bell to diver Tony Bliss in 1986, yet she still remains a mystery. The large brass bell bore no clue to her origin—perhaps she will forever be known only as the "Linda" wreck.

On occasion a lost ship can be identified by its cargo, still in evidence on the wreck site. The wreck of the three-masted schooner *Cornelia Soule* is commonly known as the "Granite Wreck," so called because of the cargo of granite slabs that litter the bottom amongst her bones. Another case is that of the *Adonis*, an iron paddle schooner lying off the New Jersey coast, which was identified by her cargo of grindstones and lead ingots.

But for every one of these vessels that has been identified, a score more remain as challenges to the shipwreck historian. A handful of scattered and worm-eaten timbers provide cozy homes for the northern lobster, but few clues for the historian. Time and shifting sands have caused most to continue sinking into the soft ocean bottom. Wrecks such as the "Happy Days" and the "59-Pounder" have sunk so deeply that all that remain are a few timbers lying half-buried in the sand—even the best boat captain has difficulty finding these wrecks today. Perhaps some tell-tale clue lies buried deep in the sand, amongst broken ribs and ballast stones, but for now each remains nearly as enigmatic as the *Flying Dutchman*.

3

THE ASCENDANCY OF THE STEAMSHIP

When the tiny, smoke-belching *Savannah* appeared off the coast of Ireland on June 17, 1819, she was greeted by a Royal Navy revenue cutter—sent out to assist the vessel that was presumed to be on fire. But the fires on board the *Savannah* were set by design, and posed no danger to ship or crew. The *Savannah* was the first steamship to cross an ocean and, although she employed her engine for only 100 hours during the 29-day passage from New York to Liverpool, she introduced an idea that would revolutionize the shipping industry and eventually lead to the virtual extinction of the sailing ship. Powered by a 75 horse-power, single-cylinder steam engine driving two collapsible paddle wheels, the *Savannah* was actually an auxiliary steamship, with her primary means of propulsion being the sails set upon her three masts. While the *Savannah* had opened the door to the age of the ocean steamship, she was little more than an experimental oddity at the time of her pioneering voyage. After traversing the Atlantic and attracting great curiosity in visits to both Sweden and Russia, she returned to the United States and found herself unwanted—a burden to her financially ailing owners. Sold at auction in Washington, D.C., her steam engine was callously removed and she was converted into an ordinary sailing packet. On November 5, 1821, the ex-steamship *Savannah* went aground on the outer bar off Fire Island, at a spot three miles west of Smith's Point Beach. A week of pounding by the surf split her hull wide open, ending all hope of salvage. She eventually disappeared into the sands of Fire Island, joining the countless ships that have met a similar fate along this shoreline.

It wasn't long before other steamships began to venture out into the open Atlantic. Step by pioneering step, adventurous entrepreneurs began to expand upon the *Savannah*'s feat. In 1833 the *Royal William* made the first passage across the Atlantic powered primarily by steam. Her sails were used only when the engine was stopped to clean out the accumulation of salt in the boilers, a process that was necessary every few days since early steamships used salt water rather than fresh. This was a time-consuming task, requiring the boilers to be shut down for approximately 24 hours every four days. The constant stopping certainly contributed to her rather long crossing time of 18 days, from Quebec to the Isle of Wight, on the southern coast of England.

The continuous impunctuality of sailing packets provided the impetus for establishing a regular transatlantic steamship service. During the first half of the nineteenth century, these fast sailing ships were the only way to cross the Atlantic. One year prior to the historic adventure of the *Savannah*, the packet *James Monroe* made the first *scheduled* transatlantic departure, beginning a revolution in the passenger trade. Competition between shipping lines soon caused the scheduled departure to become the norm. The packets carried every stitch of canvas possible in a quest for speed to outdistance their rivals, while below decks lush and elegant accommodations became a matter of rivalry as well. If the oceangoing steamship became a practical reality, its independence from the vagaries and whims of the wind would make it a natural replacement for the packets. The steady and predictable speed of steamships would allow adherence to a schedule of both departures *and arrivals*. One of the most important cargoes to be carried, first by the sailing packets and then by the steamships that replaced them, were the mails. Prior to the invention of the telegraph and the laying of the first transatlantic cable by the steamship *Great Eastern* in 1866, mail sent by oceangoing ships was the only means of communication between the Old and New Worlds. It is hard to imagine in this day of instant satellite and telephone communication that news from Europe could reach America only after a month's passage on a sailing packet—the steamship promised to shorten this time lag to weeks or even days.

In 1838, the age of the Atlantic steamer was ushered in by a great race between the steamships *Sirius* and *Great Western*. Both desired to be the first steamship to make an east-to-west crossing, as well as to capitalize on the expected market for a regular transatlantic steamship service. Their voyages improved on that of the *Royal William*, perhaps largely because they were aided by use of the surface condenser, invented in 1834 by Samuel Hall. This important device was actually a complete feed-water system, supplying the boilers with fresh water rather than salt, therefore eliminating the time-consuming blow down of the boilers for cleaning every few days. Both the *Sirius* and *Great Western* were paddle-wheelers powered by side-lever steam engines. The *Sirius* arrived in New York first, thus "winning" the race, but only after the advantage of a four-day head start when the *Great Western* was delayed by a boiler fire during her trials. The smaller *Sirius*'s crossing time was actually longer, taking 18 days 10 hours compared to the *Great Western*'s time of 15 days 5 hours.

Despite the achievements of the *Sirius* and the *Great Western*, neither of their owners managed to turn a profit and soon went out of business. In 1840, however, Samuel Cunard founded the British and North American Royal Mail Steam Packet Company, later known simply as the Cunard Line. The secret to Cunard's success over that of his rivals was in securing a contract with the British Post Office for carrying the mails between Britain and North America. This contract effectively subsidized the steamship line, guaranteeing the company profit even when its ships were not filled to capacity with passengers. Although she would have many rivals over the years, none would outlast the Cunard Line, whose ships still sail today.

THE *BLACK WARRIOR*

The employment of the oceangoing steamship was by no means limited to the transatlantic trade. For years coastal packets had been an attractive means of travel along the Eastern Seaboard, as well as an economical method of shipping cargo. Steamships simply took over the work of their predecessors, carrying passengers, merchant cargoes and the ever important mails. The paddle-wheeler *Black Warrior* was one of these early steamers. Built in 1852 at New York, she was powered by a single-cylinder, overhead-beam engine driving two paddle wheels. It was typical for American-built paddle-wheelers to employ overhead, or "walking beam" engines, while British engineers preferred the side-lever engine, like that used in the *Great Western*. The *Black Warrior* was also a fully rigged, two-masted barkentine, for it would be many years before steam power became reliable enough to do away with sails.

The *Black Warrior* proved herself a workhorse during her short seven-year career. She ran almost continuously along her appointed route between New York, Havana and New Orleans. In February 1854, she found herself in the midst of a customs controversy in Havana. Claiming that her cargo of cotton, destined for a port in the United States, was improperly missing from the cargo manifest presented to them, Cuban officials confiscated both the cotton and the *Black Warrior*. The American public was outraged—some went so far as to demand war with Spain. Eventually, the Cuban government bowed to public pressure and returned the steamship and made reparations for the seized cargo.

Three years later, during the *(Continued on page 42)*

In June 1819 the Savannah *became the first steamship to cross an ocean, beginning what would soon become a revolution in world shipping. Courtesy of The Steamship Historical Society of America.*

The paddle steamer Black Warrior *was built in 1852. Note the diamond-shaped walking beam high above the deck, between the paddle wheel and the smoke stack. Courtesy of the Long Island Maritime Museum, West Sayville, NY.*

FROM PADDLE WHEELS TO PROPELLERS

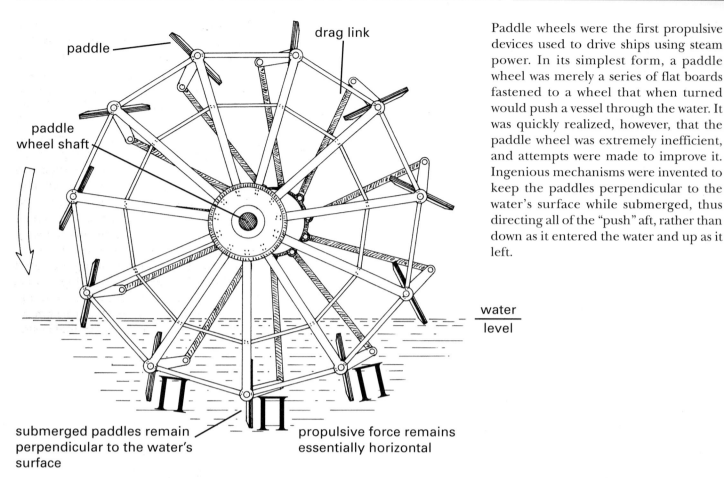

paddle

drag link

paddle wheel shaft

water level

submerged paddles remain perpendicular to the water's surface

propulsive force remains essentially horizontal

Paddle wheels were the first propulsive devices used to drive ships using steam power. In its simplest form, a paddle wheel was merely a series of flat boards fastened to a wheel that when turned would push a vessel through the water. It was quickly realized, however, that the paddle wheel was extremely inefficient, and attempts were made to improve it. Ingenious mechanisms were invented to keep the paddles perpendicular to the water's surface while submerged, thus directing all of the "push" aft, rather than down as it entered the water and up as it left.

The paddle wheels of early steamships were generally driven by single cylinder steam engines. British designers preferred the side lever engine (right), while Americans preferred the overhead, or "walking beam" engine. Both engines operated on the same principle, using a single oscillating steam cylinder to drive a beam and connecting rods, which turned the paddle shaft via a crank. The engine was made more efficient by means of an air pump, which increased the available propulsive force by drawing a vacuum in the low pressure side of the steam cylinder. The combination of paddle wheels and single expansion steam engines consumed coal at an enormous rate, however, and ships powered by this means were generally limited to passages of three weeks or less.

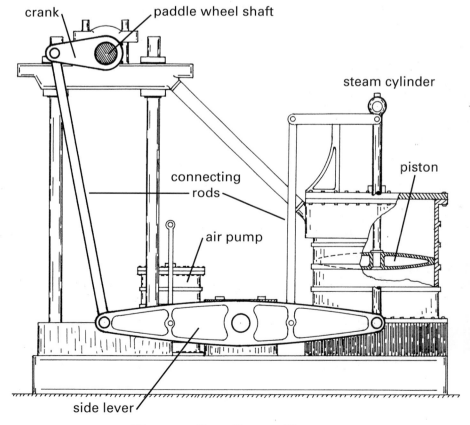

crank

paddle wheel shaft

steam cylinder

piston

connecting rods

air pump

side lever

TYPICAL SIDE LEVER ENGINE

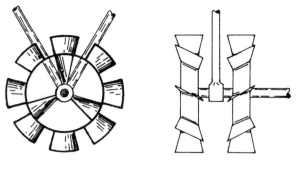

John Ericsson's propeller, 1837

Typical steamship propeller, late 19th century

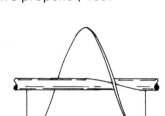

Francis Pettit Smith's propeller, 1836

It was the combination of the screw propeller and the compound engine that made the steamship economically viable for efficient, long distance ocean travel. Screw propellers were patented by both John Ericsson and Francis Smith in the early nineteenth century, although neither could claim to be their inventor. Since the propeller was submerged at all times, all of its motion was converted into propulsive force and it was more efficient than the paddle wheel. The compound engine expanded high pressure steam in stages using a series of pistons, allowing more energy to be extracted for the same amount of fuel. The resulting increased engine efficiency provided ship owners with a dramatic savings in fuel consumption, allowing their vessels to carry more paying cargo while saving on fuel costs.

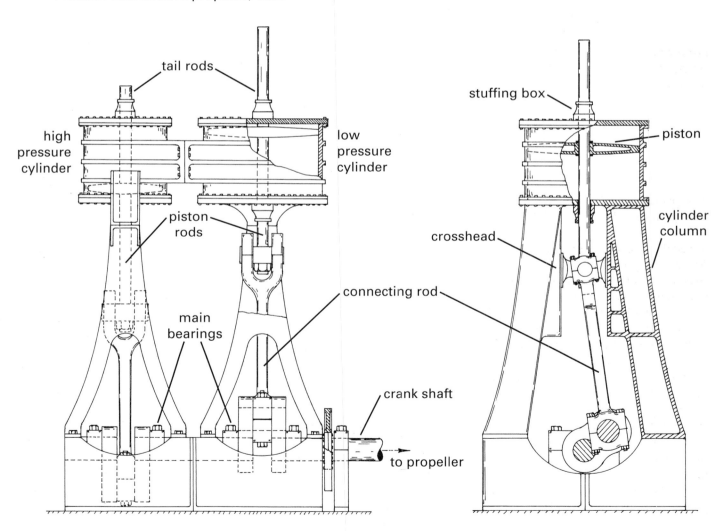

TYPICAL INVERTED COMPOUND ENGINE (DOUBLE EXPANSION)

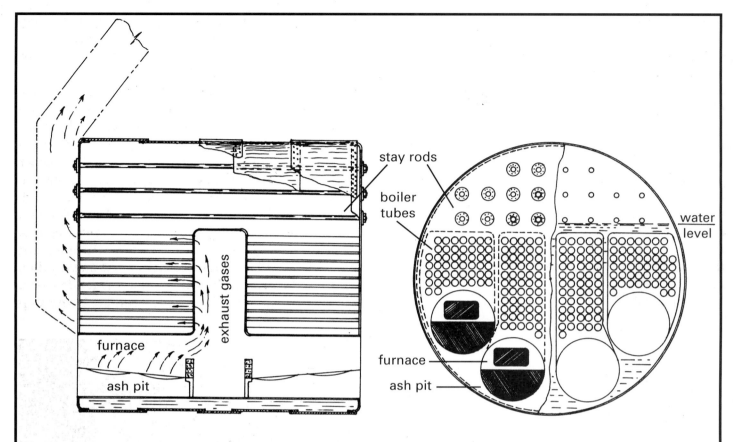

TYPICAL DOUBLE-ENDED SCOTCH BOILER

The marine "Scotch" boiler was introduced in 1862 and quickly became the standard boiler for ocean-going steamships. Its cylindrical design allowed the generation of higher steam pressures than its box-shaped predecessors, but stay rods were still required to hold the flat ends in place. Boiler tubes (also called "fire tubes") allowed hot gases from the furnace to circulate through the boiler water, providing additional heat transfer and more efficient steam production. It was the wide-spread availability of steel for boiler production in the 1870s that finally allowed the use of steam pressures high enough to make the compound steam engine practical.

stormy month of January 1857, the hardy ship very nearly met her end in a furious gale near Cape Hatteras. Mountainous seas swept away her bulwarks, deckhouses and lifeboats. Ice clogged the rigging as the ship battled to keep her head into the wind. Unable to support the additional weight of the ice, her masts came crashing down. For hours she drifted at the mercy of the terrific gale, too heavily iced to respond to her helm. When the winds finally slackened, the *Warrior*'s captain was informed that the coal bunkers were nearly empty. The ship was scoured for anything combustible; cabin woodwork was torn out and taken down to the stokers, along with furniture, spars and even the vessel's cargo. Miraculously, she managed to make it to Cape Henry at the mouth of the Chesapeake Bay, where she secured assistance and a fresh supply of coal. The dead of winter, however, seemed

to spell bad luck for the *Black Warrior*, and two years later on February 20, 1859, the shoals off Fire Island did what the storms of Cape Hatteras could not. Having made the long voyage from Havana to New York one last time, the paddle-wheeler was in the charge of a harbor pilot for the final leg of her journey when she went aground on the bar south of Rockaway Beach in a dense fog. Efforts to pull her off the bar over the next several days proved fruitless, and the wreckers settled for the salvage of her cargo. Her hull was left to disintegrate in the winter gales that followed.

THE STEAM REVOLUTION

Despite the apparent advantages of steam propulsion, it would require serious improvement before it was ready to replace the sailing ship on the world's trade routes. Paddle wheel steamships of the mid-nineteenth century consumed enormous amounts of coal, and for every ton of coal carried there was room for one less ton of paying cargo. The primitive steam engines of the era, combined with the inherent inefficiency of the paddle wheel as a propulsion device, made it impractical to carry more coal than was needed for about three weeks of continuous steaming. It was this limitation, along with the expense of feeding its engines, that prevented these early steamships from entering long-distance trade routes. Fortunately, both the transatlantic and coastal trade routes fell within their practical range, allowing the profitable employment of these early steamers and their subsequent development.

It would take two major innovations coupled together to overcome the steamship's costly inefficiencies. The first of these inventions was the screw propeller, first experimented with in the late 1830's by both John Ericsson and Francis Pettit Smith. Paddle wheels were not very effective for a number of reasons. A properly designed paddle wheel could operate at optimum efficiency only at one particular draft; but as a ship consumed coal during its voyage, it became lighter and its draft varied continuously. Another problem peculiar to ocean-going steamships was the action of the paddles in a rough sea. As the ship rolled, the paddle wheels on either side of the hull would constantly be immersed in the sea to differing degrees. This not only robbed the ship of fuel efficiency, but when one paddle was immersed deeper than the other, causing it to push harder, the vessel would tend to turn, much like a canoe with a single paddler. As the ship

The fire tubes of old steamship boilers provide a fascinating marine habitat. Forming a honeycomb-like structure much like a beehive (left), these banks of boiler tubes amount to an underwater apartment complex for a wide variety of fish and invertebrate life. Measuring two to four inches in diameter, each tube is the perfect size for a small animal or fish. While one tube may contain a small ocean pout (above), the tube next door might contain a juvenile lobster (below).

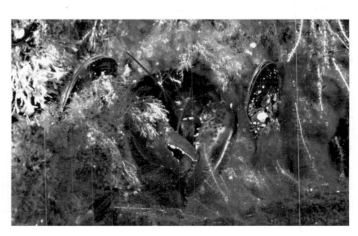

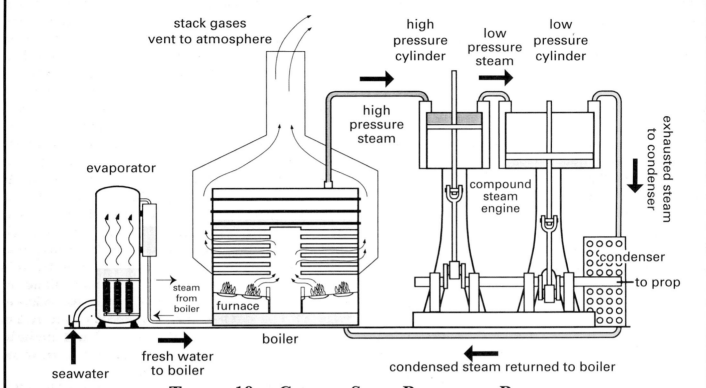

stack gases
vent to atmosphere

high pressure cylinder

low pressure steam

low pressure cylinder

high pressure steam

exhausted steam to condenser

evaporator

compound steam engine

condenser

steam from boiler

to prop

furnace

boiler

seawater

fresh water to boiler

condensed steam returned to boiler

TYPICAL 19TH CENTURY STEAM PROPULSION PLANT

In this operational schematic of a typical 19th century steam propulsion plant with a compound engine, a coal fired boiler was used to heat fresh water and produce steam. The fresh water was supplied by an evaporator, which used steam from the boiler to convert sea water to fresh. High pressure steam from the boiler drives the piston in the high pressure cylinder as it undergoes the first expansion cycle. Steam exiting the high pressure cylinder, now at a reduced pressure, enters the low pressure cylinder where it undergoes a second expansion while driving the low pressure piston. The now exhausted steam enters the condenser where it is converted back to water and returned to the boiler. A triple expansion engine would use three pistons to expand the steam in three successive cycles.

rolled back and forth in the ocean swell, it would constantly be turning one way and then the other, making it difficult to control. The screw propeller solved all of these problems since it was always completely submerged. The advantages of the screw propeller were dramatically demonstrated by the British Admiralty in 1845. In a famous trial intended to test the relative merits of the two propulsion methods, two ships, one propelled by screw and one by paddles, performed a stern-to-stern tug-of-war. The *Rattler*, powered by a screw propeller, proceeded to tow the *Alecto*, powered by paddle wheel, *backward* at a speed of 2.8 knots! This effectively spelled the end for the paddle wheel.

The second important advancement was the reintroduction of the compound engine. Originally invented in 1781 by Jonathan Hornblower, it was John Elder who put this concept to effective use for marine propulsion. By expanding the high pressure steam in

stages in separate cylinders, the compound engine effectively got twice the amount of work from the available steam.[1] High pressure steam was first expanded to an intermediate pressure in the high pressure cylinder; the steam exiting the first cylinder was then expanded a second time in a low pressure cylinder. This compound expansion of the steam required higher initial pressures in order to work, however. While it had long been known that better engine efficiency could be achieved by using higher steam pressures, it had proven difficult to build iron boilers capable of withstanding such high pressures. It was the availability of high quality steel for boiler construction that finally allowed the use of higher steam pressures and permitted the efficient use of the compound engine. The net result was that the compound engine provided increased fuel efficiency, amounting to a saving of more than 60 percent over a comparable single-expansion engine. In 1853, John Elder was granted a patent for a compound engine adapted to drive a screw propeller. It was the combination of these two advancements, along with high pressure boilers, that would finally bring the steamship into its own.

THE LOSS OF THE *HYLTON CASTLE*

It now became economically feasible to employ steam in the world's long-distance freight carriers. The members of this new fleet of merchant ships were built for cargo capacity rather than speed; they generally had small, economical engines combined with spars and sails in case the machinery broke down. The British freight steamer *Hylton Castle* was a typical working-class steamship. Built at Sunderland, England in 1871 by

Oswald & Co., she had a cargo capacity of 795 net tons and was powered by a compound engine of 150 horsepower driving a screw propeller. She was rigged aloft as a three-masted schooner, and her iron hull was constructed with seven separate watertight compartments. In early January 1886, the steamer was in New York Harbor loading a cargo of corn destined for Rouen, France. Although it was apparently common practice to load freight vessels in excess of their net registered tonnage, the 1,400 tons of corn stowed in the *Hylton Castle*'s hold was more than excessive. As she departed New York on Friday, January 8th, her stern was dragging deep in the water. Perhaps it was her overloaded condition that doomed the small steamship; perhaps it was the winds that would soon develop into a furious gale; or perhaps the old sailor's superstition about never sailing on Friday was more than just folklore. One thing was certain—the *Hylton Castle*'s destiny did not include delivering her cargo of corn to its buyers in France.

The *Hylton Castle* traveled 80 miles east of New York that first day. Shortly before midnight the wind began to blow out of the northeast at gale force. Thick snow formed a white curtain in the dark night, and the barometer fell steadily. At midnight, the wind suddenly swung around to the southwest and began to blow harder. The sea turned ugly as huge seas swept over the steamship's decks. The fierce wind continued its circle and began blowing from the west, forcing the *Hylton Castle*'s captain to come about 180 degrees and head into the relentless waves. Her bow buried itself as sea after sea crashed on board

The steam cylinders in this typical compound steam engine can be seen at the top of the engine, supported by enormous iron "legs." At the lower right is a geared flywheel, used to maintain momentum between piston strokes. In a ship, the propeller shaft would bolt to the flywheel. Courtesy of The Steamship Historical Society of America.

and carried away everything movable—providence alone left two of the lifeboats untouched. Captain Colvin and the helmsman remained alone on the bridge, lashing themselves in place to avoid being swept overboard. Snow and ice covered the ship from stem to stern and from deck to masthead as she took on the appearance of a ghostly iceberg. The stern, already perilously low in the water, was pushed down even further by the additional weight of the accumulated ice.

The arrival of daylight on Saturday morning revealed the magnitude of the mountainous seas that the crew had faced during the night. The helmsman, nearly frozen to the wheel, lost all remaining control when the rudder was torn away by the vicious ocean. Soon water was discovered in the cargo holds. The men found the hatches still tightly battened down, indicating that the ship must have sprung a leak. Captain Colvin ordered the steam-driven pumps started, but the water continued to rise. Seawater spouted furiously overboard as the powerful pumps labored to empty the ship. Slowly at first, but then at an ever-increasing rate, kernels of corn began spouting from the pumps. Soon more corn than water poured forth until finally the pumps quit altogether, literally choked with corn. The crew worked continuously throughout Saturday night trying to clear the pumps and save their ship; all night long the *Hylton Castle* drifted at the mercy of the wind and waves.

By Sunday morning the furnaces were flooded and all steam power was lost. All day Sunday and throughout the cold night they worked the pumps by hand—frostbitten and exhausted, they toiled for their very lives. At dawn on Monday, the men sighted the Fire Island lighthouse. With the steamship's starboard railing already under water, they made plans to abandon ship. Captain Colvin divided the ship's company between the two boats; nine men filled the boat commanded by First Mate Marshall, while another thirteen occupied the second boat under the command of Captain Colvin. Both boats stood by the sinking ship for half an hour, waiting for the *Hylton Castle* to go under. Finally, a huge wave lifted her stern high into the air and the battered steamship plunged to the bottom, bow first. As she disappeared from sight, the suction very nearly took Captain Colvin's boat with her—so furiously did the men pull at their oars that two of them snapped like matchsticks.

Finding his boat overcrowded, Captain Colvin ordered two of the men transferred to the mate's boat—no small feat in the rough seas that surrounded them. Waves breaking over the small boats froze almost in-

stantly in the cold January wind. The lifeboats were soon coated inside and out with a thick layer of ice. The men in both boats rowed steadily, but the mate's boat pulled ahead. In Captain Colvin's boat, two more oars were broken pulling against the mountainous seas and the remaining two were hardly enough to make any headway. The second mate, manning the tiller, was continually drenched by breaking seas and soon found himself frozen to both the tiller and his seat. Undaunted, he continued his vigilant duty without relief. By this time the other boat had pulled so far ahead that it was only visible occasionally, bobbing on the top of a distant wave crest. The lighthouse seemed an eternity away.

Meanwhile, the crew of Marshall's boat had pulled to within sight of the breakers on the beach. They had already been spotted from shore, and a boat crew from the Point O'Woods Life-Saving Station put out to meet them. Exhausted and frozen, the men were helped ashore and put up in the warm quarters of the Life-Saving station. But with little more rest than required to extricate themselves from their frozen clothing, the men donned dry clothes provided by the lifesavers and went out to walk the beach in search of their comrades in the other boat. At dawn, with no sign of the other boat, the eleven crewmen from the *Hylton Castle* were finally persuaded to start their long journey to New York—and a trying journey it was. The men walked nine miles along an icy, surf-pounded beach, and then another four miles across the thinly frozen Great South Bay, before reaching the Patchogue train station. Here they took shelter from the freezing wind and then boarded a train to New York.

As night fell, the eleven crewmen still aboard Captain Colvin's boat found themselves alone on a vast and dark ocean, with only the distant lighthouse to give them any hope. They could make little progress with their two remaining oars, so they quit rowing and allowed themselves to drift. Then, shortly before 9 o'clock a small light appeared in the distance. With their hopes of rescue rekindled, they once again set to work rowing, managing to come within hailing distance of what proved to be the fishing smack *Stephen Woolsey*. The frostbitten captain and crew were taken on board and revived below decks by a hot meal and a hot stove.

Amazingly, despite their terrible ordeal in the teeth of that winter gale, there was no loss of life associated with the sinking of the *Hylton Castle*. Two months later, however, the wreck would come under suspicion as a possible culprit in the dramatic sinking of the passenger steamer *Oregon*.

SUNK BY A SCHOONER: THE CUNARD LINER *OREGON*

During the second half of the nineteenth century an intense rivalry developed in the transatlantic passenger trade. Numerous steamship lines sprang forth to transport passengers comprising both society's elite and the thousands of emigrants leaving Europe for the hope and opportunity represented by America. Competition for these paying passengers, combined with the ship owner's competitive spirit, led to a continuing quest for speed. Each steamship line longed to own the fastest passenger liner afloat; records were kept and the prize for the fastest transatlantic passage became known as the *Blue Riband*. To a public fascinated by such adventures, it must have seemed a new steamer was launched every week—with every one bigger, faster and more luxurious than its predecessor. The transports that delivered these emigrants to America were principally owned and operated by Europeans. One notable exception was the Liverpool & Great Western Steamship Company, Limited, founded chiefly by Stephen Barker Guion in 1866. Guion was an American, born in the States in 1819, and the steamship line he founded became known as the Guion Line.

The Guion Line's first steamships were aimed at the immigrant trade, and were not the speedy ships of the record-breaking class she would acquire later. With the exception of the company's first two steamers, the *Manhattan* and the *Chicago*, both built in 1866, all of the company's vessels were named after States of the Union. Following these first two steamers came vessels such as the *Minnesota, Nebraska* and *Colorado* in 1867, the *Nevada* and the *Idaho* in 1869, and the *Wisconsin* and *Wyoming* in 1870. The *Wisconsin* was significant in that she was the first Atlantic steamer designed

A contemporary scene showing the Arizona *at the Guion Line pier in New York before departure. Note the posted schedule, an innovation made possible by the steamship. Courtesy of The Steamship Historical Society.*

In 1879 the Arizona *crashed headlong into an iceberg off the Grand Banks, smashing her bow for 20 feet. With her survival, subsequent passenger bookings actually increased! Courtesy of The Steamship Historical Society.*

from the outset to employ a compound engine. In 1871, now well established in the trade, the Guion Line ordered a pair of vessels aimed at breaking the Atlantic record and winning the *Blue Riband* that Guion longed for. Unfortunately for Guion, both the *Montana* and *Dakota* turned in disappointing performances and proved no faster than the line's previous ships. But Guion was determined to enter the race for speed, and ordered yet another vessel, this time from John Elder & Company of Fairfield, Scotland, to be named *Arizona*. Launched in March 1879, the *Arizona* lived up to her owner's expectations and her first crossing proved to be the fastest maiden voyage on record. The coveted *Blue Riband* did not elude her for long, and on her second eastward crossing in July she bested the record. Her outstanding speed made the *Arizona* very popular with the public, along with a curious ac-

cident that occurred in November of 1879. Racing through a dense fog at very nearly full speed, she collided head on with an immense iceberg off the Grand Banks. Her bow was crumpled some 20 feet back from her stem, but her collision bulkhead held and she limped into St. John's, Newfoundland under her own power. Although her master's license was suspended for his reckless speed under hazardous conditions, the *Arizona*'s bookings actually increased—the public apparently felt any ship that could withstand such an impact was nearly unsinkable. The *Arizona*'s success led her owners to order a second "Atlantic Greyhound," the *Alaska*, which was launched in 1881. She quickly captured the record by besting her sister's time from Queenstown to New York in April 1882. Now owning the two fastest liners on the Atlantic, Guion ordered a third "greyhound" so that a balanced crossing schedule could be maintained. To be named *Oregon*, the new ship was ordered despite already strained finances at Guion.

The *Oregon* was to be a refinement of her sister ships, with John Elder & Company building on the experience gained with the *Arizona* and *Alaska*. The *Oregon*'s lines retained the same 501-foot length as the *Alaska*, but added 4 feet to her breadth to give her a beam of 54 feet. Her hull, built of iron, was an oddity, since the use of steel plate had come into common usage for ship hulls by this time. Her compound steam engine was nothing short of gigantic, its 13,575 indicated horsepower (ihp) outclassing anything afloat at that time. Nine double-ended boilers provided steam for the mammoth engine, whose working pressure had been increased from the 100 pounds-per-square-inch (psi) of the *Alaska* to 110. Each boiler had eight furnaces, giving a total of 72 fires for the stokers to feed! This enormous heating capacity accounted for a coal consumption of some 280 tons per day. An article in the *New York Times* on October 8, 1883, described this luxurious new arrival to the Atlantic passenger trade as follows:

She has four masts, two having yards, and the steam steering gear, of improved construction, is in the wheel-house under the after turtle-deck. She has a promenade-deck extending the whole length and breadth of the vessel, with the exception of the parts that form the turtle-deck at the ends. Her ladies' boudoir is on this deck amidships, and the cabins for passengers are on the third or main deck, where the dining saloons, retiring and other rooms are situated. The fourth deck is constructed for steerage passengers or cargo, as may be required. The steamer is lighted with Edison's incandescent lamps, a separate switch being supplied for each state-room. The fittings are novel in several respects. The grand saloon is placed in the fore part of the vessel, and is laid with a parquetry floor. The paneling is of polished satinwood, the pilasters of walnut, with gilt capitals. The saloon is 65 by 54 feet and 9 feet in height at its lowest part. The cupola, which gives light and ventilation, is so arranged that the large skylight at the top can be opened during the stormiest weather. The ladies' drawing-room is a singularly elegant apartment, furnished with a rich pile carpet and upholstered in peacock blue velvet. It is built, as is the Captain's room and the principal entrance to the saloon, of cedar, ash, oak, and maple, grown in the American

State of Oregon. The steaming power of the vessel is enormous; the engines represent a capacity beyond anything that has ever been put on board a vessel, the boiler power being correspondingly large. . . .

Built with speed in mind, as well as luxury, the *Oregon* would not disappoint her owners. On her first crossing, the best day's run of 456 miles, achieved on her captain's birthday, bested the previous record by 20 miles. This was to improve as her machinery was broken in; six months later, in April 1884, she crossed from Queenstown to New York in 6 days, 10 hours and 10 minutes, capturing the *Blue Riband* for the fastest Atlantic passage. On this crossing, her *worst* day's run was 440 miles—an average speed of over 18 knots. She was only to make four round trip voyages for the Guion Line, however, and in May 1884, what was then the fastest vessel on the Atlantic was sold to the Cunard Line to ease the financial strain on her former owners. With their new acquisition the Cunard Line would soon recapture the coveted *Blue Riband*, which it had not held since losing it to the Inman Line's *City of Paris* back in November 1867. Two months after changing hands, the *Oregon* regained the title for Cunard by beating the record for the fastest passage in *both* directions. She first lowered the crossing time from Queenstown to Sandy Hook to 6 days, 12 hours and 54 minutes, then followed this feat by making a passage from Sandy Hook to Queenstown in 6 days 9 hours and 22 minutes, also setting a record for the fastest round trip voyage ever accomplished up to that time. Cunard had at long last recaptured the record with a steamship designed and built as a rival for her own "greyhounds," the *Umbria* and soon to be completed *Etruria*, whom she would now run alongside.

In the spring of 1885 the British Government, fearing a war with Russia over events on the Balkan Peninsula, authorized the Admiralty to charter the *Oregon*, along with her former running mates *Arizona* and *Alaska*, to be fitted out as auxiliary cruisers. One hundred of her cabins were stripped and filled with bags of coal to provide protection for her boilers and engines, and she was fitted with six 64-pounder muzzleloaders, four 5-inch Armstrong breech loaders and a number of machine guns. She was also provided with eight torpedo-carrying steam launches. By the time her conversion to a cruiser was completed, however, the war scare was over; she did, however, join the Navy for fleet exercises and proved herself the fastest large ship available. She was soon reconverted to a liner and returned to Cunard, having proved to the Admiralty's satisfaction the advantage of converting passenger liners into auxiliary cruisers and high-speed scout vessels in times of emergency.

With the *Oregon* back in the service she was designed for, Cunard found herself operating the three fastest vessels on the Atlantic, for the *Etruria* had broken the *Oregon*'s record for the fastest westward passage in May 1885. Two years later, in the spring of 1887, the *Etruria* would also break the *Oregon*'s eastward record, while the *Umbria* bested the *Etruria*'s westward passage. Cunard was in an enviable position with regard to the *Blue Riband*. This fast trio of liners was not destined to remain together, however.

On the morning of March 6, 1886, the *Oregon* departed Liverpool, England, on what all believed would be another routine passage across the vast Atlantic. A crew of 205 men was on board in order to ensure a safe and comfortable voyage for the 186 first class, 66 second class and 395 steerage passengers. Other than large swells and brisk southwest winds while off the Newfoundland Banks, the passengers enjoyed fine weather during their crossing. After rounding Nantucket, the *Oregon* headed westward on the final leg of her voyage to New York. Baggage was removed from the hold and piled on deck in anticipation of docking the following morning. About 4:00 A.M. on March 14th,

Chief Officer William George Matthews came up on the bridge and took charge of the ship. Also on the bridge was the *Oregon*'s fourth officer, standing watch on the port side while Matthews watched on the starboard side. Additionally, two men were on watch on the turtle deck in the stern and one more on the forward part of the promenade deck. The night was reasonably clear but dark, and at 4:30 A.M. dawn had still not broken.

Suddenly a white light appeared in the darkness. "A bright light a little on the port bow!" sang out the fourth officer. Simultaneously, the bow lookout reported seeing the light. Immediately Chief Officer Matthews ordered the helm hard aport, but the 500-foot length of the *Oregon*'s rapidly moving hull would not respond in time to avoid the collision. Seconds later the sails and hull of a large schooner loomed out of the darkness, striking the *Oregon* on her port side only a few feet forward of the bridge where Matthews stood helplessly watching. The darkened schooner glanced off the *Oregon*'s hull and careened off into the darkness. Matthews immediately ordered the ship's engines stopped, then turned his attention to the surrounding darkness. Searching a full 360 degrees around the horizon, he could find no trace of the mysterious schooner that had so suddenly appeared.

Meanwhile, the clang of the ship's telegraph quickly brought Captain Philip Cottier, the *Oregon*'s master, on deck where he resumed command of his vessel.

Word soon reached the bridge that the steamer was taking on water. Investigation revealed three holes in the *Oregon*'s hull plating where she had been struck. While the largest, 12 feet by 9 feet, was above the waterline, seawater was pouring into the ship's hold through one of the smaller holes. The pumps were quickly put into action and orders were given to awaken the passengers and prepare them for

The Cunard liner Umbria *served briefly alongside the* Oregon *before the* Oregon *was lost to collision; later the* Umbria *was involved in a collision of her own. Courtesy of The Steamship Historical Society of America.*

The Oregon *was built for both speed and luxury, and attained both. In April 1884, she captured the coveted* Blue Riband *for the Guion Line. Drawing by Dan Brissenden courtesy of Ralph Ziobrowski.*

abandoning ship while the crew prepared the lifeboats for launching. Just before dawn distress rockets were sent up. A short while later a big outbound steamer was seen in the distance, but continued on its way. No other vessels were sighted until after daybreak, when pilot boat No. 11 appeared with the apparent intention of dispatching a pilot on board the *Oregon*! One of the ship's officers then made an announcement to the passengers: "Here's a pilot boat, and there will be other boats here soon. I think the *Oregon* is safe, but I want to be sure of the safety of everybody. I want you to go on board the pilot boat or into the lifeboats for about half an hour, until we can assure ourselves of our condition."[3]

The stricken steamship had begun listing to starboard and was slowly settling lower in the water. The *Oregon*'s ten lifeboats were lowered and filled with pas-

sengers, women and children first, who were transferred to the pilot boat until about 400 had been put aboard that small boat. Although Captain Cottier later told the papers that "There were no scenes on board the *Oregon*. I never expected to see such an affair go off so easily,"[4] not all of the passengers agreed. Some told of confusion and disorder on deck, with some of the passengers crying, screaming or praying, obviously frightened for their lives. A group of firemen, apparently scared out of the boiler rooms by torrents of steam as the rising sea water extinguished the boiler fires, commandeered one of the lifeboats and attempted to make their escape with a half-empty boat. A more compassionate sailor beat the intended escapees with a large stick until they agreed to take some passengers aboard the boat. Even so, when the lifeboat was lowered and began pulling away from the

Oregon's side it was still not filled to capacity. It took a spirited, white-haired old man, who pulled a revolver and threatened to shoot the leader of the cowardly pack of firemen, to force the boat to return and take on enough passengers to fill her.

Some two hours after the arrival of the pilot boat, the schooner *Fannie A. Gorham* hove to, and the remainder of the passengers and crew—over 400—were transferred to her decks. Undoubtedly, it was quite a crowd aboard these two rather small vessels. Around noon the North German Lloyd Line steamship *Fulda* arrived on the scene, and most of the passengers were transferred to her for the short remaining leg of their voyage to New York. The *Fulda* stood by, however, to watch the *Oregon*'s last hours. As one passenger would later relate, "While the disappearance of the beautiful steamer we had learned to love was in one respect an awful sight, it was at the same time one of the most picturesque things I ever saw."[5]

Five minutes before the end, the great liner began to rock and pitch uneasily as she continued to list over toward port. Her foremast fell as her bow took one last dip and then reared up as though in defiance, where it poised for an instant, then plunged beneath the waves. Her stern lifted skyward until the blades of her immense propeller were exposed before they, too, disappeared from sight in a frothy, boiling mass of water. The "unchallenged mistress of the seas"[6] was gone. Throughout the entire eight-hour ordeal not a single human life was lost—even three dogs on board were saved. The sole loss of life reported in the newspapers amounted to two magpies lost by a man from Chicago.

Speculation as to the cause of the disaster quickly became the hot topic of discussion in the New York papers. Officer Matthews continued to claim that the mysterious schooner that had "run down" the fast steamship displayed no sidelights, thus exonerating him of blame. Mrs. W.H. Hurst, a passenger occupying stateroom No. 54 on the port side, just *aft* of the collision point, told a different story, however. "I had passed a sleepless night and was looking out through the deadlight into the almost impenetrable darkness," her story went, when "Suddenly the stars were shut out from view by some passing object. Then a brilliant red light shot by my cabin window."[7] Seconds later Mrs. Hurst was nearly thrown off her feet by the impact of the collision that would ultimately sink the *Oregon*. The problem with Mrs. Hurst's story, however, is that her cabin was *aft* of the collision point. It is not possible for the schooner to have passed by the porthole of cabin 54, showing Mrs. Hurst her port (red) light, and

then collide with the *Oregon* at a point *forward* of cabin 54—not unless the *Oregon* was traveling backwards! It is quite possible that the schooner was displaying sidelights but that they were hidden from view by her sails, as the following explanation, which appeared in the *New York Times* two days following the collision, points out. As the *Oregon* was heading west, into the wind, and was struck on the port side by the schooner, it is apparent that the schooner was sailing on the port tack, with the wind coming over her port side. Her head sails would have been billowing out to starboard, and would have likely concealed the starboard (green) light from an observer on board the *Oregon*.

The fate and identity of the schooner was unknown. Officer Matthews and the lookouts on duty at the time claimed that the schooner must have sunk instantly, for they could see no sign of her following the collision. (Of course, they didn't see her before the collision, either.) Others on board claimed that she had drifted slowly away, and could be seen for some ten minutes before disappearing. Up and down the coast every overdue coal schooner quickly became a suspect in the *Oregon*'s demise. Three days after the tragic collision, on March 17th, the *New York Times* reported the *Abbott F. Lawrence*, a coal schooner overdue in the port of Taunton, Massachusetts, as a possible culprit. On March 19th, the coal schooner *Hudson*, overdue in Boston from Philadelphia, was considered a suspect.

In the meantime, many other theories were advanced to explain the sinking of the great Cunard steamship. One source suggested that the *Oregon* had struck a stray, floating torpedo, or possibly was sunk by an internal explosion of dynamite or some other explosives on board. Another conjectured cause was a coal gas explosion in the ship's bunkers. A lawyer representing several of the *Oregon*'s passengers in claims against the Cunard line offered the speculation that the ship had indeed struck another vessel, but a sunken one! He claimed that the liner had struck the wreck of the steamship *Hylton Castle*, which had sunk two months earlier in the same vicinity. A Lieutenant in the Hydrographic Office later discounted this theory, determining after careful study that the *Oregon* was never closer than nine miles to the wreck of the *Hylton Castle*. On March 20th, when a fishing boat captain turned up at Sandy Hook with a schooner's yawl boat he had found floating bottom-up some 25 miles southeast of the *Oregon* wreck—advocates of the schooner theory gained more credence.

In New England, the owners of the coal schooner *Charles H. Morse* began to fear that it was their vessel that had run down the *Oregon*. (Continued on page 61)

NINETEENTH CENTURY ELEGANCE: SS *OREGON*

Designed to carry passengers in the rich transatlantic passenger trade, the *Oregon* was originally built for the Guion Line and later sold to Cunard. Sunk in a mysterious collision without loss of life on March 14, 1886, the once grand liner was identified by divers in the 1960s by the plethora of china found on the site, variously bearing the crests of both steamship lines. Clockwise from left: China with the Guion and Cunard crests, as well as silverware and bottles; chamberpots tell of a time before modern conveniences; portholes studded the sleek sides of the *Oregon's* hull (courtesy of John Lachenmeyer); many elegant vases have been recovered from the wreck (courtesy of Patrick Rooney).

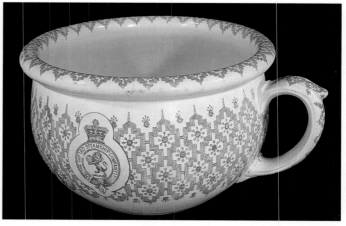

SS OREGON

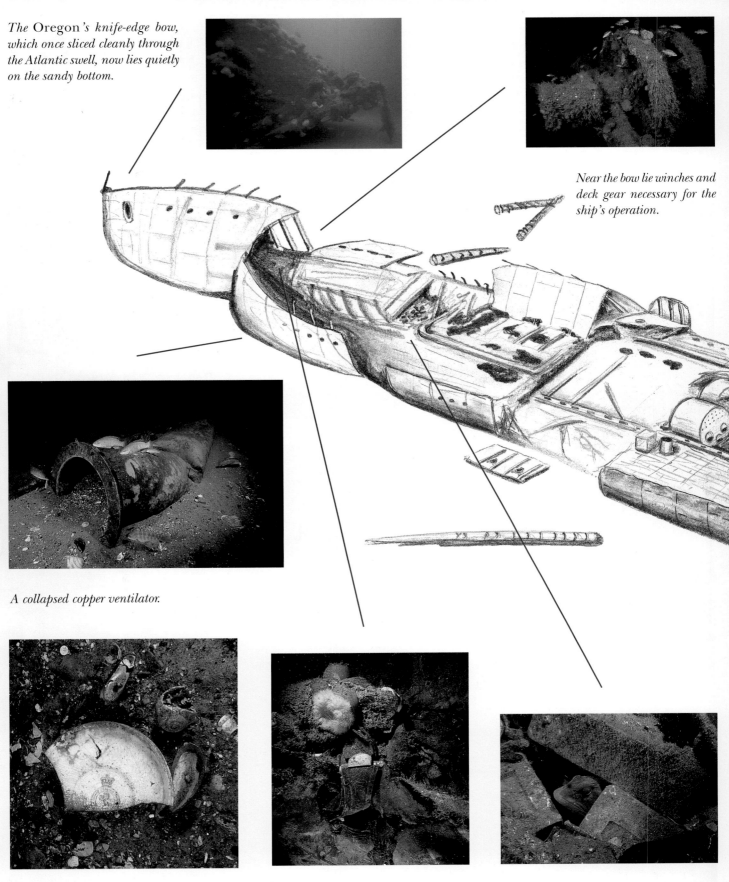

The Oregon's knife-edge bow, which once sliced cleanly through the Atlantic swell, now lies quietly on the sandy bottom.

Near the bow lie winches and deck gear necessary for the ship's operation.

A collapsed copper ventilator.

Bits of once-elegant china, bearing the Guion or Cunard crests, can still be found all over the wreck site.

Pieces of luggage are found buried in the ship's cargo holds—remnants of passengers coming to America.

An ocean pout hides among a mound of firebrick, possibly from the ship's galley.

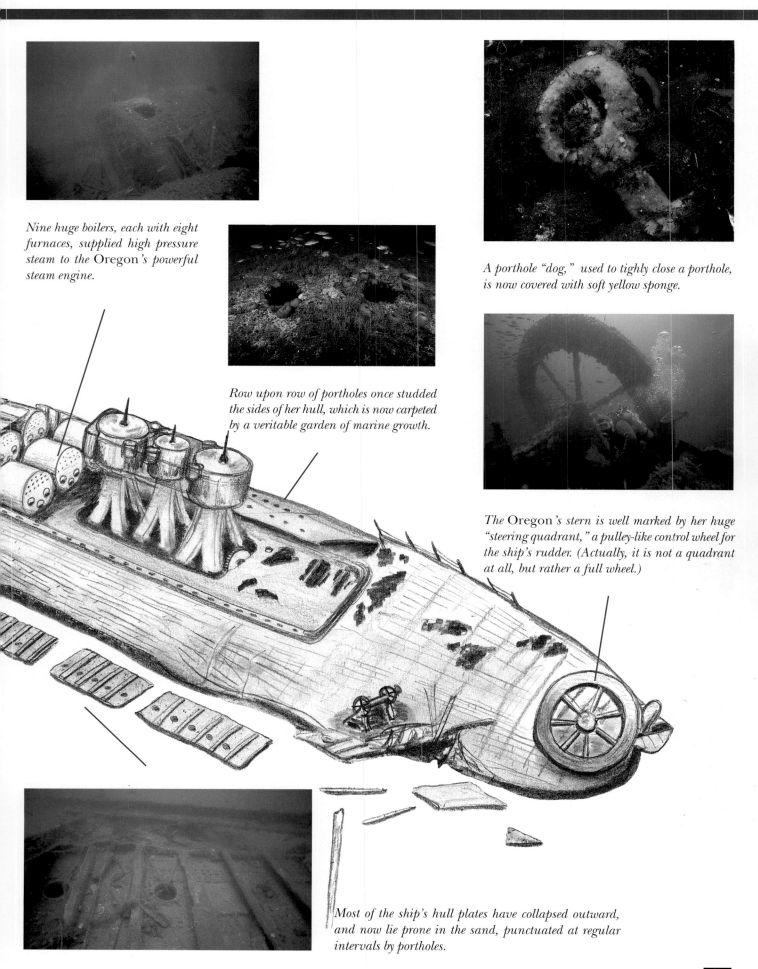

Nine huge boilers, each with eight furnaces, supplied high pressure steam to the Oregon's powerful steam engine.

A porthole "dog," used to tighly close a porthole, is now covered with soft yellow sponge.

Row upon row of portholes once studded the sides of her hull, which is now carpeted by a veritable garden of marine growth.

The Oregon's stern is well marked by her huge "steering quadrant," a pulley-like control wheel for the ship's rudder. (Actually, it is not a quadrant at all, but rather a full wheel.)

Most of the ship's hull plates have collapsed outward, and now lie prone in the sand, punctuated at regular intervals by portholes.

55

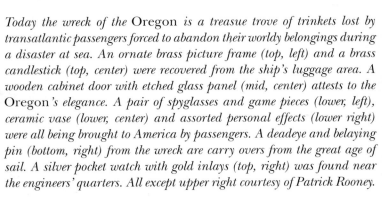

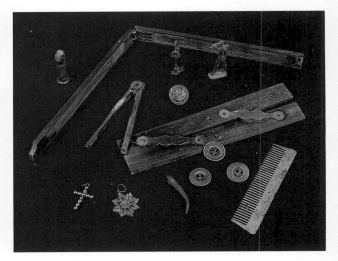

Today the wreck of the Oregon *is a treasue trove of trinkets lost by transatlantic passengers forced to abandon their worldy belongings during a disaster at sea. An ornate brass picture frame (top, left) and a brass candlestick (top, center) were recovered from the ship's luggage area. A wooden cabinet door with etched glass panel (mid, center) attests to the* Oregon's *elegance. A pair of spyglasses and game pieces (lower, left), ceramic vase (lower, center) and assorted personal effects (lower right) were all being brought to America by passengers. A deadeye and belaying pin (bottom, right) from the wreck are carry overs from the great age of sail. A silver pocket watch with gold inlays (top, right) was found near the engineers' quarters. All except upper right courtesy of Patrick Rooney.*

The *Oregon* was designed for speed. To achieve that aim, John Elder fitted her with the most powerful steam machinery afloat (at the time of her building). Her compound engine was similar to that of the *Arizona* before her, but bigger. Two low pressure cylinders, 104 inches in diameter, straddled a single high pressure cylinder 70 inches in diameter. Steam was supplied at 110 pounds per square inch (psi) by nine double-ended scotch boilers. In her trials, the *Oregon*'s engine developed 12,382 indicated horse power (ihp), driving the fast liner to average speeds of 20 knots. On her third return crossing of the Atlantic, she captured the coveted *Blue Riband* with an average speed of 18.05 knots—the *Oregon* had achieved her goal.

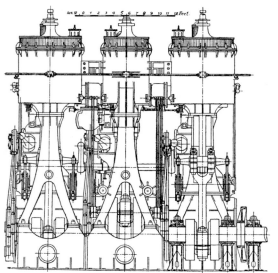

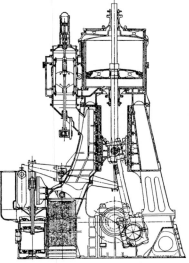

ORIGINALLY PUBLISHED IN THE MARINE ENGINEER, SEPTEMBER 1, 1881

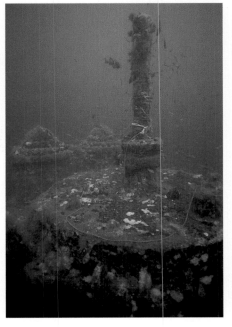

An engineering drawing (above) of the Arizona *'s compound engine—the* Oregon *'s engine was very similar, only larger. Today, the ship's mammoth engine towers over the collapsed wreckage of her hull (top, right).*

The top of one of the Oregon *'s two low pressure cylinders covered with marine growth. Note the piston tail rod protruding from the top of the cylinder, and the two steam valves in the background (middle, right).*

Steam valves were used to regulate the flow of high pressure steam into and out of the engine cylinders. The motion of these steam valves is now frozen in time—one in the down position (below, left), and one in the up position (below, center). A cylinder tail rod (below, right) is covered with mussels and fishing line.

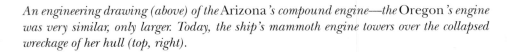

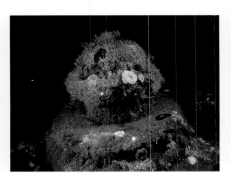

OVERLOADED WITH CORN: THE *HYLTON CASTLE*

The *Hylton Castle* was a typical nineteenth century tramp steamship designed to carry cargo economically and earn a profit for her owners. It was this desire to make a profit that led to her demise, for she was loaded with more corn than she could safely carry, and foundered in a gale south of Long Island on January 11, 1886. Her remains were rediscovered in 1958 by legendary wreck fisherman Jay Porter.[2] Built of iron plate in 1871, she was equipped with a two-cylinder compound steam engine driving an iron propeller. The high pressure cylinder measured 28 inches in diameter and the low pressure 55 inches. Steam was provided by twin boilers fed with fresh water from evaporators. The *Hylton Castle's* hull is broken up and consists largely of scattered iron hull plates and broken ribs. Her small engine is still standing upright near the stern, as are the twin boilers that supplied it with steam. Forward of the boilers are two cylindrical tanks, one standing upright and the other toppled over on its side—these were the evaporators that fed the boilers with fresh water made from salt. One of these is badly corroded, exposing what remains of its inner workings. Astern of the engine one squarish blade of the ship's iron propeller stands erect above the sand, while the oval cutout in the ship's keel that housed it can be seen lying nearby. At the bow lies a small crane or lifeboat davit, nearby a capstan and fused pile of anchor chain. Cargo winches are strewn randomly about the wreck.

A capstan, once used to raise and lower the ship's anchor, lies on its side near the bow.

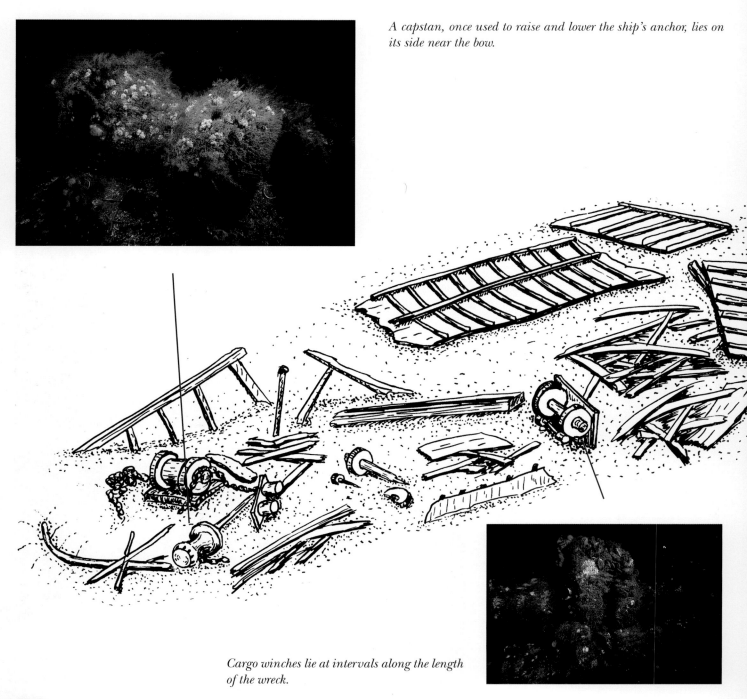

Cargo winches lie at intervals along the length of the wreck.

The tops of the engine's steam cylinders are covered with a living veil of color and often surrounded with schooling fish. Note the piston tail rod extending vertically above the steam cylinder.

Sea anemones crowding a pipe on the face of one of the boilers extend their tentacles to snare plankton.

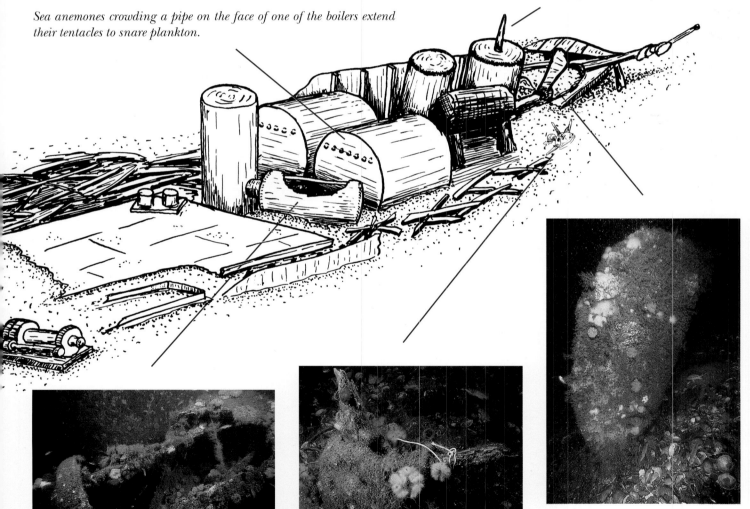

The blades of the Hylton Castle's *iron propeller are squarish in shape, typical of nineteenth century steam propellers.*

In front of the ship's boilers are the remains of two evaporators that manufactured fresh water from salt water. The outer casing of one is broken up, exposing the badly corroded interior.

The hub of the helm can still be seen along-side the engine. According to Captain John Larsen, the recovered helm stand was the key to the wreck's identification.

A DECAYING WOODEN STEAMSHIP: *KENOSHA*

The *Kenosha* was originally built as a Great Lakes ore carrier and named *Madagascar*, but was later sold, renamed and put into service along the Eastern Seaboard as a collier. In contrast to the relatively well preserved iron- and steel-hulled steamships she shares the ocean floor with, the *Kenosha*'s wooden hull has deteriorated under the severe ocean environment, leaving her hull collapsed and largely buried. A single boiler and an overturned steam engine mark her stern, along with a half-buried, square-bladed iron propeller.

The wreck's identity remained a mystery for many years, and she was known as the "Fire Island Wreck," or erroneously as the "Fire Island Lightship." The mystery was finally solved in August 1989, when diver Marc Weiss recovered a capstan cover from the wreck with the name "MADAGASCAR" emblazoned across it.

An upside-down windlass near the bow.

Sawn timber ribs, cut from the forests surrounding Saginaw Bay on Lake Huron, are all that remain of the Kenosha's *stoutly built hull.*

An ocean pout peers out curiously from a barely recognizable mound of anchor chain.

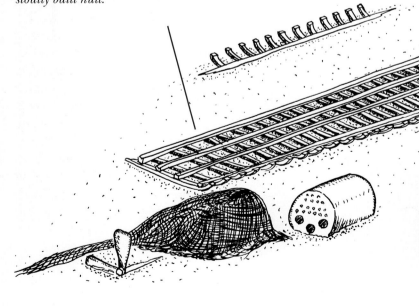

Its flukes buried in the sand, an anchor marks the location of the ship's bow.

The 152-foot long, three-masted schooner had left Baltimore on March 6th, bound for Boston with 200 tons of coal. She had sailed in company with a second schooner, the *Florence J. Allen*, which had left her on the night of the collision near where the *Oregon* had sunk. While the *Florence J. Allen* arrived in Boston two days later, ten days after the collision, the *Charles H. Morse* had still not been heard from. A full two weeks after the *Oregon*'s sinking, a steamer arriving in Philadelphia reported a sunken wreck with three masts protruding from the sea 16.5 miles southwest of the *Oregon*. Speculation soon led to the widespread belief that this was the remains of the *Charles H. Morse*, and that she was indeed the *Oregon*'s destroyer.

One month after the sinking, the Merritt Wrecking Company released a report based on examination of the wreck by a diver. The diver reported that the ship was broken in two between hatches No. 2 and 3, the result of the ship's collision with the ocean bottom. Twenty-five feet aft of where the hull was broken, on her port side, the diver found the hole that had sunk the great liner. Still covered with the canvas patch the crew had used in an attempt to stop the influx of sea water, the opening was reportedly 12 feet below the main deck and measured 6 feet long by 3.5 feet wide. The hull plates surrounding the opening bulged inward, and stretching aft of the hole were long scratches in the *Oregon*'s hull paint, which the diver reported appeared to have been made by the fluke of an anchor. For some time after the sinking, the tips of two of the *Oregon*'s four masts still protruded above the ocean's surface. While these were later cleared away, the wreck was still considered a hazard to navigation, and on April 10th the lightship *LV20* was established approximately 600 yards east of the wreck. Seven months later soundings indicated that there was at least 60 feet of water over the wreck, and the lightship was removed from its station.

The *Oregon* and her record-setting transatlantic passages would soon be forgotten as ever-faster steamships captured the public eye. The record of the *Etruria* soon fell to *Umbria*, completing the circuit of the *Blue Riband* among the three fast Cunard liners that had so briefly run alongside one another. But the *Umbria* would soon make headlines with a collision of her own.

THE END OF THE TRAMP STEAMER *IBERIA*

As the ocean greyhounds became both faster and increasingly elegant, attracting a larger share of the transatlantic passenger trade, they necessarily became more expensive to build, own and operate. These steadily rising costs could only be offset by increased revenue. What could not be made up in increased passenger volume was partly recovered by charging higher fares for cargo. Thus it became increasingly expensive to ship cargo overseas—due in part to the great rivalry among the steamship lines. A demand for cheaper ocean freight service was met by a fleet of small steamers dedicated to carrying cargo economically and with no great emphasis on speed. These small steamships had much lower operating costs than the huge ocean steamships. Their simple, functional appointments made them cheaper to build, their slower speed reduced their coal consumption per ton of cargo to less than half that of the fast liners, and they required a much smaller crew in comparison to their larger relatives. The lower overhead costs enabled these small ships to carry freight at a fraction of the cost that their rivals could, and still earn a profit.

The term "tramp" steamship was coined for small freight steamers that did not run a regular route, but rather went wherever a paying cargo took them. Such vessels worked their way from port-to-port, often circling the globe on a seemingly random, haphazard course. A tramp might be found carrying cotton or tobacco from the American south to Europe, where it might pick up a cargo of manufactured goods for transport to the Far East. Here she would do her best to pick up a cargo that would pay her way to another port of call, where she would find yet another cargo, and the cycle continued.

The French steamship *Iberia* was built in 1881 at Leith, Scotland, on the Firth of Forth for La Compagnie Francaise de Navigation a Vapeur, based in Marseilles. Rigged as a hermaphrodite brig in addition to her steam engine, the 943-ton *Iberia* measured only 254 feet long. She made a career as a tramp steamer, plodding from port to port. September 21, 1888 found her leaving the port of Busreh in the Persian Gulf, bound for New York with a cargo of coffee, dates, hides and wool. Her voyage took her through the Red Sea and into the Mediterranean by way of the 19-year-old Suez Canal, then westward until she reached the Strait of Gibraltar on October 17th. Here she finally pointed her bow into the Atlantic swell and headed for her appointment in the New World.

The *Iberia* was not a fast ship; it took her three and one-half weeks to transit the Red Sea, Suez Canal and the Mediterranean, and another three weeks to cross the same ocean that the fast passenger steamers were now crossing in less than a week. Arriving in the coastal waters outside New York Harbor (*Continued on page 64*)

NINETEENTH CENTURY TRAMP: *IBERIA*

Built at Leith on the Firth of Forth in Scotland in 1881, the *Iberia* was meant to carry cargo economically for her French owners. In this capacity, she traveled around the world in search of paying cargoes. While inbound for New York Harbor in November 1888, the *Iberia* was struck by the large Cunard liner *Umbria* in a dense fog. The tiny *Iberia* had no chance against the huge liner, which witnesses claimed cut off the last 14 feet of the tramp steamer's stern; the following day her bulkheads gave way and the *Iberia* went to the bottom only three miles off the beach. Divers soon set to work recovering her cargo for the insurance agents. Although witnesses claim that the after part of the *Iberia* was completely severed in the collision, the steamship's propeller is still attached to its shaft, along with the after part of her keel. If the *Umbria* did cut off the *Iberia*'s stern, it must have been the overhanging "counter stern" only. Except for the steamship's bow, which lists on its port side, the *Iberia* sits upright on the bottom. Her hull has almost completely collapsed after more than 100 years on the bottom, but her steam engine and boilers still stand above the wreckage.

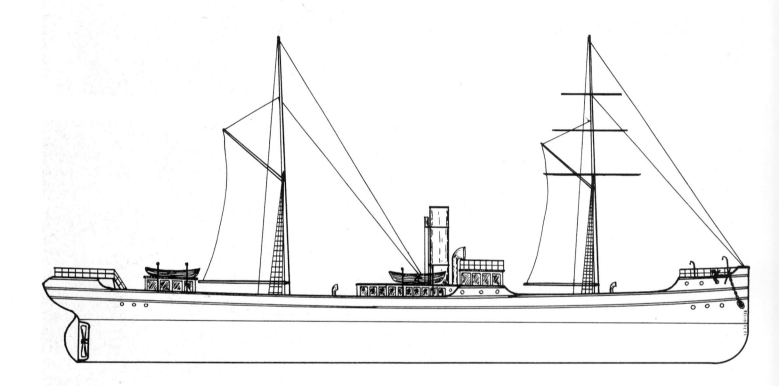

The *Iberia*'s propeller, with two blades broken off, is still attached to its shaft.

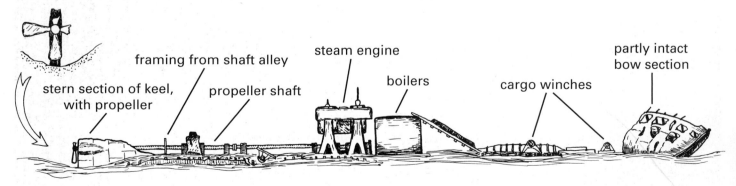

stern section of keel, with propeller

framing from shaft alley

propeller shaft

steam engine

boilers

cargo winches

partly intact bow section

A tramp steamship designed to carry cargo for profit, the *Iberia* was in no hurry to get to her destination. She was powered by a simple compound engine with one high pressure cylinder (above, right) and a single low pressure cylinder (above, left). A pair of boilers supplied steam to her engine; the boiler face is now overgrown and the boiler tubes provide homes for tiny crabs (right). Some of the *Iberia*'s cargo was salvaged by divers after she sank. But the salvors made no attempt to save the dates and coffee she carried—previous experience had proved these perishable items not worth the effort. Today, crates of dates can still be seen on the wreck, mostly buried in the sand (below, right). The frozen links of her anchor chain spill out across the sand near the ship's bow (below, left).

on the morning of November 9th, the *Iberia* dropped anchor and lay to for some 30 hours while her engineers repaired her machinery. After the repairs were completed, the *Iberia* was gotten under way once again. During the time she had been at anchor, however, a dense fog had fallen over the ocean. The *Iberia* was forced to proceed at a speed of only three and one-half knots, on a course of west-northwest, toward New York Harbor. Captain Sagois of the *Iberia* could hear the fog whistles of other vessels all around him, and ordered his ship's whistle sounded at short intervals to warn them of his presence. A passenger aboard the liner *Umbria* would later recount to the newspapers that the *Iberia*'s fog horn sounded like a "penny whistle"; indeed, it would not save the small tramp from the huge and famous Cunarder.

The *Umbria*, which had eighteen months earlier broken the *Oregon*'s record for the fastest westbound Atlantic passage (and since lost it to her sister ship, the *Etruria*), had cleared Sandy Hook just past noon on November 10th, bound for Liverpool. As she proceeded eastward a dense fog began to settle over the ocean; at ten minutes past one o'clock she was forced to slow down to half speed. Five minutes later a fog whistle which seemed to be coming from ahead on the starboard bow was heard by the *Umbria*'s captain. The big steamship was ordered slowed down even further as the whistle was heard again, this time closer. Suddenly, a small steamer materialized out of the fog ahead, cutting directly across the *Umbria*'s path. Captain McMickan ordered the Cunarder's engine full speed astern, but the momentum of the *Umbria*'s 7,798-ton hulk carried her forward and she sliced through the stern of the tiny tramp steamer. Passengers on board the *Umbria* reported seeing the last 14 feet of the *Iberia*'s stern floating away with the ship's colors still flying from the flagstaff, while the remainder of the vessel drifted away in the opposite direction.

As the *Umbria* slowly came to a stop, the steamer she had just cut in two disappeared once again into the dense fog. It took Captain McMickan a good 20 minutes to relocate the unfortunate *Iberia*, whose identity he learned only after sending an officer over to her in one of the ship's boats. The *Umbria*'s Chief engineer, upon examining the crippled vessel, declared she would float long enough to be towed into port, but recommended that the 30-man crew abandon the vessel as a precaution. Captain Sagois refused to leave his vessel, however, and the two ships spent the night anchored a short distance apart. After daybreak, Captain McMickan finally managed to persuade the *Iberia*'s crew to abandon the slowly settling hull for their own

safety. After taking them on board, the *Umbria* headed back into port.

Meanwhile, the pilot boat *Caldwell H. Colt* pulled alongside the anchored *Iberia*. Finding that the bulkheads were still holding against the sea, a salvage crew of three was put on board while the pilot boat went to fetch tugboats to tow her into port. Two tugs left for the *Iberia* that afternoon, but before they reached her the hapless ship's bulkheads gave way and she went to the bottom only three miles off Long Beach. The Merritt Wrecking Company was later hired by the National Board of Underwriters to attempt a salvage of the *Iberia*'s cargo. Divers found the little steamer relatively undamaged save her missing stern, and managed to salvage 840 bales of wool from her cargo holds over a three-month period. Several bales of hides were also brought up, but had to be thrown overboard due to the horrible stink they created. The coffee and dates were abandoned as worthless due to their submergence in salt water.

STEAMSHIPS WERE MADE OF WOOD, TOO: *KENOSHA*

Although iron, and then steel, gradually replaced wood as a shipbuilding material during the second half of the nineteenth century, it by no means eliminated the traditional shipbuilding material from use. In the mid 1800's, "Many national factors added up to the circumstance that British shipyards could build iron vessels more cheaply than wooden ones, while American yards for about half a century would continue to rely upon wood as cheaper and more readily available."[8] However, as America's seemingly endless timber resources began to slowly dwindle, suitable lumber for shipbuilding became harder to obtain and more expensive. There was also the question of mechanical strength as larger and larger ships were desired for economical shipping. "How large a structure, fit to ride out a hurricane, could be fastened together out of multitudinous sticks of wood?"[9]

The Great Lakes represented a major shipping industry that found wooden steamships in service through the end of the nineteenth century. The five lakes making up this enormous inland sea, along with the Illinois Waterway, Mississippi River, New York State barge canal and the modern St. Lawrence Seaway, form a massive interstate transportation network. Three-quarters of the iron ore found in the United States surrounds Lake Superior. These reserves and the rich coal deposits of the Allegheny mountains provided the two essential raw materials for the production of steel.

Ships built for use on the Great Lakes evolved into a distinct type, with the navigation bridge far forward and the machinery aft. The Madagascar *was later renamed* Kenosha *and put into service along the East Coast. Courtesy of the Dossin Great Lakes Museum, Detroit, MI.*

The Great Lakes provided a natural transportation "highway" linking these two resources, and formed the foundation for the American steel industry. Copper ore and limestone, also found in the region, and grain from the heartland of America, were also important cargoes for ships plying the lakes.

While there were waterways linking the lakes to the oceans, the channels connecting the lakes and rivers were of limited size, making large ships essentially land-locked until the St. Lawrence Seaway was created in the 1950's. This relative isolation from saltwater shipping, combined with the bulk cargoes carried and the unique conditions found on the lakes, provided the evolutionary force for the development of ships distinctly different from their seagoing cousins. The *R.J. Hackett*, built in Cleveland in 1869, became the model upon which subsequent Great Lakes ore boats were based. The ship's boilers and engine were placed in the extreme stern and her navigation bridge in the forecastle in the extreme bow; in between these two superstructures stretched one long, continuous cargo hold, accessed through the deck by many hatches. This large single hold facilitated loading and unloading the bulk cargoes of ore and grain she carried.

When first discovered by Europeans, the Great Lakes lay among immense stands of virgin forest. Huge timber reserves of excellent quality oak and pine stood waiting to be exploited. It was the lumber industry that gave rise to Bay City, Michigan, located on Saginaw Bay (the gap in Michigan's mitten) in Lake Huron. At the height of the trade, during the 1880's, over a *billion feet* of lumber was cut annually. First schooners and then the steamships that replaced them were invariably built of the fine timber available locally. It was perhaps ironic that the iron ore and coal feeding the nation's steel mills were carried down the lakes for years in wooden ships, but it was economical. Toward the end of the nineteenth century the Great Lakes' shipping industry underwent great change. During the 1890's the lumber trade was rapidly declining while the demand for iron ore grew tremendously. Larger and larger ships were needed for economical transport of the heavy ore, and it seemed that every ship built was larger than its predecessor. Some of the smaller, and now nearly obsolete, wooden ore boats were sold and found their way into the saltwater cargo trade. Such was the fate of the Lake steamer *Kenosha*.

The wooden-hulled steamship *Madagascar* was built in West Bay City, Michigan, on Saginaw Bay, in 1894. Built of stout Saginaw timber, she was a typical Great Lakes ore boat, with a tiny superstructure far forward, engines and deckhouse located in the stern and a great open cargo hold in between. In 1907 she was sold to the F.B. Cheseborough Company, who renamed her *Kenosha* and put her into the coastal coal trade along the Atlantic Seaboard. Although her design made the *Kenosha* well suited for her new duties, she did not last long. Bound from Baltimore to Boston with a cargo of coal, the 15-year-old ship encountered heavy weather south of Long Island on July 24, 1909. The seas were apparently more than the stoutly built ship could handle, for she sprang a leak and foundered despite all efforts to save her. There was no loss of life in the sinking, and no records of assistance rendered by either the Revenue Cutter Service or the Life-Saving Service exist—apparently the crew of the *Kenosha* made shore themselves. The value of the vessel at the time of loss was estimated at $35,000.

For years the wreck of the *Kenosha*, lying twelve miles south of the Fire Island lighthouse, was an unidentified wooden hulk commonly referred to as the "Fire Island Wreck," or mistakenly, as the *Fire Island* lightship (which never sank). On August 13, 1986, however, the wreck was correctly identified when diver Marc Weiss brought up a brass capstan cover bearing the name *Madagascar*.

RIPE FOR FIRE: LONG ISLAND SOUND STEAMBOATS— THE *LEXINGTON, GENERAL SLOCUM* AND *GLEN ISLAND*

The successful application of steam power to ocean-going ships was preceded by its use on inland vessels operating on rivers and sounds. A steamboat had the ability to easily travel upstream against a river's considerable current. This unique ability soon led to the development of steamboat lines carrying passengers and freight along the Hudson and other navigable rivers in the early and mid-1800's. In an age before the introduction of the automobile, what we now term mass transportation was virtually the only way to travel relatively long distances. The river steamboats running along the Hudson River soon expanded into the Long Island Sound, connecting New York with cities in southern New England such as Hartford, New London, Providence, Fall River and New Bedford.

The steamboats traveling these routes were derived from the river craft plying the Hudson's waters, and were very different from oceangoing steamships. Designed for calmer waters rather than the rigors of the open ocean, inland steamboats generally had low freeboard and wide, open decks that overhung their narrow hulls to nearly twice the hull's beam. Large square windows provided light and a view for the interior compartments, as opposed to the smaller, but stronger, portholes found on ocean steamers. Almost to the end of the nineteenth century they were powered by huge paddle wheels located amidships. The paddle wheels were generally driven by an overhead, walking beam engine employing a vertical steam cylinder. The diamond-shaped walking beam towered above the superstructure near the paddle wheels and could be seen rocking back-and-forth steadily when the vessel was under way. The calmer inland waters of rivers and sounds were more suited to the operation of paddle wheels than was the open ocean, and there was no drive to replace the devices with the screw propeller until late in the century. Indeed, many of these paddlewheelers could easily cruise along at nearly 20 knots, more than adequate for their owners to make a profit.

In addition to serving as coastal passenger liners, many paddle wheel steamboats found employment as excursion steamers after the Civil War. The boats would carry passengers on weekend cruises from Manhattan to vacation areas such as Coney Island, Rockaway Beach, New Rochelle or Glen Island in Long Island Sound. Even at the turn of the century it was a treat to escape the bustle of life in New York City for a weekend picnic along the shores of the Long Island Sound.

However, these inland steamboats were plagued with a remarkable propensity to catch fire. Often, flammable cargo was stored too close to the hot machinery spaces, as in the case of the *Lexington* in January 1840. Bales of cotton were stowed on deck near the smokestack and ignited while the ship was off Eaton's Neck. Built of wood, fire was a steamboat's worst enemy and in minutes the *Lexington* was burning out of control. Her pilot, Stephen Manchester, tried to run her toward shore but never made it—the tiller ropes burned through and the ship was left drifting out of control. A strong southwest wind fed the furious flames and many tried to escape in the ship's boats or by jumping overboard. In a panic bred of an innate human fear of fire, the boats were capsized upon launching, forcing their occupants to endure the same icy death as those who voluntarily jumped overboard. Of more than 100 persons aboard the *Lexington*, the only four to survive had flung bales of cotton from the cargo overboard and used them as improvised life rafts.

A steamboat's wooden construction provided ample fuel for a fire once ignited; in addition, the boats were designed with elegant accommodations, thick carpeting and luxurious wood paneling in order to better compete for passengers. All this flammable material left them ripe for devastation by fire. In June 1880, the steamer *Seawanhaka* caught fire in the East River just south of the entrance into Hell's Gate and more than 100 lost their lives. In May 1883, an exploding lamp in the engine room set fire to the Hartford Line's *Granite State,* and she burned to the waterline with the loss of four lives. In April 1884, the International Line's *Falmouth* caught fire at the pier in Portland, Maine, and was burned beyond repair. And in late December 1888, the Fall River Line's *Bristol* burned to embers at the pier in Newport.

Perhaps the most famous steamboat fire was the burning of the *General Slocum* on June 15, 1904. The 264-foot-long excursion steamer had left her pier on East Third Street about 9:00 A.M. headed for Locust Point on Long Island Sound. More than 1,300 members of the St. Mark's German Lutheran Church, many of them children, were on board the steamboat that morning for a Sunday picnic. As the *General Slocum* headed up the East River the band played a lively German hymn for the passengers. The steamer had just passed through the treacherous Hell's Gate and was

opposite the Bronx shore when the first wisps of smoke were noticed. A passing vessel saw the danger and tooted a warning on her whistle. The crew tried to fight the fire, but the wind created by the ship's motion quickly spread the flames through the old, tinder-dry wooden vessel and the firefighting equipment proved inadequate. Although only 100 yards off the Bronx shoreline, her captain, William Van Schaick, ordered the *General Slocum* beached on North Brother Island, still one-half mile away. The panic-stricken passengers fled to the ship's stern to escape the growing inferno, but the flames swept aft as well. Passengers began jumping overboard, some with their clothing ablaze. Just as the steamer came crashing ashore on North Brother Island, the burning upper decks came cascading down, trapping passengers in the flaming cauldron or throwing them into the water. Some 1,021 persons were killed in one of the worst maritime disasters in the history of the port of New York. Captain Van Schaick was sentenced to ten years in prison on charges of criminal negligence.

The Steamboat Inspection Service ordered a reinspection of every steamboat in New York Harbor two weeks after the disaster. This inspection was intended to preempt a repeat of the *Slocum* affair. The Steamboat Inspectors requested a list of operating vessels from each steamboat line and then arranged the inspections so that there would be minimal inter-

Steamboats like the Glen Island *were built for inland waterways and usually powered by paddle wheels. These wooden vessels were ripe for fire and were at the heart of a number of marine tragedies. Courtesy of The Steamship Historical Society of America.*

ference with the line's operations. A number of vessels were in the shipyard for repairs at the time and were thus reported as being out of commission. The inspectors were already overworked complying with the emergency order and concentrated on the working boats; those laid up for repairs slipped through the cracks.

Two excursion boats of the Starin Line, the *Glen Island* and the *Erastus Corning*, both escaped the emergency reinspection for this reason. The Starin Line ran its excursion steamers between Manhattan and their own amusement park located on Glen Island, just off New Rochelle on Long Island Sound. The *Glen Island*'s history is a fascinating and foreboding one.

The 239-foot-long steamboat was originally named *City of Richmond*, and was bought by the Hartford Line in 1886. Her new owners put her into service on their run from Manhattan to Hartford, on the Connecticut River. Five years later on March 5, 1891, while sitting alongside the pier in the East River, a fire began amidst a cargo of cotton bales and spread to the steamboat's superstructure. When the fire was finally brought under control there was little left but her hull and smoldering superstructure. The gutted hulk that had been the *City of Richmond* was towed to the Erie Basin in Brooklyn, where the Starin Line purchased her remains at a good price. She was completely rebuilt and given a new name—*William G. Egerton;* sometime later she was again renamed, this time *Glen Island*, after her new owner's amusement park.

On a given summer weekend hundreds of passengers were crowded aboard the decks of the Starin Line's steamers as they made their way up the East River and into Long Island Sound. But during the winter, the boats were put on night freight runs from Manhattan to New Haven. On December 17, 1904, while on the Connecticut side of Long Island Sound and east of Execution Light, the ex-*City of Richmond* caught fire once again. The flames spread quickly through her wooden superstructure. Fortunately, there were relatively few people on board, amounting to ten passengers and 21 crew; still, nine persons were lost in the fire. Had it occurred during the busy summer excursion season, the incident would likely have been a repeat of the *General Slocum* disaster.

The first sign of trouble was the sudden loss of the electric lights about midnight. Two minutes later the helm locked up and shortly thereafter the fire alarm bells sounded. As flames and dense smoke spread through the ship's superstructure and cargo it was obvious to Captain Charles MacAllister that his ship was lost. Both passengers and crew were ordered to the lifeboats with all possible haste. One of the passengers, a Mrs. Silken, was about to climb into one of the lifeboats when she suddenly remembered she had left her money in her stateroom. She insisted on returning to retrieve it, and both she and a fireman, who was later sent to search for her when she failed to return, perished in the fire below decks. Residents on both sides of Long Island Sound gathered to watch the burning spectacle, and it was reported that she burned so brightly "that it was possible to read a newspaper at Rye, possibly two miles away."[10]

One of the lifeboats began leaking profusely immediately after launching, and the occupants were forced to bail the cold seawater with their hats. It was soon discovered that the plug was missing from the drain hole in the boat's bottom and the leak was finally stopped with a handkerchief stuffed in the drain. The two lifeboats stood by the burning steamer in the hope that she would serve as a distress signal. A passing tug, the *Bully*, cast off its tow and took the cold survivors on board until the Starin Line's other steamer, the *Erastus Corning*, happened along and the passengers and crew were transferred to that boat.

Meanwhile, the burning *Glen Island* had drifted ashore on Captain's Island off Greenwich, where she burned to the waterline before the flames extinguished themselves. Later, she broke free and drifted across the Sound, finally coming to rest off Glen Cove. At high tide only the smokestack and the ship's whistle were visible. A diver was sent down to the wreck in search of bodies, but none were found.

An inquiry board later concluded that the fire was most likely caused by defective wiring in the steamboat's electrical lighting system. At that time the Steamboat Inspection Service had no provisions for inspecting electrical equipment on board vessels. The *Glen Island* affair reinforced the lesson of the *General Slocum* disaster, and two days afterward an official of the Steamboat Inspection Service had this to say: "Neither the *General Slocum* nor the *Glen Island* would be permitted to house a single human being if they were brought ashore and an attempt made to use them for that purpose. Yet they are permitted to carry upon the waters thousands of people every day when every minute there is danger of just such a catastrophe as that of the *Slocum*. It was only because the *Glen Island* had a small passenger list that the loss of life was so small, and yet in proportion to the number carried it was nearly as large as that of the *Slocum*. The *Glen Island* burned as fast as the *Slocum*, and there was just as small an opportunity for the passengers and crew to escape."[11]

4

Aground on the Beach!

Throughout history the trackless expanse of the open ocean has overwhelmed the oceangoing sailor. The largest vessel ever built is but a tiny speck upon this colossal wilderness. On a clear, calm, sun-drenched day far from shore the ocean presents us with a peaceful facade; her surface appears as a smooth, flat plane stretching seemingly to infinity. This perception of the enormity of the ocean seems to magnify the insignificance we feel as human beings— it makes us feel *small*. Yet, as powerful as this feeling of inconsequence is, it provides only a vague recognition, a tiny awareness, of the raw power hiding beneath the ocean's calm. Men who have ventured far from shore for any length of time inevitably learn her true capabilities and those who have experienced her full fury have come to both fear and respect her.

In the face of the enormous power wielded by the ocean, man has slowly learned how to build ships so that they might survive the tempests. He has crafted stout vessels that are at home on the surface of the open ocean, far from land, in their intended domain. The men who entrust their very existence to these rugged ships are well aware of their crafts' abilities, as well as their liabilities, and although they rightfully fear the sea, what terrorizes them most is the land. For while the open ocean has taken many vessels, it is the terrible cauldron of destructive energy at the interface of land and sea that has consumed most ships.

It is a curious irony that during a violent storm the safest place for a ship is as far from land as possible. Heavy weather often reduces a ship's ability to maneuver. The more ferocious storms can leave a vessel at nature's mercy, drifting out of control before the wind and sea. The worst possible place for a ship to be during heavy weather is off a lee shore. (A lee shore is one downwind of a ship, hence the action of the wind tends to blow the vessel towards shore.) This was particularly true of sailing vessels during the nineteenth century. Unable to sail well, if at all, to windward, these ships found it difficult or impossible to make headway into a gale. If that gale was blowing them towards the beach, it often spelled disaster. By necessity, shipping routes bring vessels into close proximity with the shoreline, and hence closer to danger.

To gain entrance into the large, well-sheltered port of New York, a ship had to travel along either of two treacherous stretches of coastline. Traveling northward, ships paralleled the barrier islands along the coast of New Jersey, while ships coming from Boston and points north, or coming from Europe, were forced to round Montauk Point at Long Island's eastern end and sail along some 100 miles of desolate beach. Both coastlines took their share of ships.

Long Island's southern shore is characterized by a series of long, narrow, low-lying barrier islands running parallel to the mainland. Only a few hundred yards wide and ten to twenty feet high, these strips of wind-swept sand dunes are held together by an assortment of beach grasses, sea oats and scrub pine. During the nineteenth century the islands were sparsely inhabited, and the closest civilization lay on the mainland to the north, across a series of wide bays and salt marshes. Offshore, a few hundred yards to seaward and running parallel to the barrier islands lies a series of constantly shifting sand bars. On a dark night or during a storm, the islands were nearly invisible from seaward, and often a ship's first sign of danger was the sound of the surf breaking on the beach. It is hard to envision a better ship trap.

And trap ships is just what these beaches did. At least 300 ships are known to have run aground along the south shore of Long Island, from Rockaway Point to Montauk Point, during the nineteenth century, which equates to an average of three wrecks per mile. There were undoubtedly many other wrecks whose histories remain obscure. Just imagine the sight if all these weathered hulks were still visible today—a ghostly fleet of beached ships lined up along Long Island's southern shore. This is not so far from what a visitor to Fire Island would have found (Continued on page 72)

AGROUND ON THE BEACH

Long Island's sandy southern beaches have proved an incredibly efficient "ship trap" over the years. The low-lying barrier islands have snared hundreds upon hundreds of ships in their deadly embrace. The crews of these stranded vessels often found themselves helpless in the face of a raging winter gale, and loss of life was common. The loss of both ships and men became such a problem that a series of life-saving stations was established along the Long Island coast and most of the Atlantic Seaboard in the latter part of the nineteenth century. Shown here is a selection of ships that were stranded and/or lost along the southern beaches during the nineteenth and early twentieth centuries, along with the stations of the United States Life-Saving Service. The wrecks shown are only a partial listing; there were hundreds more documented wrecks, as well as many undocumented ones. Note that the wreck locations are approximate. Early records are often incomplete and imprecise, and the sheer number of wrecks shown cannot be plotted with any accuracy due to space limitations alone.

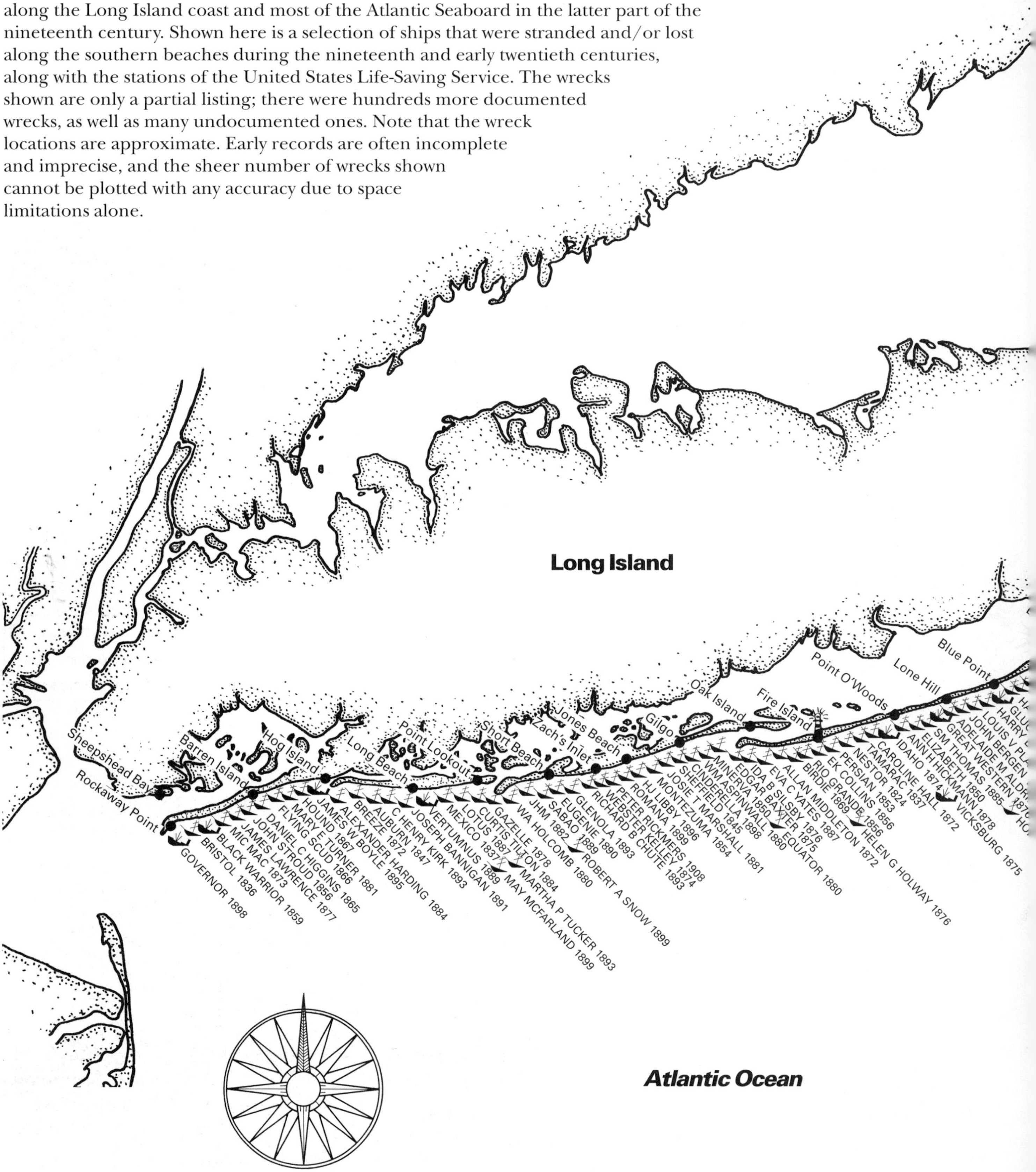

Long Island

Atlantic Ocean

Blue Point

Lone Hill

Point O'Woods

Oak Island

Fire Island

Gilgo

Jones Beach

Zach's Inlet

Short Beach

Point Lookout

Long Beach

Hog Island

Barren Island

Sheepshead Bay

Rockaway Point

GOVERNOR 1836
BRISTOL 1836
BLACK WARRIOR 1859
MIC MAC 1873
JAMES LAWRENCE
JOHN STROUD 1873
DANIEL COLLINS
FLYING SCUD 1856
MARY E HIGGINS 1877
HOUND 1865
JAMES W BOYLE 1867
ALEXANDER 1881
BREEZE 1872
AUBURN HARDING 1895
C HENRY KIRK 1893
JOSEPH BANNIGAN 1884
VERTUMNUS 1847
LOTUS 1887
MEXICO 1889
CURTIS TILTON 1891
GAZELLE 1878
JHN 1882
WA HOLCOMB 1884
MARTHA P TUCKER 1893
MAY MCFARLAND 1899
SABAO 1889
EUGENIE 1880
GLENOLA 1890
RICHARD B CHUTE 1893
HJ LIBBY 1896
WEBSTER B KELLEY
ROMANA 1899
PETER RICKMERS 1908
MONTEZUMA 1874
JOSIE T MARSHALL 1854
ROBERT A SNOW 1899
CINDERELLA 1845
SHEFFIELD 1881
WM ASPINWALL 1898
MINERVA 1850
EDGAR BAXTER 1880
EIA C YATES 1875
EDA B SILSBY 1876
ALLAN MIDDLETON 1872
EQUATOR 1880
RIO GRANDE 1869
BIRDIE 1887
EK COLLINS 1872
PERSIAN 1853
NESTOR 1824
TAMARAC 1856
HELEN G HOLWAY 1872
CAROLINE 1856
IDAHO 1878
ANN HICKMANN 1872
ELIZABETH 1850
SM THOMAS 1885
GREAT WESTERN
ADELAIDE M ALDRICH
LOUIS V PL...
JOHN BERGEN 1870
HARRY L ...
VICKSBURG 1875
H...

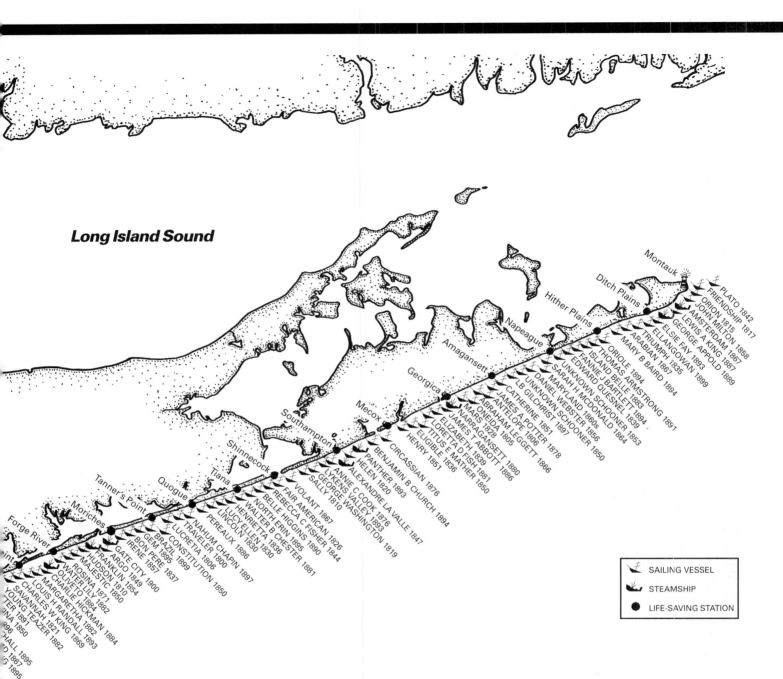

The German ship Peter Rickmers *was driven ashore at Zach's Inlet by a heavy storm on April 30, 1908. Wreckers attempted to salvage the ship and her cargo of kerosene and crude oil, carried in 5-gallon cans, but the* Rickmers *was a total loss. Much of the cargo was thrown overboard, while some was salvaged—both by wrecking crews and local inhabitants. The cans were shipped in wooden crates, and at least one barn was reportedly shingled with wood from the crates. It was a long time before the local inhabitants had to purchase kerosene again. Courtesy of The Mariners' Museum, Newport News, Virginia.*

Above: The bark Hougomont *was stranded on Fire Island on February 7, 1915. Shown here with sails set, she was later pulled off the beach. Courtesy of the Long Island Maritime Museum, West Sayville, NY.*

Left: The four-masted schooner Bessie A. White *came ashore one-half mile west of Smith's Point on February 6, 1922. A storm uncovered what may have been her remains in 1987. Courtesy of the Long Island Maritime Museum, West Sayville, NY.*

at the turn of the century, when broken wooden hulks lay scattered along the base of the dunes. Some would have been newly beached, intact in form and still bearing vestiges of paint, while others would be bleached wooden ribs, half buried by decades of shifting sands. The vast majority of these wrecks were sailing vessels— schooners, brigs, brigantines, barks and sloops—that had fallen victim to the great ship trap. But rusting iron steamers lay in the surf line as well, long defying the destructive power of the breakers. While many of these grounded ships were pulled off and refloated by wrecking crews, an equal number became total wrecks. Their backs broken by the relentless surf, they were abandoned and left for the sea to dismantle.

Aground and helplessly caught in a winter storm's pounding breakers, the human crews of these vessels often found themselves stranded only a few hundred yards from the safety of the beach. Inexperienced at handling a small boat in the breaking surf, these men were often unable to escape their ships for the dry land only a stone's throw away. For those lucky enough to reach shore, there remained the challenge of survival on the sparsely inhabited islands. Low-lying sand

dunes carpeted with razor-sharp grasses and tightly knit, wind-sculpted shrubs provided little shelter from the biting cold winds of a winter storm. After struggling ashore through mountainous breakers, it was all too easy for the salt-drenched and exhausted men to perish from exposure.

During the first half of the nineteenth century, most of those who did survive shipwrecks along the south shore owed their lives to the few local inhabitants who had made their homes along the beach. Mostly fishermen, the residents were experts at handling small boats in the surf, and out of human compassion, lent a helping hand to those unfortunates cast upon the shore. There was, of course, also the prospect of material gain surrounding such wrecks. As the sea tore these ships apart and spit their remains up on the beach, their valuable cargoes lay prey to the many local inhabitants who literally made a living collecting these spoils, or at least supplemented their otherwise meager incomes. Local legend along the outer islands claims that many of the older beach houses are partly built from the timbers of such wrecks. Shipwrecks also provided a source of employment for local surfmen, who were often hired as wreckers by salvage companies who needed a few extra hands to extricate a grounded ship or salvage her cargo.

There are also darker stories concerning the locals that have persisted over the years. Exactly how often the line was crossed between wishing a ship would come ashore and attempting to lure one to its death is largely speculation, but stories of just such occurrences have persisted all along the Atlantic Coast. Nags Head, on the Outer Banks of North Carolina, supposedly takes its name from the legendary practice of hanging a lantern around a horse's head. The horse was marched up and down the beach and the bobbing lantern was supposed to appear as another ship when seen from seaward, misleading sailors into believing that they were a safe distance from shore. There are stories of "Barnegat pirates" who lured ships ashore along the coast of New Jersey, and Long Island has its own tales of treachery as well. One explanation often given for the origin of the name "Fire Island" is the fabled custom of building fires on the beach to lure ships to their doom. While there is undoubtedly some truth to these stories, it is likely that they have been largely exaggerated over the years. For the most part, the local inhabitants were honorable, courageous men who often risked their lives to save those stranded off the beach. There has always been a kind of kinship among those who make their living by the sea and the rescuers knew very well that they could be the rescued tomorrow.

THE UNITED STATES LIFE-SAVING SERVICE

With the increase in traffic caused by the boom in American merchant shipping, there was a corresponding increase in the number of shipwrecks. As the nineteenth century progressed, the sight of grounded ships along the south shore of Long Island became more and more common. While most were sailing vessels, blown ashore or grounded in fog and snowstorms, the "modern" steamship was far from immune to the same fate. Occasionally such wrecks were accompanied by terrible loss of life, and this invariably caught the public's attention. In 1847, the newly elected Congressional Representative of New Jersey, Doctor William A. Newell, personally witnessed the terrible wreck of the Austrian brig *Terasto* on the Jersey shore. Thirteen of her crew perished during the winter storm that destroyed the vessel. Doctor Newell was so moved by the plight of the poor crew that he persuaded Congress to enact a bill authorizing $10,000 for the con-

struction and equipping of eight life-saving stations along the coast of his district.

In 1849, the Life-Saving Benevolent Association of New York was incorporated in the Legislature of New York and successfully lobbied Congress for a similar appropriation to establish stations along Long Island's coast. The result of the two Congressional bills was a series of twenty-four life-saving stations, spaced approximately ten miles apart, along the Long Island and New Jersey shorelines. Ten stations were built on Long Island, located at Eaton's Neck and Fisher's Island on Long Island Sound, and Amagansett, Bridgehampton (Mecox), Quogue, Moriches, Mastic (Bellport), Fire Island, Long Beach, and Barren Island (Rockaway) along the south shore.

At first the stations were manned entirely by volunteers, and a local resident was entrusted with overseeing both the station and its equipment. But the residents of the barrier islands had more than enough of their own chores to do, and as a result the equipment often deteriorated badly for lack of maintenance. In addition, the stations being on average some ten miles apart, left a long stretch of beach to be covered by a single all-volunteer crew. Ships and lives continued to be lost.

In April 1854, the ship *Powhattan* was wrecked on the New Jersey coast, resulting in 354 lives lost. This disaster helped prompt Congress to appropriate more funds for additional life-saving stations and provided for salaried officials. Two superintendents, to be paid $1,500 per year, were appointed to supervise life-saving operations along the two coasts. In addition, each station was assigned a full-time keeper, to be paid an annual salary of $200. Although the station crews continued to be all volunteer, a true organization was beginning to emerge.

With the funds provided by the appropriation of 1854, fourteen new stations were established on Long Island, as well as additional stations on the New Jersey coast, bringing the total number along the two coasts to 56. The new Long Island stations were located at Montauk Point, Ditch Plains, Napeague, Georgica, Shinnecock, Petunk, Smith's Point, Blue Point, Lone Hill, Point O'Woods, Oak Island, Zach's Inlet, Rockaway Point, and Sheepshead Bay. The average distance between stations was narrowed to approximately five miles—a much more manageable stretch of beach to be covered by a single station.

In 1871, $200,000 was appropriated to establish permanent paid crews during the stormy months of the year. Each station was to have a resident crew consisting of a keeper and six surfmen (a seventh was added in 1885). Regular drills with both surfboat and breeches buoy were begun, and nightly beach patrols between stations were instituted to ensure the earliest possible discovery of wrecks. In 1875, Congress passed a bill requiring detailed records to be kept of the stations' activities. Finally, in 1878, the United States Life-Saving Service (U.S.L.S.S.) was formally established as a separate entity, to be headed by Sumner I. Kimball. While the already established United States Revenue Cutter Service patrolled the offshore waters, the new United States Life-Saving Service would patrol the beaches.

THE STATIONS

The original stations consisted of two-story wooden buildings designed to house the surfboat and life-saving gear provided by Congress. In essence, each was a boathouse with living quarters for the surfmen. The stations were set back into the dunes far enough to provide some protection from surf and storm, yet near enough to the ocean to allow the men to watch for wrecks. A lookout tower was provided on top of each boathouse to facilitate searching the long stretch of desolate beach assigned to each station. A government standard "Francis" galvanized iron lifeboat was furnished to each station, as well as a wagon for transporting the boat along the beach to the scene of a wreck. A host of other equipment was supplied as well: a mortar and shot for throwing lines; manila hawser, shot line and coiling frame; assorted blocks, shovels,

Life-saving stations were established along the beach approximately five miles apart. A typical station included a lookout tower to watch for wrecks, a boathouse for the surfboat, and quarters for the crew. Courtesy of Harry Huson.

OLD COAST GUARD STA., DESTROYED IN 1938 HURRICANE

lanterns, and axes; as well as a stove and fuel for the boathouse. The first floor of the station was for the lifeboat and equipment storage, and had a mess room for the men; the second floor provided sleeping quarters.

Once a wreck was sighted there were two means of rendering assistance. The most obvious method, and the one preferred if conditions permitted, was to launch the surfboat and row directly out to the stranded ship. The passengers and crew could then be taken off and transported to shore. The station crews were expert surfmen, and they trained often in the complex art of launching and landing small boats through heavy surf. Quite often, however, the very conditions that brought a ship ashore made it impossible to launch the small boats and another method of rescue was needed.

Mortars were used along the English coast as early as 1791 to fire lines out to stranded vessels. This same technique was adopted along the United States coast after some experimentation. The original appropriations made by Congress provided funds for supplying "rockets, surfboats and carronades"[1] to the new stations of the Life-Saving Service. The idea was to use either a rocket or mortar (carronade) to fire a light line across the rigging of the stranded vessel. Once this contact with the ship was established, a system of heavier lines and pulleys, resembling an endless clothesline, was stretched taut between the ship and shore. A breeches buoy or lifecar could then be used to evacuate the passengers and crew of the vessel, one by one. A breeches buoy was nothing more than a cork ring buoy with a pair of canvas trousers attached, suspended from a pulley. The occupant would literally sit in the pair of trousers, clinging to the ring buoy that now encircled his waist, while the life-saving crew pulled him along the "clothesline" to the safety of the beach. A lifecar was used in really heavy weather, and consisted of a covered iron surfboat that was suspended from the "clothesline" and used in the same fashion as the breeches buoy. A hatch in the top of the closed boat allowed several passengers at once to enter the device, where they would be protected from the seas during their short journey to the beach. Simple and ingenious means of rescue, both the breeches buoy and the lifecar were responsible for saving many lives. Getting that first line out to the stranded ship, however, was a rather tricky operation.

One of the earliest problems encountered was that the line constantly broke at the instant of firing, right at the attachment to the projectile. This problem was finally overcome when it was discovered that a spring-

A surfboat makes its way out to the North German Lloyd liner Prinzess Irene, *which came ashore near Lone Hill on April 6, 1911. At lower right a second boat is ready for launching by the crew of the life-saving station. Courtesy of the Long Island Maritime Museum, West Sayville, NY.*

The breeches buoy was put into action when the freighter Vincenzo Bonanno *came ashore with a cargo of lemons on June 17, 1906, off Point O'Woods. To the delight of the local residents, the jettisoned cargo was strewn along the beach for miles. Courtesy of the Long Island Maritime Museum, West Sayville, NY.*

like coil of wire, placed between the mortar shot and the line, acted as a sort of shock absorber and prevented the line from parting. Conditions during rescues were often extremely windy, with gale force winds or worse, and allowance for windage had to be made while aiming the mortar. Often, it took many attempts before the line was successfully put across the ship's rigging. During winter rescues, blinding snowstorms made it a challenge just to see the ship off the beach and take aim, while freezing temperatures made working the tackle both painful and difficult. Despite the difficulties associated with using both the breeches buoy and the surfboat, they were to prove indispensable. From 1850 to 1870, before accurate records were kept by the station crews, 272 vessels are known to have wrecked on the New Jersey and Long Island shores, and 4,163 lives were saved. From 1871 through 1914, when Congress mandated that official records be kept at each of the life-saving stations, 178,741 persons were assisted by the U.S. Life-Saving Service.

THE WRECK OF THE BARK ELIZABETH

One of the first shipwrecks to occur on the Long Island coastline after the life-saving stations were established was that of the three-masted bark *Elizabeth*. The *Elizabeth* had left Leghorn, Italy under the command of Captain Hasty in May 1850, bound for the United States. In the *Elizabeth*'s cargo hold was a huge marble statue of the famous South Carolina Senator John C. Calhoun, while in her passenger accommodations was the equally famous Margaret Fuller. Margaret Fuller was one of the first outspoken advocates of women's rights, as well as a writer and past literary critic for the New York *Tribune*. Mrs. Fuller and her Italian husband, Count Giovanni Ossoli, along with their young son Angelino, had chosen the *Elizabeth* on which to make their journey to America. In an ominous sign two days after sailing, Captain Hasty fell ill with confluent smallpox and expired before the *Elizabeth* reached Gibraltar. Only after being quarantined for a week by the local authorities, with no further outbreak of the dreaded disease, was the ship allowed to set sail for America under the command of the former first mate, Mr. Bangs.

Two days after setting sail for America Margaret's son, Angelino, came down with the dreaded disease that had cost Captain Hasty his life. For seven long days Angelino suffered while under the constant care of his mother. Finally, nine days out from Gibraltar, Margaret's son began to recover from his brush with smallpox. Relieved by her son's improving health, Mrs. Fuller was able to relax and enjoy the pleasant weather that blessed the remainder of the voyage. As the *Elizabeth* approached the coast of the New World on July 18, Mr. Bangs announced to the ship's five passengers that they would dock in New York the following morning. But by 9:00 P.M. the wind had increased to gale force, and it appeared that Mother Nature had another plan in mind.

Depth soundings showed only 21 fathoms under the ship's keel; still, Mr. Bangs retired to his cabin, believing there was little danger of grounding on the New Jersey coast. Although the wind, which was now approaching hurricane force, had been driving the *Elizabeth* steadily northward, Mr. Bangs showed little concern for the dreaded sand bars along the Long Island shore. At 3:30 A.M. on July 19, however, the passengers were thrown from their bunks as the wooden bark grounded hard on the outer bar off Fire Island, near Point O'Woods.

By daybreak a considerable crowd had gathered on the beach opposite the wreck, but mysteriously no attempt was made to rescue those stranded on board. There was a new life-saving station nearby that was equipped with a sturdy iron surfboat, but there was no regular crew to man it. Unaware of this situation, two sailors on board the *Elizabeth* decided to brave the heavy surf in an attempt to obtain help. Since the ship's boats had been lost or smashed to pieces, one of the men jumped in clinging to a life preserver while the other rode the waves on a spar. Those on board the *Elizabeth* watched their progress intently, and were temporarily encouraged when the men eventually reached the beach. Next to try was a passenger, Horace Sumner, who grabbed a plank and jumped into the sea. The spirits of those watching were quickly doused, however, as Sumner was lost in the churning sea almost immediately.

After a time, the officers urged the remaining passengers to abandon the *Elizabeth*, arguing that their only chance for survival lay in making their own way to shore. The crew built makeshift "lifeboats" by attaching rope handles to heavy wooden planks, but the passengers were frightened and refused to leave the ship. Finally Mrs. Hasty, the former captain's wife, and Davis, the second mate, grabbed one of the planks and gave it a try. They endured a long struggle through cold, tempestuous seas, and finally managed to reach the beach safely. Despite their success, Margaret Fuller and the other passengers steadfastly refused to attempt the only escape available. Mr. Bangs offered to take young Angelino ashore himself, (*Continued on page 81*)

LONG ISLAND'S TREACHEROUS SOUTHERN BEACHES

Lighthouses were often erected along hazardous shorelines to warn shipping traffic of danger. Long Island has operated its share of lighthouses over the years, the two largest and most famous located at Montauk Point and Fire Island Inlet. Montauk Point thrusts its rocky finger out into the Atlantic and has claimed many wrecked ships. The lighthouse at Montauk Point (above, left) was authorized by President George Washington in January 1796, and was originally located some 300 feet from the edge of the cliff. Today, severe erosion has moved the face of the cliff more than halfway to the lighthouse, endangering the old structure. This important navigational aid still serves as a beacon, lighting the way for shipping through the worst storms.

The lighthouse at Fire Island Inlet was originally erected at the extreme western end of the barrier island known variously as the Great South Beach or Fire Island. A long, low-lying stretch of sand dunes covered with beach grass and scrub pines, the island was both inhospitable and treacherous to coastal shipping traffic. The lighthouse (above, right) was built to help guide shipping along the dangerous shoreline, and was in operation by late 1826; one of the original ten life-saving stations established on Long Island was located adjacent to the lighthouse and was appropriately designated Fire Island Station. Over the past 150 years, the inlet has migrated westward and the lighthouse now lies some five miles from the inlet. The lighthouse was extinguished in 1974 and fell into disrepair, but has since been refurbished and relit, and is now part of the Fire Island National Seashore.

Today, Fire Island is a summer playground for young and old alike. Her sandy ocean beaches rank among the finest in the world and modern access draws visitors by the thousands. The island is dotted with tiny communities of beach houses, while the remainder is made up of two parks and the Fire Island National Seashore. Within the National Seashore lies a seven-mile stretch that is New York State's only designated wilderness area. Many of the communities can trace their histories back to the nineteenth century, and some of the older houses are said to be partly constructed of timbers from ships that came ashore and wrecked. Huge driftwood timbers are constantly found along these beaches; most are probably just modern driftwood, but a visitor can't help but wonder if an occasional piece may be from an old shipwreck (right)—note the "scarf" in the end of the timber.

Long Buried Shipwrecks Exposed by Winter Storms

The number of ships that have wrecked along Fire Island's ocean beaches and sand bars is almost countless. The lucky ones sustained little damage, and were unloaded and hauled off the beach and returned to service; most became total wrecks, however, and were left to be dismantled by the sea. The constantly shifting sands of this barrier island quickly covered what was not totally destroyed by the ocean, creating a time capsule for future discovery. Today, it is a rare occurrence when a ship comes ashore along these beaches, yet the furious winter storms that have pummeled the region for centuries continue. From time to time, these storms uncover the bones of an old ship, and for a short time we can see and touch a piece of history. Before long, however, the relentless ocean quickly buries the past once again.

A tremendous nor'easter in December 1992 uncovered a series of old ships along the Great South Beach. At the Fire Island Pines, near the site of the old Lone Hill Life-Saving Station, the storm cut deeply into the dune, exposing this old ship (above, left) as well as toppling beach houses. Iron drift pins can be seen securing knees, ribs and hull planking (above, right). The same nor'easter uncovered the remains of another ship at Water Island (left) near the site of the old Blue Point Life-Saving Station, as well as a third in the wilderness area of the Fire Island National Seashore (below), not far from the old Bellport Life-Saving Station.

Later in the spring of 1992 a series of storms continued the work of the December nor'easter. In early April the bow section of this wooden ship washed ashore at Jones Beach (right). Photo by Henry Keatts.

A portion of the hull of what was likely a small coast schooner washed ashore at Robert Moses Park, at the western end of Fire Island later that same month (middle, left). Two iron chainplates that once secured deadeyes to the hull were still fastened to the ship's outer planking.

Sometimes single timbers are found on the beach that may or may not be from old ships, such as this one that washed ashore at Smith's Point (middle, right, with Joe Gallo). This may be part of a deck support beam.

In October 1995, yet another section of wooden ship was freed from the sand dunes at Robert Moses Park (right). The upside-down section of hull clearly revealed the keel, outer hull planking, and numerous ribs and floor timbers. Succeeding storms quickly tore those remains apart and scattered the timbers.

SCATTERED REMNANTS OF BROKEN SHIPS

This needlelike marble monument (above) was erected in East Hampton to honor the men lost aboard the ship John Milton *off Montauk in 1858. Signs of shipwreck are often subtle, like these bits of coal collected along a quarter-mile stretch of beach near East Hampton (left), undoubtedly washed ashore from the wreck of an old steamship. Wreckage from ships washed ashore has been collected and put to use by local inhabitants for centuries; today it is often used for decorative purposes, such as this ship's rudder displayed on a local resident's lawn in Moriches (below).*

Remnants of Long Island's maritime heritage lie scattered everywhere. In Patchogue, eight stones memorialize the men who died (and one who survived) aboard the schooner Louis V. Place *in 1895 (below, top). Only four men are actually buried there, however—Captain Squires is buried in Southold (below, bottom), John Horton's body was never found, Soren Nelson died in a hospital in Brooklyn and was buried locally, and Claus Stuvens was the lone survivor of the ordeal.*

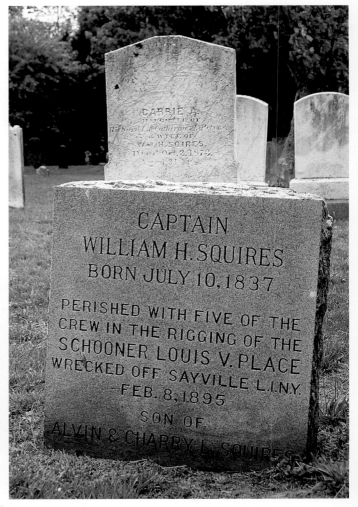

The four-masted bark Clan Galbraith *came aground near Shinnecock, Long Island, on July 22, 1916. Surfboats and onlookers can be seen on the beach. The ship was later refloated. Courtesy of the Long Island Maritime Museum, West Sayville, NY.*

The Lady Napier *came ashore at Sandy Hook, New Jersey, November 30, 1907. At the extreme right the Sandy Hook lighthouse is visible—apparently ineffective as far as the* Napier*'s captain was concerned. Courtesy of the Long Island Maritime Museum, West Sayville, NY.*

but Margaret would not allow it. His patience exhausted, Bangs finally declared that it was every man for himself, and he and the majority of the crew left the ship. Left remaining on board the *Elizabeth* were four passengers and four of the crew who also refused to leave.

That afternoon the ship began to break up. One of the sailors was finally able to convince Mrs. Fuller to part with Angelino, but just as he scooped him up in preparation for making his way to the beach, a huge sea swept over the ship's decks, carrying everyone into the surf. There was a brief struggle, but there would be no more survivors from the *Elizabeth*. Shortly after-

wards the bodies of Angelino and the steward were washed up on the dunes of Fire Island; Margaret Fuller and her husband were among the missing.

THE STEAMSHIP *FRANKLIN*

While the majority of ships that stranded on the beach were sailing vessels, occasionally steamships met the same fate. During the transition from sail to steam in the mid- and late nineteenth century, many vessels could qualify as either. The SS *Franklin* was built in 1850 for the New York and Havre Steam Navigation

Company, and had cost her new owners $310,000. The 263-foot-long vessel was rigged with three masts and a full complement of sails, as well as a set of paddle wheels driven by an auxiliary steam engine. Designed for the booming transatlantic trade in mails, cargo and passengers, she was built with a sleek bow that boasted a full-height figurehead of her famous namesake, Benjamin Franklin.

She had left the port of Havre, France in July 1854, packed with foreign mail and one-half million dollars worth of assorted cargo, as well as 150 passengers and a crew of 50. Among the many passengers on board was the widow of Commodore Issac Hull, late commander of the United States warship *Constitution*. The *Franklin*, under the command of Captain James Wooten, made the Atlantic crossing in a respectable 12 days before running into trouble. Caught unawares by a thick fog opposite Center Moriches, the *Franklin* grounded one-half mile west of present day Moriches Inlet on July 17th. A heavy surf was running and threatened to pound the steamer to pieces. Captain Wooten dropped three anchors in an attempt to hold her, but the chains let go and the *Franklin* soon found herself stuck fast on the bar.

The steamship *Leviathan*, on her way to New York, passed close enough to see the *Franklin*'s predicament and soon notified the authorities. Meanwhile, Captain Wooten fired guns to summon the local inhabitants

On September 8, 1934, the Ward Line steamer Morro Castle *caught fire off New Jersey. While under tow during rough seas, the towline broke and she came ashore at Asbury Park. There were 134 casualties resulting from the accident. Curious onlookers flocked to the beach to see the grounded liner. Courtesy of The Steamship Historical Society of America.*

to the ship's aid. Crossing Moriches Bay by small boat, the alerted residents soon arrived at the scene of the latest wreck on their shore. There was little these spectators could do, however, other than help pull passengers and boats out of the surf and up onto the beach. The *Franklin* herself was lying broadside to the beach and was taking a pounding from the rough seas. Of the 200 persons on board, 190 were safely evacuated, while 10 perished in the rough surf. The survivors were transported across the bay by boat to the mainland, where they were lodged overnight in Mr. J. H. Bishop's boarding house.

The following day three steam tugs and two sloops were dispatched from New York to assist the grounded *Franklin*. The seas were running too high to make a salvage attempt, however, and when the ocean finally subsided several days later there was little they could do. The *Franklin* lay so close to the beach that at low tide it was possible to unload much of her cargo by cart and wagon, and nearly all of it was saved over a period of several weeks. The ship herself was given up as a total loss and abandoned on the beach. Her figurehead was rescued by Thomas Conklin, a resident of Bellport, who was employed as a diver during the salvage operations. The figurehead was sold to Emmett J. Howell after Conklin's death, and stood on his front lawn opposite the Bellport Episcopal Church for years. It was later moved to the city of Philadelphia, and finally ended up in a private collection in Small Point, Maine.

The *Franklin* herself remained just off the beach and was still visible for over a century. During World War II, army pilots used her hulk for target practice, pummeling her with machine gun fire during training exercises. Part of the engine was still exposed at high tide until December 1952, when it finally succumbed to a storm and disappeared from sight. Lying so close to Moriches Inlet, however, the wreck remained a serious menace to navigation. In October 1956, a team of Navy demolition divers blasted the wreck in an attempt to clear her. The job wasn't finished until 1979, however, when another team of divers blasted away the remains of the old steamship's boilers, and the wreck symbol marking the final resting place of the steamship *Franklin* was finally removed from NOAA's charts.

THE BITTER COLD FATE OF THE SHIP *JOHN MILTON*

While nearly all of the passengers and crew of the *Franklin* were saved, many wrecks involved a large loss of life—sometimes there were no survivors at all. The first sighting of the wreck of the sailing ship *John Milton* was not encouraging. A member of the Stratton family, who operated the Third House Inn at Montauk, was the first to notice her shattered hulk lying on the rocks on the morning of February 20, 1858. The weather was bitter cold and a blinding snowstorm had been raging since the previous day. The ship had apparently run headlong onto the rocky beach under full sail, unable to discern the low lying shoreline through the heavy snow.

Frozen solid in blocks of sea ice, the men who had brought the *John Milton* safely around treacherous Cape Horn, up the Eastern Seaboard and within a few days sail of home, began to wash ashore that evening. Some were entombed alone, lying stiff on the beach as the howling winter winds froze ocean spray over their lifeless bodies. Others washed up in ghastly embraces with shipmates, or frozen in a jumbled heap with oars, timbers and assorted debris. Riding his horse along the beach that afternoon, the keeper of the Napeague Life-Saving Station came across the only survivor of the vessel capable of telling her tale: inside the wreckage of the ship's long boat he found a seaman's chest containing the *John Milton*'s logbook.

The *John Milton* had cleared Hampton Roads, Virginia on February 16th, bound for her home port of New Bedford after having rounded Cape Horn from a trading voyage through the Pacific. Her logbook told of "strong gales and thick snowstorms"[2] for several days preceding the wreck. She had last obtained a navigational fix on February 18th, recording her latitude as 36° 56'N. Thereafter she had groped along using only dead reckoning as the gales and snowstorms grew worse. The remainder of her story remains a mystery, frozen in time much as her crew were frozen in blocks of ice.

Twenty-two men and one boy, the captain's son, were found frozen and washed up on the beach—four other bodies disappeared in the sea, never to be found. Two weeks later a beachcomber, Mr. Aleck Gould, found a heavy pea jacket half buried in the sand—in the pocket he found $400 in gold coins! This honest soul turned the money over to the coroner's office in the hope that its rightful owner might be found. The jacket belonged to none other than the *Milton*'s captain, Ephraim Harding; the coins were returned to his widow, but were little solace for her loss. The ship's bell was taken from the wreck and hung in the belfry of the Presbyterian chapel erected in East Hampton in 1859. A single marble stone in East Hampton's South End Burying Ground marks the common grave

of the *John Milton*'s crew. The marker bears the following inscription, written by Mr. John Wallace of East Hampton:

This stone was erected by individual subscriptions from various places to mark the spot where, with peculiar solemnity, were deposited the mortal remains of the three mates and eighteen of the crew of the ship *John Milton* of New Bedford, wrecked on the coast of Montauk, while returning from the Chincha Islands on the 20 February 1858 where together with those who rest beneath, Ephraim Harding, the Captain, and four others of the mariners, being the whole ship's company, were drowned in the waves.
The way, O God, is in the Sea

THE *AMSTERDAM*

On June 21, 1970, a spear fisherman named Donald Dalbora brought a 2°-foot-long brass nameplate to the surface while snorkeling, positively identifying a shipwreck lying some two miles west of Montauk Point. The wreck lies in only 15 feet of water, and is little more than scattered and half-buried debris, except for her engine, which still protrudes from the ocean's surface at low tide. The location is just offshore of an area the locals refer to as Amsterdam. There is good reason for the location's nickname, for the nameplate Dalbora recovered was inscribed with the following legend:

AMSTERDAM
Andrew Leslie & Co.
Iron Ship Builders
New Castle on Tyne
1866

Intrigued by his find, Mr. Dalbora wrote to Lloyd's of London to find out more about the ship he had identified. He found that the *Amsterdam* "was a screw-propeller, iron ship with two decks, two masts, pole-rigged, elliptic stern, clinker-built . . ."[3] The steamship measured 211 feet long and was owned by Donald Robert MacGregor of Leith, Scotland, while the engine that can sometimes be seen protruding from the surf was built by Stephenson & Co. of Newcastle.

Her story is a familiar one, for she came ashore on the rocky beach near Montauk Point on October 21, 1867, while lost in a dense fog. The *Amsterdam* was bound for New York from Malaga, on the Spanish coast of the Mediterranean Sea, just west of Gibraltar. In her cargo holds was an assortment of raisins, grapes, lemons, Malaga wine and Spanish lead. The ship was only one year old at the time of her loss and, fortunately for her owners, was insured at Lloyd's; her value was estimated at 25,000 to 30,000 pounds, while her cargo was reportedly worth some 6,000 pounds and was also insured.

TEN LOST INDIANS: THE SALVAGE OF THE *CIRCASSIAN*

Thick snowstorms were the cause of many wrecks along Long Island beaches over the years. Near-zero visibility combined with a heavy northeast gale proved a deadly combination, particularly for sailing vessels with their limited maneuverability. The night of December 11, 1876, presented just this set of conditions to Captain Robert Wilson, commanding the full-rigged iron ship *Circassian*. The 255-foot-long vessel was originally built as a steamship by S.S. DeWolf & Company, of Belfast, in 1857. Sixteen years later, her iron hull having outlived her engines and boilers, she was stripped of her machinery and converted to a sailing ship. She had seen her share of near-disasters during a 19-year career at sea, being captured as a blockade runner during the Civil War and grounding once off Cape Sable, Nova Scotia, and later off Squan Beach on the New Jersey coast. On all occasions she had escaped relatively unscathed, but her luck was about to run out.

Captain Wilson later claimed that this particular grounding was caused by compass error, although running aground on Long Island's south shore during a blinding snowstorm and northeast gale hardly needed further explanation. She came ashore only 20 yards west of the Mecox Life-Saving Station and 400 yards off the beach, and was promptly discovered by the life-savers on their nightly patrol. The weather was particularly nasty, the tide was high, and the wreck lay near the extreme range of the mortar, so the life-savers decided to postpone the rescue attempt until dawn. Crews from the two adjacent stations, Georgica and Southampton, were summoned to assist, and preparations were made for firing a line out to the ship.

At dawn the tide had fallen considerably, reducing the distance between the beach and the *Circassian*. Placing the mortar as close to the surf line as they dared, the life-savers managed to land the mortar shot on the *Circassian*'s deck on the first try. The required lines were rigged between the beach and the stranded ship to evacuate the crew with the lifecar. By the time this was accomplished, however, the seas had calmed considerably and the men chose to use the surfboat for the rescue instead. It took seven trips through the breakers to remove the 49 crew from the iron ship, and most were sent safely on their way toward New York. Sixteen of the crew, including the captain and officers, however, remained behind to assist in the salvage operations. This loyalty to duty would cost them their lives.

On December 12th, the Coast Wrecking Company took charge of the wreck under contract to the ship's owners. The salvage operation was to be directed by Captains Perrin and Pierson of the wrecking company, who remained on shore. Aboard the *Circassian*, the operation was being run by Captain John Lewis of New York, along with three engineers, also employees of the wrecking company. Twelve more men were hired locally to assist in the operations, ten of whom were Indians from the Shinnecock Reservation. Together

The Circassian *was built as a steamship in 1872 and later converted to a sailing vessel. She grounded near Mecox in 1876; the entire crew of 49 was safely rescued, but 28 were killed in the subsequent salvage attempt. Courtesy of The Steamship Historical Society of America.*

with the 16 original crew of the iron ship, the total salvage crew amounted to 32. For more than two weeks the operation continued unabated. Most of her cargo of soda ash, caustic soda, baking powder and bath bricks had been removed, and all the water pumped out of the ship's holds by December 29th. All efforts to lighten her had been completed—she was ready to be refloated. That night an extraordinarily high tide was expected; the wind began to blow out of the east and the barometer began to plummet, announcing an approaching nor'easter. The high tides would help in the attempt to get the ship off the bar—the strong gale force winds would not.

That Friday morning, the crew on board the *Circassian* requested that an emergency lifeline be rigged between the ship and beach in view of the coming blow. Captain Pierson, however, was apparently fearful that the men might desert the ship, and refused. The seas rose steadily, and by afternoon Captain Lewis was forced to slacken the two anchor cables holding the *Circassian* in position to ease her motion. Not long afterward the lightened ship swung around toward the west and the seas, which had grown mountainous, began to break over the helpless vessel. Snow and sleet started to fall heavily. The seas continued to build, and the wind increased to near hurricane force. Around 4:00 P.M., Captain Lewis ordered the anchor cables cut, leaving the *Circassian*, and the men stranded on board her, at the mercy of the wind and sea.

At 7:00 P.M., the life-savers were once again summoned to the wreck of the *Circassian* by a distress signal. The men began setting up the beach apparatus immediately, and were set to fire a mortar by 8:00 P.M. Just then, the wind swung around to the southwest, forcing the surfmen to redeploy their gear in a new position further down the beach. After the mortar was repositioned, the men made several attempts to get a line on board the wreck, but the darkness, combined with a heavy current, foiled their efforts. Before midnight fell, the *Circassian*'s mainmast fell into the sea.

By 2:00 A.M. the 32 men had been forced to climb the foremast rigging to escape the seething cauldron of wave and foam that had become the ship's deck. As the ship began to break up in the pounding surf, the men abandoned the foremast for the mizzen mast. Distress rockets were launched in a vain attempt to summon help from those watching the scene from the beach. The life-saving crew tried fruitlessly to get a line to the vessel. Shot after shot from the mortar fell short or drifted downwind. The seamen's wailing cries could be heard by those on the beach throughout the night. The end came swiftly about 4:30 Saturday morning,

as a tremendous swell lifted the vessel and then dropped her heavily on the bar. The mizzen mast parted from the shock and fell into the sea, carrying the entire crew with it. Four men managed to make it to shore alive—the remaining 28 men, frozen and stiff, washed ashore over the course of the next several weeks, some as far away as Montauk. None of the Shinnecock Indians were among the survivors, and it was said that the loss of these ten young men was a severe blow to the Shinnecock tribe. Their bodies were buried on the Shinnecock Reservation; Captain Lewis and the three engineers were taken to New York; the 14 remaining bodies were buried in the Old South End Cemetery in East Hampton, near the common grave of the sailors from the *John Milton*.

FROZEN IN THE RIGGING: THE *LOUIS V. PLACE*

During the winter of 1977-78, a tremendous ice storm covered Long Island with a glistening coat of frozen sleet. Leafless trees became beautiful, multi-fingered statues with every minute detail encased in a thick sheath of clear ice. Telephone and power lines broke under the crushing weight of accumulated ice, while fence posts, mailboxes, flagpoles and any other protuberance exposed to the driving sleet became a shimmering ice sculpture decorating an eerie winter landscape. The days of sailing ships with their towering masts and intricate rigging had long since passed; only the imagination could bring forth the spectacle of such a vessel encased in a gleaming coat of ice. But eighty-two years earlier this dramatic scene existed in more than the imagination, and brought with it tragic human consequences.

The three-masted schooner *Louis V. Place* set sail from Baltimore, Maryland on January 28, 1895 with a cargo of 1,100 tons of coal to be delivered to Fall River, Massachussets. As the 163-foot-long ship sailed northward, the weather began to thicken and the air grew colder. On February 5th the wind began to blow with gale force, and Captain William H. Squires ordered the sails reefed. In an ominous sign of events to come, the men were unable to furl the foresail—it was frozen nearly solid with a heavy coating of ice. For the next two days the eight men on board the schooner were locked in a relentless battle with the icy gale. The *Louis V. Place* began drifting before the storm, barely under the control of her human occupants. On the 7th, the wind veered around to the northeast; on the 8th the wind again shifted, this time blowing from the west. Although the wind seemed to constantly shift direction, it blew steadily. The crew was exhausted from days of battling the storm without sleep; the ship's sails and rigging were thickly encrusted with ice, as were her nearly impassable decks. The *Place* had become a drifting iceberg, frozen, out of control, and tossed before the tempestuous sea.

The ship's position was a matter of speculation—the best navigator could do little more than guess at their location after days of being blown before the icy gale. The lead line showed only eight fathoms of water under the schooner's keel—the treacherous beach must be close at hand. The mate reported that there was water in the hold and it was gaining faster than it could be pumped out. Captain Squires called his men together and told them his last, desperate plan. "I am going to beach her. All hands go below and dress as warmly as possible. Put on all your clothes. Stuff your pockets with food. When she strikes, we'll jump into the rigging. And may God help us."[4]

At 8:15 A.M., the ship crashed onto the outer bar of Fire Island, an eighth mile east of the Lone Hill Life-Saving Station. Donning every stitch of clothing they could wear the men scrambled up into the rigging to escape the icy surf, for the heavy seas now broke over the ship's decks.

Just before the *Louis V. Place* had grounded, she was sighted by surfman Frederick Saunders of the Lone Hill Station. Saunders's fellow life-savers were already at work with another victim of the winter storm two miles east of the *Louis V. Place*. The nine men on board the four-masted schooner *John B. Manning* were successfully brought ashore with the breeches buoy that day, and the ship was later refloated. Unable to help the crew of this new wreck alone, Saunders contacted the two life-saving stations adjacent to Lone Hill, at Point O' Woods and Blue Point, in search of assistance. The men from the Blue Point Station responded by picking up the same Lyle gun used in the rescue of the *John B. Manning*'s crew, and after hauling it two miles down the beach, set up the apparatus opposite the wreck of the *Louis V. Place*. Conditions were nothing short of horrible. The beach was covered with deep snow; large cakes of ice were piled six to eight feet high at the water's edge. It was impossible to launch the surfboats as a porridge of slush and ice filled the ocean between the ship and the beach. The air temperature was below zero with gale force winds blowing at 30 to 50 miles per hour. Periodic snow squalls lashed the stricken ship. The wind chill must have been unbearable for the crew. The sole remaining hope for the men slowly freezing to death in the *Place*'s rigging lay in the breeches buoy.

As the surfmen on the beach set up the Lyle gun opposite the wreck, they watched helplessly as Captain Squires and the cook, John J. Horton, fell into the sea, unable to hold on to their icy perches any longer. They disappeared into a grinding maelstrom of ice and slush and sea. The body of the captain washed up on the beach at Southampton a few days later.

Three times the Lyle gun fired a line across the decks of the schooner; three times the action of the sea washed it away before the men in the rigging could even move toward it. After the third try by the surfmen, a heavy snow squall moved in, obscuring the *Louis V. Place* in a white shroud. When the squall subsided three hours later, there were only four men visible in the rigging—Charles Allen and Fritz Oscar Mard had succumbed to the bitter cold and fallen into the sea. Those remaining had lashed themselves in place in order to avoid the same fate. Two more lines were fired across the *Place*'s rigging before darkness fell, but again the men in the rigging were unable to reach them. The life-savers built huge fires on the beach that night, extending a symbol of hope to those clinging desperately to life only a few hundred yards to seaward. The fires also served to warm the life-savers in the freezing conditions, many of whom were suffering severely from frostbite.

At dawn, it was clear to those on the beach that only two of the four men in the *Place*'s rigging were still alive. George Oelson and Lars Gioby swung lifelessly at the end of the ropes they had lashed themselves in place with. The two remaining survivors, Claus Stuvens and Soren Nelson, shook, pounded and beat each other in order to keep their blood circulating despite the biting cold. They wrapped themselves in sailcloth, attempting to hide from the icy wind that was slowly robbing them of life. At one point, Stuvens climbed down onto the ship's deck and attempted to haul aboard one of the shot lines that had been placed across the wreck by the Lyle gun. Exhausted and cold, he was unable to haul the heavy, ice-covered line aboard, and he dragged himself back into the rigging. Again and again he and Nelson beat each other, sometimes with ropes, while dodging the swinging body of George Oelson.

Finally, around midnight on February 9th, the seas subsided and the terrible wind eased. With a falling tide the men managed to launch the surfboat through the heavy ice. Once past the breakers, the surfmen glided alongside the hull of the *Louis V. Place* and rescued the two men left alive by the winter gale. Stuvens, the stronger of the two, was badly frostbitten on the

L.V. Place.

The Louis V. Place *came ashore near the Lone Hill Station in February 1895, and became a testimony to human suffering. Eight men clung desperately to the ship's frozen rigging (left and below, left) for 39 hours before rescue came. Claus Stuvens (below, right) was the only survivor. Courtesy of The Mariners' Museum, Newport News, Virginia (left) and the Long Island Maritime Museum, West Sayville, NY (below, left and right).*

face, ears, neck, hands and feet, but unshaken in spirit. Shipwrecked several times before, he claimed he could have lasted a while longer given only some tobacco and a can of beans! Nelson, however, had fared much worse. His boots had filled with water and his feet were frozen solid in large blocks of ice. Both men were taken to the hospital the following day. Both of Nelson's legs were amputated; a few weeks later he died of tetanus, still in the hospital. Stuvens apparently recovered fully, and undeterred by his 39-hour ordeal in the rigging of the *Louis V. Place*, again went to sea.

Eight tombstones were placed in the Lakeview Cemetery in Patchogue to commemorate the seven who perished aboard the schooner *Louis V. Place*, as well as the lone survivor. The mate, Lars Gioby, was buried with a piece of rope still in his grasp, for it could not be removed from his frozen hand. It is said that only four of the sailors' bodies lie here, for Captain Squires was buried in Southold beside his first wife and two daughters, Nelson was buried in Brooklyn, and the body of the cook, John Horton, was never found.

THE FIRST MODERN TANKER: *GLUCKAUF*

The remains of a wooden sailing ship often lasted only

a few weeks on the beach; some were smashed to pieces in a matter of days or even hours; a few were stout enough that their hulks remained visible for several months before disappearing into the sea of shifting sands along the beach. With the arrival of the iron- or steel-hulled steamship, however, shipwrecks often became lasting monuments upon the landscape. Those left abandoned on the beach often remained visible spectacles for years, even decades.

One of the more famous wrecks along the Great

South Beach came aground near the Blue Point Life-Saving Station on March 24, 1893. Three years after grounding there the *Gluckauf* still lay in the surf, heeled over on her port side, bow on the beach and stern slowly sinking into a quagmire of sand at the water's edge. Once a bold and pioneering engineering effort as the world's first steamship designed and built expressly for the purpose of carrying oil in bulk, she had become but a curiosity for the summer tourist. Her bow and masts rose so high above the sur-

The German steamship Gluckauf *wrecked near the Blue Point Station on March 24, 1893. The first steamship expressly built to carry bulk oil, the* Gluckauf *was left to decay on the beach for decades (below) before she was partially salvaged at the turn of the century. The salvagers left much of her hull and machinery behind, however, and she remained partly visible until at least 1975 (right). Below courtesy of the Long Island Maritime Museum, West Sayville, NY.*

rounding landscape that they were easily visible from the Long Island Railroad on the mainland, as well as ten miles down the beach in either direction. Each summer tourists would come to see her. Those adventurous enough to pull themselves up over her crazily canted railing and onto her deck could explore her sand-filled interior. Souvenir hunters quickly stripped her of anything not bolted down—the big brass letters spelling out her name on the bow began to slowly disappear, one letter at a time. The posts from her deck railing were reportedly used as horse hitching posts in the town of Patchogue for many years. The *Gluckauf* also found herself afflicted with a curious predecessor of a common twentieth century problem—graffiti. Visitors scrawled their names all over her hull, on her masts and decks, cabin walls and any other surface sure to be seen by later visitors.

The *Gluckauf* struck the outer bar early on the evening of March 24th, driven ashore by a tremendous southerly gale. Huge breakers pounded the iron-hulled steamer throughout the long night. The lifesavers from the Blue Point Station, who had watched helplessly as she came ashore, built fires on the beach with driftwood to buoy the spirits of the men trapped on board the *Gluckauf*. At daybreak, the Lyle gun was fired and a breeches buoy was established between the beach and the wreck. The entire crew of the steamer was evacuated safely, although they were dragged through the breaking seas rather than over them.

A wrecking tug, summoned by telegraph, had arrived during the night to assist the stranded *Gluckauf*. For days the wreckers toiled preparing the tanker for the salvage attempt. Heavy hawsers were fastened to her stern so that the tug could attempt to pull her off the bar when the tide was right. On April 7th the tide they needed arrived, but it was accompanied by another southerly gale. As the seas grew in size, the tug began to pull on the hawsers. Ever so slowly the iron grip of sand loosened its hold on the big steamship, until at last she was free. But as the tug began to tow her toward New York, the storm's wrath increased and the hawsers parted; the tug's crew could only watch in frustration as two week's work was picked up by the breaking seas and tossed across the outer bar and up onto the beach—the *Gluckauf* would sail no more. Sometime around the turn of the century, a salvage firm broke up the *Gluckauf*'s exposed hull and hauled away the iron scrap. But much of her hull and machinery had already sunk beneath the sand and could not be salvaged. Even today part of her hulk can sometimes be seen standing amongst the breakers just off the beach between Water Island and Davis Park.

DESTINED FOR DISASTER: SS *GATE CITY*

When the Ocean Steamship Company accepted delivery of the new passenger steamship *Gate City* from her builders, John Roach & Son of Chester, Pennsylvania in 1878, little did they know that she was not destined to be a lucky ship. Her rather short iron hull, full length promenade deck and long after-deckhouse did not make her a particularly pretty vessel. Her two masts and single funnel were raked aft in an attempt to give her the look of speed, but she lacked the elegant beauty of her larger cousins, the big transatlantic passenger steamers. What her outward appearance failed to convey, however, her lavish interior provided. Her elaborately furnished saloons and staterooms provided all the luxury a prospective passenger required for a journey along the Atlantic Seaboard.

The *Gate City*'s first mishap occurred eight years after her launching, in July 1886. While carefully navigating Vineyard Sound in a heavy fog, she ran aground on the shores of Naushon Island, just northwest of

The passenger steamship Gate City *grounded near Moriches during a dense fog in February 1900. Most of the passengers and crew were removed by breeches buoy (above). The breeches buoy A-frame can be seen at the extreme right. The wreck was later partly salvaged (below) before being abandoned. Courtesy of the Long Island Maritime Museum, West Sayville, NY.*

Martha's Vineyard. Her hull was badly damaged on the rocky bottom, and it was widely believed that she would be a total loss. Forty-three thousand watermelons from the *Gate City*'s cargo were jettisoned overboard in an attempt to lighten her, causing local residents to take to their boats. Imagine the sight of some forty-thousand watermelons floating on the waves of Vineyard Sound! Although her owners quickly abandoned the vessel to the insurance agents, a canvas patch was fitted over the hole in her damaged hull. She was ultimately brought into Boston Harbor under her own power, where she was repaired in dry dock.

Eleven years later, in September 1897, she again limped into port bearing a canvas patch over her side. In a collision hauntingly reminiscent of that suffered by the Cunard steamer *Oregon* eleven years earlier, the Ocean Steamship Company's liner was rammed by an unidentified, unlighted schooner on a dark, starless night off the coast of New Jersey. The schooner's bowsprit stove a huge hole in the *Gate City*'s 7/8-inch-thick iron hull before disappearing into the night. Water began pouring into the steamer through the gaping hole in her side, but the quick work of twelve men, who shoveled several tons of coal from the starboard to the port bunkers in only fifteen minutes, gave the vessel a list to port and brought the wound above sea level. The canvas patch was rigged and she was once again saved, but only temporarily.

On the night of February 8, 1900, a dense fog blanketed the Long Island coastline. The men of the U.S. Life-Saving Service were, as always, ready for the inevitable accidents such weather brings. About 8 o'clock that evening the beach patrol, then 1˙ miles west of the Moriches Station, heard a steamer's whistle just offshore. Repeated attempts to signal the steamer were futile, the fog being too dense for signal lanterns, and the unfortunate vessel soon grounded hard on the outer bar. The steamship was the *Gate City*.

Word of the grounded ship was quickly sent to the Moriches Station. Since the sea was relatively calm, the surfboat was launched directly from the station and rowed down the beach toward the sound of the *Gate City*'s whistle. The surfmen found the steamship aground but in no immediate danger. When transportation to the beach was offered to as many passengers and crew as the surfboat could hold, only the three women on board accepted. However, during the night the surf began to rise, and at high water the next morning the *Gate City* bounced over the outer bar and grounded fast only 200 yards from the beach. The life-savers used the breeches buoy to bring the rest of the passengers ashore, as well as those crew whose services

were not immediately required on board. That afternoon brought the arrival of the wrecking tug *William E. Chapman,* of the Meritt and Chapman Derrick & Wrecking Company, and work began immediately to salvage both the ship and her cargo of cotton and general merchandise.

The salvage work continued for three days, as both the crew and wreckers worked to lighten the vessel. Several attempts were made to pull the steamship off the bar, but to no avail. The surf continued to build and on February 12th the captain and crew abandoned the *Gate City*, leaving her in the hands of the Chapman wrecking crew. Although the surf conditions were severe, the wreckers managed to salvage much of her cargo and transport it to New York. Further attempts to pull the ship herself off the bar proved unsuccessful, and she was abandoned to the sea on April 17th. Today her remains lie just east of Moriches Inlet, a short distance off the beach. On calm days the ocean's gentle swells surge through the remains of the *Gate City*, leaving swirls on the glassy surface to mark her location.

THE "TEA WRECK"

Very early on the morning of March 1, 1902, the lookout at the Short Beach Life-Saving Station sighted a ship among the breakers on the Jones Beach bar. The sea was running high, driven by a strong south-southeast wind and it was clear that the stranded ship was in trouble. The keeper of the Short Beach Station lit a Coston signal (a type of signal flare) to let the ship know that help was on the way, and then telephoned the Zach's Inlet Station for assistance. Both stations launched surfboats and met at the outer point of the beach. Here they rearranged crews in order to put a full complement in the larger of the two surfboats, which proceeded to the wreck. It was daylight by the time the life-savers reached the stranded steamship. Once there, they stood by waiting for the flood tide. While they waited, they observed a small boat launched from the wreck. The boat was too small for the large breakers, however, and capsized on the way in, throwing 17 men into the water. The crew of the large surfboat picked up 13, while the remaining men were picked up by a boat from the Point Lookout Station which had just arrived on the scene. However, all this action in the surf didn't dissuade those still on board the steamer from launching a second, larger boat filled with 44 men. The men on the second boat were more fortunate and came through the breakers without

What is known locally as the "Tea Wreck" is really the British steamer Acara, *shown here with her back broken on the bar. Her local name was derived from her cargo of Chinese tea. Courtesy of the Long Island Maritime Museum, West Sayville, NY.*

mishap. All 61 persons on board—Captain Kilgour and his wife, 15 officers and a mixed crew of 16 Malays from Singapore, 23 Indians from Calcutta, and 5 Chinese from Hong Kong and Canton—managed to reach shore safely. A few were in bad shape after their ordeal, and two men required medical attention for two hours before they were stabilized. This latest casualty on the beach was the *Acara*, a British steamship bound from China to New York with a mixed general cargo: tin ingots, cinnamon, pepper, cassia, indigo, rubber, gum and 50,000 cases of fine Chinese tea.

Three days after the ship had come ashore, on March 4th, the wreckers were at work on her cargo, whose value was estimated at between $600,000 and $1,000,000. The ship herself, although only three years old, was a total loss, for she had broken in two amidships during the effort to get her off the bar. The Merritt and Chapman Company was hired for the salvage work, and was still at work in mid-June, three months after she had come ashore. Ultimately, 11,911 tin ingots and 30,000 of the 50,000 cases of Chinese tea on board were salvaged by the wrecking company. The local residents apparently managed to salvage their own share of the steamer's cargo, and referred to the *Acara* as "our tea wreck," a name that has stuck until this day.

LONG DISTANCE RESCUE: *DRUMELZIER*

The crew of the British tramp steamer *Drumelzier* undoubtedly thought their captain, William Nicholson, a scrooge when he insisted on setting sail Sunday morning, December 25, 1904. Early the next day, however, Captain Nicholson probably wished he'd spent Christmas in port. Captain Nicholson would later speculate that the 2,000 tons of steel billets stowed in the *Drumelzier*'s hold might have thrown the compass

off kilter which, coupled with a blinding snowstorm, caused his ship to go aground on the bar outside Fire Island Inlet at 3:00 A.M. on December 26th.

At 5:30 that morning a distress signal was sighted by a patrolman from the Oak Island Life-Saving Station. The keeper of the Fire Island Station was notified by telegraph, and both stations sent surfboats to the steamer's aid. After boarding her, the life-savers found that the *Drumelzier*'s captain had no intention of abandoning his vessel; the seas were moderate and he believed his vessel could be gotten off at the next high tide. The surfmen were thanked for their concern, but the steamer's entire 30-man crew elected to remain on board, although signal arrangements were made should assistance ultimately be needed.

High tide came and went, and still the *Drumelzier* remained stranded on the bar. The wind continued to howl out of the northeast and the seas grew ever larger. The stranded steamship was pounded relentlessly on Fire Island's infamous outer bar, while huge waves swept over her decks. The wrecking tug *William E. Chapman* stood by like a vulture, waiting for the ship's captain to abandon her, but captain Nicholson remained stubbornly on board his charge. In fact, he now had little choice, for the rising seas had made launching a surfboat nearly impossible, and the ship was too far from shore to use the breeches buoy. At daybreak on Wednesday the 28th, the *Drumelzier*'s crew was startled by a report like a cannon shot. The deck bulged up amidships, the engine was torn from its mounts and thrown six feet aft, while the boiler slid forward. The ship had broken its back on the bar.

That morning the revenue cutter *Mohawk* arrived at the scene, hoping to render assistance to the mariners from seaward, but this, too, proved impossible. What was needed was a big surfboat capable of making its way through the fierce seas pounding the vessel; the only one available, however, was located on

The British tramp steamer Drumelzier *wrecked in a blinding snowstorm west of Fire Island Inlet in December 1904 (above). Her remains now lie east of the inlet (see below). Courtesy of the Long Island Maritime Museum, West Sayville, NY.*

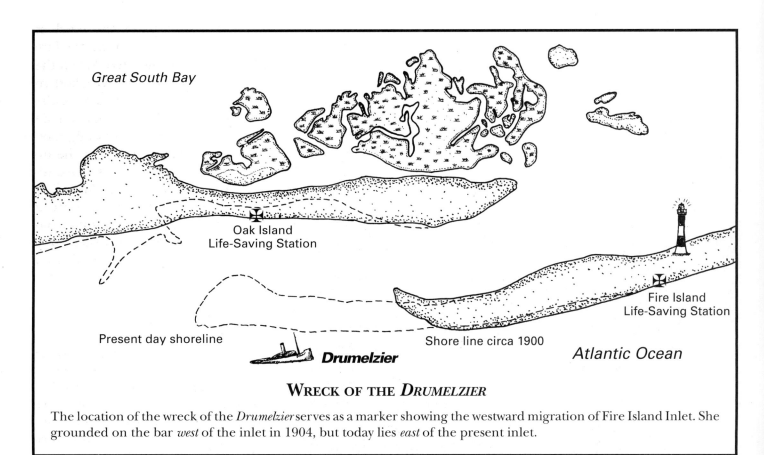

Great South Bay

Oak Island
Life-Saving Station

Fire Island
Life-Saving Station

Present day shoreline

Drumelzier

Shore line circa 1900

Atlantic Ocean

WRECK OF THE *DRUMELZIER*

The location of the wreck of the *Drumelzier* serves as a marker showing the westward migration of Fire Island Inlet. She grounded on the bar *west* of the inlet in 1904, but today lies *east* of the present inlet.

the New Jersey coast at the Sandy Hook Life-Saving Station some 42 miles away. That evening the keeper of the Sandy Hook Station was ordered to secure a tug and tow the station's big, unsinkable, self-righting, self-bailing iron surfboat to the wreck. The tug *Catherine Moran* was recruited for the job, and the crew of the Sandy Hook Station, described as "the hardiest lifesavers on the Atlantic Coast,"[5] set out for the wreck. When they arrived the next morning, they found their wonderful lifeboat and all its gear heavily encrusted with ice. Nevertheless, after chipping her free of ice the crew raised the boat's sails and set out for the *Drumelzier,* lying one-quarter mile away. They found her entire stern and bow encased in solid masses of ice, with "huge stalactites of fantastic shape"[6] hanging from her rigging. They managed to take off 16 of the crew who desired to leave the wreck. Captain Nicholson stayed on board with the remaining 13 crew and refused the offer of the exhausted crew of the Sandy Hook lifeboat to return for them. The tug turned and headed toward New York.

Perhaps the sight of the tugboat heading off into the distance changed Captain Nicholson's mind; perhaps it was the huge seas sweeping entirely across his ship; or perhaps it was the final realization that his ship, now broken in two, would never be saved. Whatever the reason, shortly after the *Catherine Moran* turned and headed for New York, the stubborn steamship captain hoisted the prearranged flag signals for the life-savers to come to the rescue. Fortunately for Captain Nicholson and the remainder of his crew, the seas had subsided enough during the previous night to enable the launching of the smaller surfboats. Boats from both the stations at Oak Island and Fire Island rescued the 14 men remaining on board the steamer, who were put up at the Oak Island Station for the night. Over the next several days the *Drumelzier* broke completely in two. The monstrous seas continued their destructive work, finally breaking her into pieces.

It is noteworthy that the wreck of the *Drumelzier* shows how far the Fire Island Inlet has migrated. When the British steamship was wrecked in 1904, she lay well to the *west* of the inlet; today her broken remains lie *east* of the inlet, which has migrated westward by several miles in the intervening years. For years she was often called the "Quadrant Wreck" by fishermen, because her steering quadrant could be seen jutting from the sea just off Robert Moses State Park. It has since disappeared from view.

After grounding, the crew of the Drumelzier *posed on the foredeck of their wrecked steamer. The ship's captain stubbornly remained on board for three days, only accepting rescue after the ship's back was broken by rough seas. Courtesy of the Long Island Maritime Museum, West Sayville, NY.*

WRECK OF THE *RODA*:
THE CAPTAIN REFUSED TO LEAVE

In a thick fog on the evening of February 13, 1908, still another ship found herself stranded on the outer bar, south of the Jones Beach Life-Saving Station. The unfortunate vessel was the British steamship *Roda*, bound for New York from Huelva, Spain, with a cargo of copper ore. She was discovered a mere half-hour after stranding by Jacob Baldwin of the Jones Beach Station while on beach patrol. The station crew launched the surfboat through a moderate sea and made their way out to the stranded vessel. After reaching the wreck and coming on board, the life-savers were informed by Captain W. J. Beaven that both he and his crew would be remaining on the *Roda*. The surfmen were asked to please send for tugs so that the ship might be pulled off the bar, and this was done after the men returned to the beach.

At 7:00 A.M. on the 14th, the crews of the stations at Jones Beach and Zach's Inlet returned to the wreck. Once again the life-savers were informed that their assistance was not wanted—the men would be staying on board their ship. This time word of the stranding was sent to the *Roda*'s owners.

That afternoon and evening the surf began to rise—heavy weather was on the way. At 1:30 A.M. on the 15th, the beach patrol returned to the station and informed the keeper that the *Roda* was sounding distress signals. The brave men of the Life-Saving Service again launched their surfboat through the breakers and pulled out to the wreck. Captain Beaven informed them that he felt the masts were ready to go and he was ready to abandon her. Twelve men were taken ashore in the boat on the first trip. A second trip

through the rapidly rising surf brought ashore another eight men. A third trip was made out through the breakers in the cold dark of night, but when the boat reached the ship's side only three men climbed on board—the captain, first mate and chief engineer still refused to leave their ship.

After a hard night's work, the crew finally returned to the Jones Beach Station about 4:30 A.M. where they made the *Roda*'s crew as comfortable as possible, breaking out dry clothing for the men and feeding them. The storm continued to build, and at 11:00 A.M. distress signals were again seen from the *Roda*. For the sixth time in two days, the surfboat was launched into the breakers and rowed through the surf to the British steamship. When the crew of the boat reached the wreck, they found the seas breaking clear over the ship; they also found a captain who had finally capitulated to the inevitable—Captain Beaven was ready to leave.

A few days later the crew of the life-saving station received a letter of appreciation signed by all of the *Roda*'s officers. Surely the men of the U.S. Life-Saving Service were deserving of their praise.

THE UNITED STATES COAST GUARD

In early April 1912, an event occurred off Montauk Point that would plant the seed for a merger between the United States Life-Saving Service and the Revenue Cutter Service. The Merchants and Miners Line steamship *Ontario* caught fire well off the south shore of Long Island while on a voyage from Baltimore to Boston. The burning ship was guided to the south side of Montauk Point by two revenue cutters. Now only a short distance off the beach, the crews of the Ditch Plains and Hither Hills Life-Saving Stations employed both the breeches buoy and surfboats, and in concert with the two revenue cutters safely evacuated 72 passengers and crew from the burning hulk, just before the ship blew up. This cooperative rescue effort caught the attention of Congress, who had been searching for ways to cut the federal budget. On January 28, 1915, the Revenue Cutter Service and the Life-Saving Service were officially merged into one service, to be called the United States Coast Guard. This new service had the combined assets and strengths of its two parent organizations, consisting of 45 cutters, 280 life-saving stations and 4,155 personnel. Later, in 1939, the United States Lighthouse Service was merged into the Coast Guard and finally, in 1942, the Bureau of Navigation and Steamboat Inspection Service was also absorbed into the service we know today.

Thick fog caused the Roda *to ground near Jones Beach Station on the night of February 13, 1908. Courtesy of the Long Island Maritime Museum, West Sayville, NY.*

5

THE WORLD GOES TO WAR: 1914-1918

By the turn of the twentieth century, the Imperial German Empire had evolved into the most powerful force on the European continent. Germany was ruled by a democratic Reichstag and an imperial chancellor, but the latter was appointed, and dismissed, by a sovereign monarch, Kaiser Wilhelm II. While Germany was generally considered to command the most powerful land army on the continent, she was not considered a major naval power. The German Emperor, however, had ambitions for a strong navy and escalated the construction of Germany's High Seas Fleet. The Kaiser's naval building program began a naval arms race between Germany and the acknowledged queen of the seas, England.

England had ruled the seas for centuries. An island nation in possession of a vast, worldwide colonial empire, a strong English Navy was imperative for survival. England had always made it her policy to maintain a navy equal to, or superior to, the combined naval strength of any two major European powers. England quickly became alarmed at Germany's large naval building program. In order to maintain her policy of naval superiority, England was forced to build new ships at nearly twice the rate of the German expansion.

Meanwhile, the continent of Europe was fraught with nationalistic rivalries and locked in a web of military alliances. In addition to the powerful German Empire, there was the geographically massive, but relatively weak, Austria-Hungary. Plagued by internal friction between her many differing nationalities, the Empire's internal unrest was further fueled by Serbia to the south, whose desire for a Greater Serbia uniting the Slavic peoples stirred nationalistic sentiments within Austria-Hungary. To the east lay the vast terri-

tory of Russia, under the rule of Tsar Nicholas II. The Russian giant stretched from the Pacific Ocean in the east to the German and Austro-Hungarian borders in the west, encompassing a huge block of territory across the top of the continent.

Germany, Austria-Hungary and Italy had long been joined in what was known as the Triple Alliance. Feeling threatened by this vast military alliance, France and Russia had created a dual alliance for their mutual protection. Of the major powers, England alone remained neutral and unaligned. By the turn of the century, with the major continental powers divided into two opposing military blocs, the stage was set for war.

While politics would provide the impetus for war, the tools were furnished by the industrial revolution, which had fueled a massive arms race between the powerful economies of the European empires. England's development of the Dreadnought class of armored battleship in 1906 had rendered the world's navies obsolete overnight. The naval arms race escalated as Britain and Germany scrambled to build modern fleets; Britain pursued her policy of maintaining control over the world's oceans, while Germany strove to build a world-class fleet and establish naval respectability.

The impetus for war came on June 28, 1914, in Sarajevo, Bosnia. An agent of the secret Black Hand organization assassinated the Archduke Francis Ferdinand, nephew of Emperor Francis Joseph and heir to the Austrian throne, along with his wife, Sophie. Austria-Hungary, long seeking an excuse to crush the troublesome Serbia, issued an ultimatum to the small country. On July 28th, exactly one month after the assassinations, Austria-Hungary declared war on

Serbia. The European alliance system quickly plunged the continent into a four-year struggle that would later be called "The Great War."

CLASH OF THE TITANS

The naval arms race between Germany and England had provided each with an enormous fleet of heavily armed capital ships. When war broke out, the world awaited the outcome of the expected titanic clash of Dreadnoughts—Germany's High Seas Fleet versus England's Grand Fleet. But England's geographic location allowed her to blockade Germany from a distance, shutting off her seaborne commerce by stopping ships from passing around the British Isles. This blockade left Germany frustrated and in short supply of vital materials needed to fuel her war effort. The High Seas Fleet remained bottled up in German ports, for both sides greatly feared a major naval confrontation, in which the entire war could be won or lost in a single afternoon. In fact, there were only two major confrontations between Dreadnoughts in the First World War—the Battle of Dogger Bank and the Battle of Jutland. Neither confrontation produced a clear victor, and the naval war appeared destined to be a campaign of avoidance. But a largely overlooked naval weapon was about to make its dramatic debut.

In the war's second month Germany's tiny U-boat fleet, then consisting of only 26 submarines and ranking fifth in size among the war's combatants, decisively demonstrated the tremendous offensive potential of the *unterseeboot*. On September 5, 1914, Korvettenkapitan Otto Hersing commanding the *U-21* found the British light cruiser *Pathfinder* steaming obligingly toward him. Submerging, Hersing merely had to wait for the enemy warship to come into range. He fired a single torpedo at his target. His aim was accurate and the barb of the revolutionary new weapon ran straight, hitting the British warship behind the bridge and igniting one of her magazines. The ship went down in only four minutes with a heavy loss of life.

But the real eye-opener came 17 days later. On September 22nd, Kapitanleutnant Otto Weddigen, commanding the obsolete kerosene-powered *U-9*, sank three 10,000-ton British armored cruisers, *Aboukir*, *Hogue* and *Cressy*, in the course of one hour using only five torpedoes. Some 1,400 British sailors lost their lives in the attack, and the loss of three capital ships was an embarrassment to the British Navy. Naval establishments throughout the world sat up and took notice—the submarine had come of age.

The sinking of the British cruisers had proved the military worth of the submarine as an offensive weapon, but it was its use against merchant shipping that would bring the weapon into its own. On February 4, 1915, in response to Britain's naval blockade of Germany's seaborne commerce, Germany declared the area around the British Isles a war zone. Germany's submarines would sink all merchant vessels found within this combat area without warning—the first employment of unrestricted submarine warfare on merchant shipping the world had ever seen.

This policy came to a halt only seven months later, following worldwide protests after the sinking of the liners *Lusitania* by the *U-20* on May 7th, and the *Arabic* by the *U-24* on August 19th. On August 30th, German submarines were prohibited from attacking passenger liners without warning, and were required to ensure the safety of the crew and passengers before sinking the ships. Shortly thereafter, Germany's U-boats were withdrawn from western waters, however, this hiatus in the German commerce war would not last long. The unrestricted submarine campaign was reinstituted on February 11, 1916, when Germany announced that enemy merchant shipping inside the war zone was again subject to attack without warning. This second campaign lasted less than two months, however, when it was again called off after the sinking of the French passenger steamer *Sussex* on March 24th. The United States had protested and issued an ultimatum to the German government: the submarine war against passenger and freight vessels must stop, or Germany would face a break in diplomatic relations.

But the land war on the European continent was not going well for Germany, and she was becoming increasingly desperate. On February 1, 1917, Germany once again began an unrestricted submarine campaign against Britain's merchant shipping, this time encompassing the North Sea, the English Channel, the Mediterranean Sea and the western approaches of the Atlantic—it was Germany's last hope for survival.

Only two months later, the United States, long reluctant to enter the conflict, ended her neutrality and declared war on Germany. The date was April 6, 1917.

ESCORTING ALLIED CONVOYS:
THE SINKING OF THE REVENUE CUTTER *MOHAWK*

On the same day that the United States declared war on Germany, a fleet of cutters commanded by the recently formed United States Coast Guard was temporarily transferred to the Navy (Continued on page 109)

SHIPWRECKS AS ARTIFICIAL REEFS

ENCRUSTING MARINE ORGANISMS

Sea anemones carpet intact hulls and scattered wreckage in northern waters. Although flowerlike in appearance, they are actually animals. With their tentacles retracted (left; left middle), they look like plump fruit; when open and feeding (right; right, middle), they take on a completely different appearance.

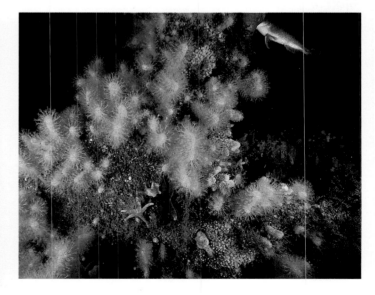

Colorful soft corals (above) are sometimes found on northern wrecks—such vivid colors are rare, however, for most creatures in these waters tend toward drab greens and browns.

Mussels (left) are another encrusting organism commonly found in abundance on northeast shipwrecks.

SHIPWRECKS AS ARTIFICIAL REEFS

CRUSTACEANS AND STARFISH

Starfish are almost always found in abundance on shipwrecks. The crimson blood star (above, left) provides a colorful addition to an often drab landscape. Starfish feed on shellfish such as mussels, and can often be found eating their way across a mussel bed like this on the top of one of the Oregon's boilers (above, middle). This starfish (above, right) seems to be reaching out for one of the terminals on a fuse panel deep inside the USS San Diego (above, right).

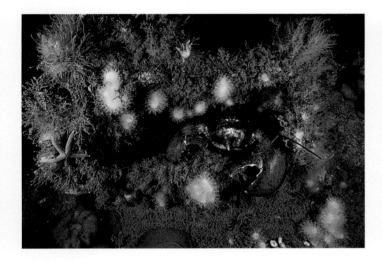 

A large lobster hides inside an orifice on a paddle wheel steam engine off the coast of New Jersey. Lobster are found in abundance on shipwrecks, and hunting them is popular among divers (above).

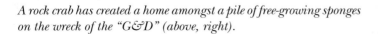

A rock crab has created a home amongst a pile of free-growing sponges on the wreck of the "G&D" (above, right).

Shipwrecks serve as congregation points for a huge variety of creatures; sand dollars are often found burrowing in the sand alongside wrecks (right).

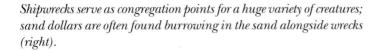

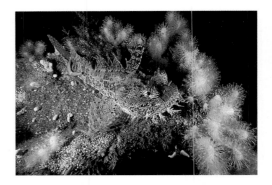

The sea raven, a particularly ugly member of the sculpin family, is a common sight on northern shipwrecks. They come in a wide variety of colors ranging from black to drab browns and greens, and often seem to blend into their surroundings (left, bottom and right, top). Sometimes, however, they seem to defy all efforts at camouflage and display bright colorations ranging from bright yellows (left, top) to reds. They are characterized by their long spines, pebbly skin and a host of fleshy tabs on their chin (right, bottom).

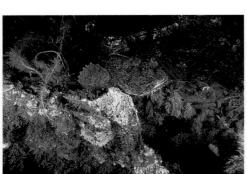

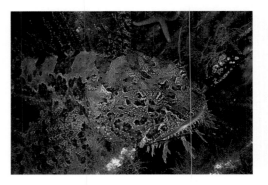

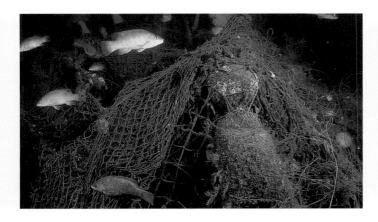

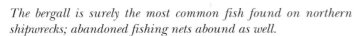

The bergall is surely the most common fish found on northern shipwrecks; abandoned fishing nets abound as well.

The strange looking and well camouflaged goosefish is sometimes seen lying in the sand alongside a wreck.

An ocean pout peers from a crevice on the Oregon (left); out in the open they appear quite different (right). Red hake often school near wrecks (above).

REVENUE CUTTER *MOHAWK*:

When the revenue cutter *Mohawk* sank in October 1917, she did not settle into a peaceful grave. Instead, the *Mohawk* had come to rest in an area that would soon bear the mark "DUMP SITE: municipal sewage sludge" on coastal navigation charts.

As early as 1925, a controversy raged between the states of New York and New Jersey over ocean garbage dumping, the latter blaming the former for the trash washing up on its beaches. A court battle finally resulted in the end of garbage dumping at sea in 1934—yet the dumping of an even more treacherous substance had already begun. In 1924, a special site was designated for the disposal of "sewage sludge" 12 miles southeast of New York Harbor. For the next 63 years, day after day, year after year, decade after decade, New York's "sludge barges" made daily trips out to the dumping grounds, and the *Mohawk*'s grave.

The environmental awareness that came with the arrival of the 1960s and '70s drew attention to this abhorrent practice. In 1973 Dr. William Harris, a Brooklyn College marine scientist, reported that a survey of the ocean bottom off Atlantic Beach, Long Island found that sewage sludge had crept to within a half mile of the beach. Seven months later, he announced that the sludge had come to within a quarter mile of the beach and predicted that the ocean currents would bring the sewage ashore by 1977. This was disputed by the National Oceanic and Atmospheric Administration (NOAA) and the Environmental Protection Agency (EPA), who claimed that the sludge "presents no threat to swimmers and may even be of natural origin."

In June 1976, 20 miles of Fire Island beaches were closed to swimmers: Dr. Harris's prediction had been off by only one year—the sludge had arrived on the beaches early. Throughout the month of June "globules of sewage-like material" washed up along Fire Island's beaches. When accusing fingers pointed to the City of New York's dumping practices, the EPA came rushing to the defense of the metropolitan giant, denying that the City was the "major cause" of the polluted beaches.

In July, commercial fishermen reported a huge fish kill off the coast of New Jersey, extending from Sandy Hook to Barnegat Inlet; the water below the thermocline was fouled a yellowish-brown color and the oxygen content was found to be below normal. Biologists later determined that offshore sewage dumping had caused an algae bloom that depleted the seawater's dissolved oxygen and subsequently killed hundreds of thousands of fish. Raw sewage continued to wash up on the beaches, and public outcry was enormous. It was the uproar of the voting public that finally caught the attention of the politicians, who had so long ignored the environmentalists. In July the EPA announced that all municipalities must end ocean dumping by 1981; EPA administrator Gerald Hansler proclaimed that the government would "not tolerate" any failure by New York and New Jersey to meet the deadline. Such threats failed to impress the City of New York, however, who sued the EPA over the issue and won—Judge Abraham Sofaer ruled that the EPA could not stop New York from dumping its sludge in the ocean unless it determined that such dumping would "unreasonably degrade the marine environment." The dumping continued.

In 1985 the EPA tried a new approach by ordering the sludge to be dumped further out to sea: 106 miles off the New Jersey coast and beyond the edge of the continental shelf. The new dumping limits were to go into effect at the end of 1987; compliance was all but assured when sewage again appeared on the beaches during the summer of 1987, this time accompanied by infectious medical waste. Dumping at the 12-mile site ceased in November 1987, but only at the expense of a previously untouched deep sea environment off the edge of the continental shelf. Before long, lobster fishermen reported that crabs and lobster caught in the area exhibited burn-like holes eaten through their shells by bacteria breeding in the sludge on the ocean floor.

The summer of 1988 brought another massive fish kill off the New Jersey coast and medical waste continued to wash ashore on the beaches, outraging a public fearful of the AIDS epidemic. While the source of the medical waste

Long Island

RC *Mohawk*

DUMP SITE
(municipal sewage sludge)

New Jersey

Atlantic Ocean

was unclear, the message wasn't. In October 1988, both the House of Representatives and the Senate passed a bill banning the dumping of sewage sludge at sea after January 1, 1992. New York City immediately protested and managed to gain a six-month extension of the deadline, but the end of ocean dumping was inevitable. On July 7, 1992, the sludge barge *The Spring Creek* released the last 450,000 cubic yards of sewage sludge to be dumped in United States waters. A long, hard-fought battle had finally been won.

But the end of 63 years of ocean dumping did not suddenly change the condition of the marine environment—the damage had been done and the recovery of the area would take time. Sewage sludge, dumped for decades, had driven almost all living creatures from the area—an area that had come to be known as "the dead sea." A few years after the close of the 12-mile dump site, however, an astounding change began to take place in the waters surrounding the wreck of the *Mohawk*. Visiting scuba divers found the murky, yellowish-brown water of years past less and less frequent. Fish and other marine life slowly began to return and, amazingly, over the course of the past several years a six-decade accumulation of sludge appears to be receding.

Today, schools of fish swarm above the *Mohawk*'s bow and stern, while sea anemones carpet the higher parts of her hull. But down below are signs that all is not well. Plastic debris of decades past can be found strewn about the bottom; glass bottles from an earlier epoch in man's dumping history abound, along with evidence of more recent disposals—scores of medical hypodermic needles. Fanning the fine layer of brownish sediment from the ocean bottom reveals a thick layer of black goo of unmistakable origin—the *Mohawk* is still not at peace with her surroundings.

The Mohawk's *bow rises above the ocean bottom, supporting a variety of life high above a bottom scarred by decades of ocean dumping.*

R.C. *MOHAWK*: LIFE ABOVE...DEATH BELOW

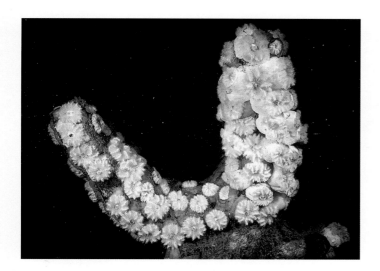

A gun mount yoke near the ship's stern once held a three-inch gun (left).

On the side of the ship's engine, a steam pipe serves as home to a colony of sea anemones (right).

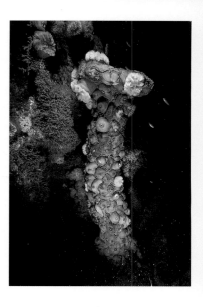

A crab hides inside an open steam valve.

Beneath the silty-gray bottom, black sludge from decades of sewage dumping can still be found.

"BETH ISRAEL MEDICAL..." reads this cloth tag littering the ocean bottom, proof positive that medical waste once found its way into our offshore waters.

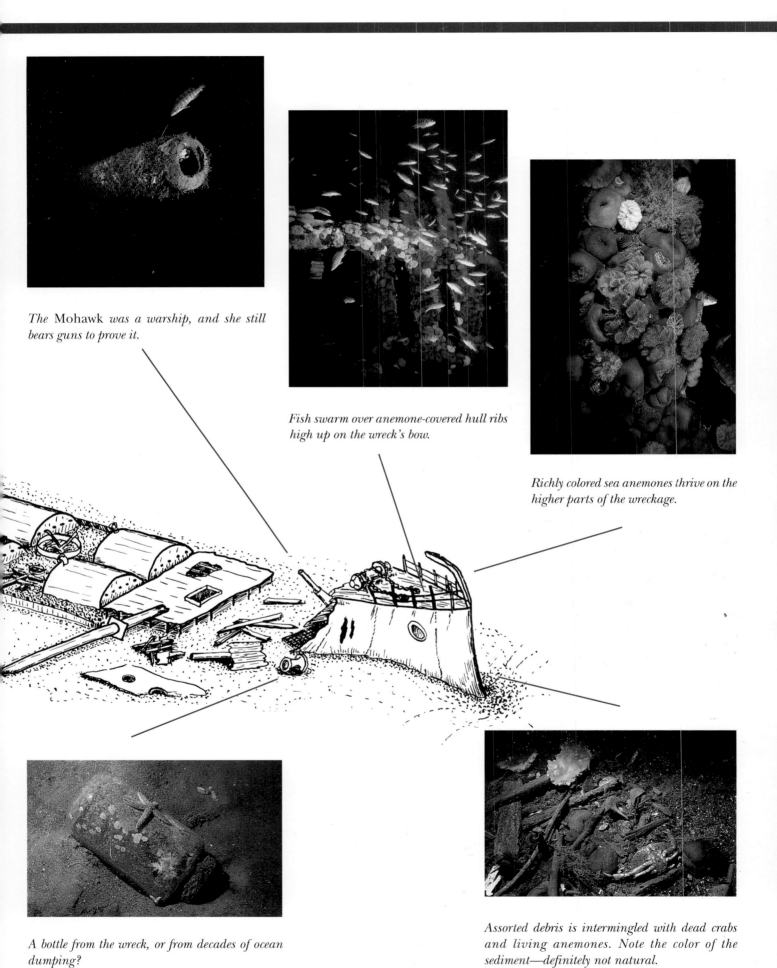

The Mohawk *was a warship, and she still bears guns to prove it.*

Fish swarm over anemone-covered hull ribs high up on the wreck's bow.

Richly colored sea anemones thrive on the higher parts of the wreckage.

A bottle from the wreck, or from decades of ocean dumping?

Assorted debris is intermingled with dead crabs and living anemones. Note the color of the sediment—definitely not natural.

THE *MOHAWK*'S ENGINE: OASIS IN A BARREN OCEAN

Rising some 15 feet above the scarred ocean floor, the *Mohawk*'s steam engine (left) forms a towering oasis for marine life trying to escape the poisoned bottom. Sea anemones and schooling fish can be found inhabiting every nook and cranny high off the bottom, but below, death and garbage bear witness to a long history of ocean dumping.

Seemingly every square inch of the Mohawk's *steam engine is carpeted with sea anemones.*

This oiler once distributed lubricating oil to the engine's moving parts; now it forms a trellis for flowerlike sea anemones.

A bergall finds refuge inside an open steam pipe.

The ocean bottom abounds in garbage and death.

USS *SAN DIEGO*: TURN-OF-THE-CENTURY WARSHIP

The USS *San Diego* was designed with one primary objective in mind—to make war on America's enemies. To that end, she was armed with a variety of heavy guns, small arms and even torpedoes. Her guns were mounted both in turrets on the main deck, and in casements in her sides, reminiscent of the days of iron cannon firing broadsides. Clockwise from top, left: 3-inch gun still mounted in its casement; thousands of rounds of small arms ammunition; 6-inch armor-piercing shells in one of the stern magazines; the breech end of a 6-inch gun; wooden rifle stocks still in their racks in the ship's armory; 6-inch powder cannisters in a bow magazine.

THE *SAN DIEGO* TODAY: A DECAYING TIME CAPSULE

The *San Diego*'s relatively intact hull, shown here as it appeared in the early 1980's, holds an almost infinite variety of items from an age nearly a century ago, when the world was at war. Every conceivable item that might be required to support a bloody battle at sea or a simple sailor's everyday life was contained aboard the *San Diego* when she went down.

Today her hull is rapidly collapsing, particularly the stern; the interior is filled with mountains of silt, falling beams and hull plates, making it dangerous for divers to explore. Yet within this collapsing time capsule a view of another era can still be glimpsed, luring divers into her labyrinth despite the danger.

The warship's knife-edged bow looms high above the sand (left).

A plethora of storerooms held supplies to cover all possible contingencies at sea (right).

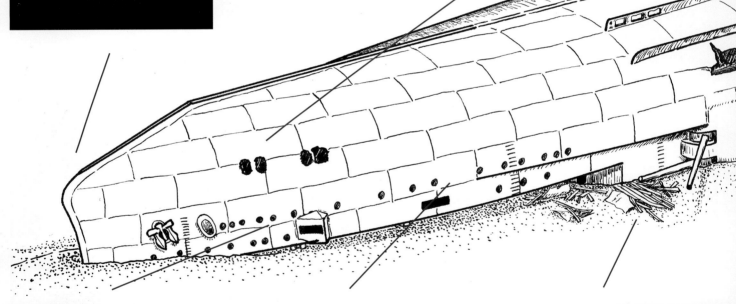

A pair of marine toilets hang down from overhead in the bow—a reminder that the ship lies upside down.

Part of an old-fashioned desk sits half-buried in silt in the ship's infirmary, providing a perfect home for lobster.

The ship's superstructure is pinned under her hull, crushed by the weight of the massive warship as it settled to the bottom.

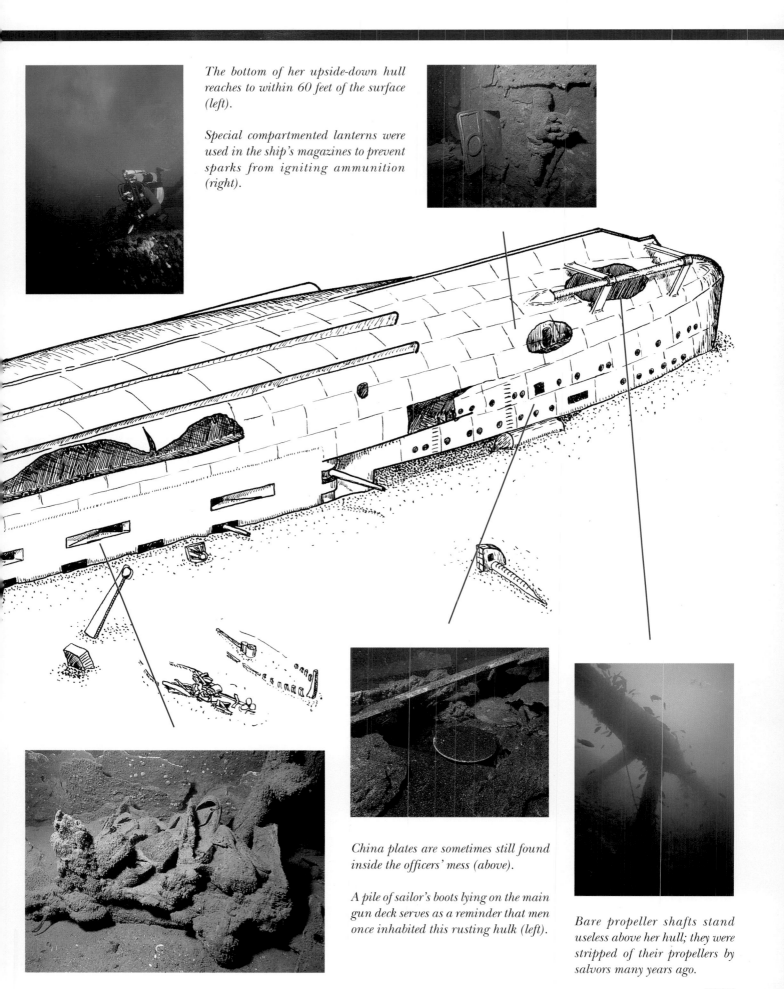

The bottom of her upside-down hull reaches to within 60 feet of the surface (left).

Special compartmented lanterns were used in the ship's magazines to prevent sparks from igniting ammunition (right).

China plates are sometimes still found inside the officers' mess (above).

A pile of sailor's boots lying on the main gun deck serves as a reminder that men once inhabited this rusting hulk (left).

Bare propeller shafts stand useless above her hull; they were stripped of their propellers by salvors many years ago.

The San Diego Beckons to Be Explored

Small Wrecks in the Warship's Shadow

The wreckage of several of the San Diego's lifeboats can be found strewn about the sand alongside her inverted hull. Clockwise, from upper left: the stem post and ribs of a wooden lifeboat; lifeboat rudder; a giant pulley on one of the lifeboat davits standing erect above the sand; bergalls swarm about one of the lifeboat's propellers.

The Gloomy Interior...

The USS San Diego offers a glimpse into another age. Surely the most popular wreck dive off the Long Island coast, the allure of exploring her remains is a siren call difficult to resist.

and the 13-year-old revenue cutter *Mohawk* suddenly found herself at war—a tiny combatant in the huge United States Navy.

Originally built for the United States Revenue Cutter Service, the *Mohawk* was part of a fleet of steel-hulled, steam-powered cutters constructed at the turn of the century. Built at the William R. Trigg Company shipyard in Richmond, Virginia, her sleek 205-foot hull was designed for extended coastal cruising in order to accomplish her primary duties of assisting vessels in distress and enforcing navigational laws. She was commissioned on May 10, 1904, and was named after one of the six Iroquois Indian nations of New York. Following her commissioning, the *Mohawk* was assigned to New York Harbor where her regular cruising grounds ranged from the Nantucket Shoals to the Delaware Breakwater. During her career in the Revenue Cutter Service, she was called upon numerous times to destroy floating derelicts blocking the shipping lanes. She was also active in assisting vessels unfortunate enough to ground on Long Island's southern beaches, such as the steamer *Drumelzier* in 1904, and the bark *Peter Rickmers* in 1908. Her duties also included assisting victims of offshore accidents. On the cold winter night of February 11, 1907, when the tragic collision between the coal schooner *Harry P. Knowlton* and the Joy Line paddle-wheel steamer *Larchmont* occurred, the *Mohawk* was ordered to sea to "do all in her power to render assistance."[1] Little could be done in one of the worst maritime tragedies ever to occur on Long Island Sound, however, and the cruel winter sea claimed the lives of all but 19 of more than 300 persons on board. On January 23, 1909, the steamship *Florida* collided with the White Star liner *Republic* some 26 miles southeast of the Nantucket lightship. The collision proved fatal for the *Republic*, but the *Mohawk* was unable to assist in this famous maritime accident, for she ran aground on Palmer's Island in New Bedford Harbor on her way to answer the distress signal. The *Mohawk* was pulled off the bar undamaged the following day. On January 28, 1915, the *Mohawk* was transferred to the newly formed United States Coast Guard.

After the outbreak of hostilities in Europe, but before the United States entry into the war, the *Mohawk* had spent her days on neutrality patrol up and down the East Coast. When the United States entered the war and the *Mohawk* became a member of the United States Navy, she was assigned to coastal patrol duty in support of convoy operations. Early in the war, England had developed the convoy system, the only effective defensive measure then available for merchant ships against the growing U-boat menace. The *Mohawk*'s new duties were to defend the assembling convoys outside the entrance to New York Harbor.

At first light on the morning of October 1, 1917, the sleek little cutter reported to the commanding officer of the USS *Gloucester*, who assigned the *Mohawk* to patrol sectors F, G and H outside the entrance to Ambrose Channel. A convoy was being assembled for the long Atlantic crossing and was nearly ready to sail. By 8:00 A.M. the *Mohawk* was busily patrolling her assigned sectors. Everything seemed in order on the bridge and it appeared to the watch officer, Lieutenant Whitbeck, that this would be just another routine patrol. The ship's commanding officer, First Lieutenant E. Barker, had left orders that the *Mohawk* be kept clear of the convoy, at a distance of at least one-half mile from the assembling ships, to avoid any possibility of collision. It was such a fine, clear morning that when Cadet Mandeville, who had been authorized by headquarters to stand a regular watch, came on deck at 8:00 A.M. to relieve Lieutenant Whitbeck, the lieutenant took the opportunity to join his fellow officers below for breakfast.

At 8:20 A.M., the *Mohawk*'s commanding officer came up on deck to check on the morning watch. He was dismayed to see a member of the convoy only a short distance off the starboard bow, headed at a right angle to the *Mohawk*'s course. It was obvious that a collision was imminent unless immediate action was taken. Rushing to the bridge, Barker startled the dazed cadet on watch by asking if he had blown any signals. The cadet replied that he had not, and quickly blew several short blasts—the marine danger signal. Barker immediately assumed command, ringing the engine room for full speed ahead and throwing the helm hard astarboard in a desperate attempt to get the *Mohawk* out of the path of the onrushing steamship. But the *Mohawk*'s reaction was too late, and the British steamship *Vennachar* slammed headlong into the side of the small revenue cutter. The *Vennachar*'s bow slipped neatly between the *Mohawk*'s starboard lifeboat davits, smashing her surfboat and slicing deeply into the engine room. The British steamer remained momentarily stuck in the *Mohawk*'s side, effectively plugging the gaping hole she had created. When she finally pulled free, the cold sea came pouring into the cutter's engine room. Lieutenant Barker climbed down below to see the damage first hand. The pumps were started immediately, but they could not keep up with the rising water in the *Mohawk*'s belly. The cut made by the *Vennachar* was so deep that the use of a collision mat was out of the question—Barker had no

The Mohawk, *down by the stern as she fills with water, is taken under tow by the USS* Bridge *(left, top). Courtesy of the National Archives. The* Mohawk *apparently broke in two as she hit the ocean bottom, for today her bow stands erect (above), while what is left of her stern lists heavily to starboard (left, below). Most of her hull plating has rusted away over the years, leaving only a skeleton of ribs behind.*

choice but to order all hands to abandon ship. The crew safely abandoned the cutter in her remaining boats, pulling well clear in case the boilers exploded. The *Mohawk* was filling rapidly and began to settle by the stern. Still, Barker returned on board a short time later to inspect his command, finding that the sea had risen to the level of the engine room gratings. It was clear she was going down.

The USS *Bridge* soon arrived and attached a hawser to the *Mohawk*'s bow, hoping to facilitate an eventual salvage operation by towing her to shallow water. But only ten minutes after she was taken under tow, the *Mohawk* began to list heavily to port. As the tow line was cut free, the *Mohawk* reared her bow skyward as her stern slowly settled to the ocean bottom. Wisps of smoke rose from her submerging boiler fires, and the sea boiled about her bow, churned by escaping air from her settling hull. Finally, at 9:39 A.M., the last of the *Mohawk* disappeared from sight. A red buoy was placed over the wreck, and along with the *Mohawk*'s mastheads still protruding from the sea, was the only visible aftermath of this relatively minor naval accident.

The possibility of raising the *Mohawk* was entertained for a short time, and salvage bids were received from three separate contractors. However, the salvage effort was estimated to cost in excess of $100,000 and was never pursued.

THE U-BOATS ARRIVE ON AMERICA'S DOORSTEP

Eleven months after the United States' entry into the war, the first hostile German U-boat appeared off the East Coast and shelled the steamship *Nyanza* on May 19, 1918. The *Nyanza* managed to escape, but those that followed would not be so fortunate. The large cruiser submarine *U-151* would return to Germany after sinking 22 vessels off the American coast, with a combined tonnage in excess of 52,000 gross tons.

The *U-151*, however, was not the first German submarine to visit the shores of the United States. During the second half of 1916, before America's entry into the war, the large mercantile submarine *Deutschland* made two trips to the Eastern Seaboard. Designed as a cargo-carrying blockade runner, she carried dyes and chemicals to the United States and returned to Germany with such scarce raw materials as rubber, copper, nickel and tin, slipping quietly *beneath* the English naval blockade. After two trading missions to the East Coast of her future adversary, the *Deutschland* was converted into a long-range warship armed with both torpedoes and two 15-cm deck guns, and redesignated

the *U-155*. (This and other large submarines came to be known as "U-cruisers.") Before long she would make a return visit to America under less amiable conditions.

Between the first and second visits of the *Deutschland*, the military submarine *U-53* also paid a visit to America. She appeared without warning outside the port of Newport, Rhode Island on October 7, 1916. Her visit was apparently meant as a warning to the United States that she would not be spared from the U-boat offensive if she entered the war. Her commander, Kapitanleutnant Hans Rose, stated to the authorities in Newport that he "had no object in entering the port except to pay his respects."[2] He stated that he would be happy to entertain visitors aboard his submarine, and in fact he proudly showed off his command to a number of officers who took him up on the offer. The *U-53* put back to sea that same afternoon. The following day she sank five steamships in the vicinity of the Nantucket lightship, but just outside American territorial waters. The U-53's victims were the British steamships *Stephano*, *Strathmore* and *West Point*, along with the Dutch *Blommersdijk* and the Norwegian *Chr. Knudson*. Ironically, American destroyers were forced to stand

The U-cruiser U-151, *as it stopped the Spanish passenger steamer* Infanta Isabel De Bourbon *on April 3, 1918 (prior to U-151's war cruise to America). Courtesy of the U.S. Naval Historical Center.*

by and watch the sinkings, unable to interfere due to the United States' neutrality in the war.

Before the war ended, six of the large, long-range U-cruisers were dispatched to the shores of America. Four of the cruisers were converted mercantile submarines; three, *U-151, U-152* and *U-156* were converted during their construction, while *U-155* was the former *Deutschland*. The two remaining submarines were designed from the outset as warships; the *U-140* was built as a cruiser while the *U-117* was designed as a mine layer. These six U-boats managed to sink a total of 99 vessels, with an aggregate tonnage of 166,907 gross tons, off the United States East Coast during a six month campaign. Besides the material loss, 421 deaths are attributed to this U-boat offensive.

THE MINE-LAYING CAMPAIGN: SINKING OF THE USS *SAN DIEGO*

An important aspect of the U-cruisers' missions to the

American coast was that of laying mines at the entrances of major shipping ports. Of the six U-cruisers sent to the American coast, all but the *U-140* carried submarine mines as part of their armament. Since the *U-152* had barely approached to within 1,000 miles of the American coast when the war ended, she never had the opportunity to plant her mines. The *U-155* laid mines off the coast of Nova Scotia, outside the entrance to the harbor at Halifax, before heading south with the intention of operating against coastal shipping. The remaining three boats planted seven minefields off the American coast.

The *U-151* was the first to arrive on the coast, and her commander was apparently eager to rid his boat of the high-explosive devices as soon as possible. On May 24th he planted a field of six mines approximately eight miles east of Cape Henry, just outside the channel entrance into Chesapeake Bay. Two days later he laid a second field consisting of eight more mines south of the Overfalls lightship, at the mouth of Delaware Bay. The mines carried by the U-boat were of

The tanker SS Herbert L. Pratt *fell victim to a mine laid by the* U-151 *in June 1918. She was later salvaged and became the USS* Herbert L. Pratt. *Courtesy of the U.S. Naval Historical Center.*

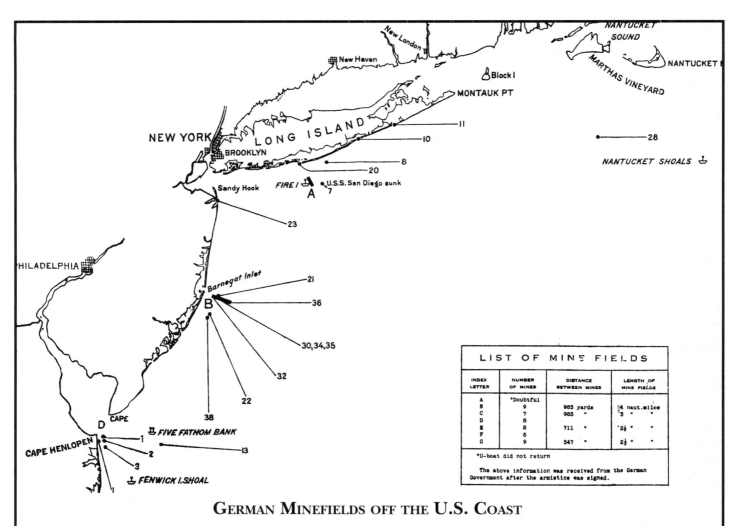

GERMAN MINEFIELDS OFF THE U.S. COAST

The above chart was compiled after the war using information supplied by the German government. Shown are the locations of seven minefields planted by German U-boats, as well as the locations of mines that were discovered by U.S. forces. Note the location of the USS *San Diego* sinking, mine field at "A," and mines later discovered to the east (numbers 8, 10, 11 & 20). From "Publication No. 1, German Submarine Activities on the Atlantic Coast of the United States and Canada," Government Printing Office, 1920.

two types: the six deposited outside Chesapeake Bay were carried outside the pressure hull on the main deck, and were thrown overboard, while the eight mines planted outside of Delaware Bay were carried inside the pressure hull, and were launched through the torpedo tubes. The latter type could be laid while the boat was submerged, while the deck-carried mines could only be launched while the boat was surfaced.

After disposing of her mines, the *U-151* embarked upon a three-week terror campaign against merchant shipping. On June 2nd her commander, Kapitan von Nostitz und Janckendorff, had a field day by sending three schooners and three steamships to the bottom some 60 miles off Atlantic City, New Jersey. The steamer *Winneconne* was first, followed by the schooners *Isabel*

B. Wiley, Jacob M. Haskell and *Edward H. Cole.* The steamer *Texel* was next, and the final prize of the day was the passenger steamer *Carolina.* Day after day, more and more ships were sent to the bottom. The schooner *Samuel C. Mengel* was sunk on the 3rd east of Assateague, Virginia, followed by the schooner *Edward R. Baird, Jr.* and the steamship *Eidsvold* on the 4th, off Cape Charles. On the 5th the steamships *Harpathian* and *Vinland* became victims of the marauding submarine as she moved south into North Carolina waters. Three days later the steamer *Pinar del Rio* was the victim. On the 10th the steamers *Vindeggan* and *Henrik Lund* were sunk, also off the coast of North Carolina. On the 14th the *U-151* shelled two sailing vessels, the barks *Samoa* and *Kringsjaa,* then turned and headed back toward Germany. In the next week she managed to destroy three more steamships while on her way home: the *Dwinsk* on the 18th, the *Chilier* on the 22nd, and finally the *Augwald* on the 23rd. In addition to those she sank in direct action, the *U-151* also is credited with sinking the tanker *Herbert L. Pratt*, who fell victim to one of the submarine's mines off the Overfalls lightship on June 3rd.

The second U-cruiser to arrive on the American coast was the *U-156*, which proceeded directly to the entrance to New York Harbor, where she had been instructed to plant her mines. Since this was the only one of the U-cruisers that did not return to Germany—she struck a mine in the North Sea on her return voyage and was sunk—her exact activities while off the American coast can only be reconstructed from circumstantial evidence. German records indicate that she was to lay a field of contact mines in the coastal shipping lane along the south shore of Long Island, just east of the Fire Island lightship. That she successfully completed her mission is evidenced by the sinking of the armored cruiser USS *San Diego*, which ran into one of her mines on the morning of July 19, 1918.

The *San Diego*, originally named *California*, was one of six armored cruisers contracted for by the United States Navy in 1901. Built by the Union Iron Works of San Francisco, she was commissioned on August 1, 1907. She spent the majority of her peace-time career operating in the Pacific theater and along the west coast. On September 1, 1914, the *California* was renamed USS *San Diego*, so that her former name could be assigned to a 32,300-ton battleship that had just been laid down. Three months after the United States entered the war, the *San Diego* was ordered to join the Atlantic fleet, where she was based at both Tompkinsville, New York, and Halifax, Nova Scotia. Her mission was to escort merchant convoys through the first leg of their Atlantic journey to Europe.

On July 19, 1918, the *San Diego* found herself zigzagging at 15 knots along the south shore of Long Island. She was returning to New York from Portsmouth, New Hampshire to pick up another convoy. Her decks were piled high with extra coal so that she could make a quick turnaround in New York without recoaling, and still have enough fuel for the Atlantic crossing. It was a fine morning; the sea was smooth except for a slight swell that lifted the cruiser slowly up and down as she steamed steadily along her course. The *San Diego* was running on a base course toward the beach, to the northwest; Captain Harley H. Christy had ordered a change in course 30 degrees to the north only a few minutes earlier. Still out of sight of

land in an era before modern electronics, Captain Christy wanted to make a landfall and confirm his ship's position before reaching the Fire Island lightship. He planned to take the cruiser inshore of the lightship, and make his way to New York as close to the beach as practical. The ship was on full wartime alert—enemy submarine activity had been reported off the coast and tensions were high. No fewer than 18 men were standing watch in addition to Captain Christy, who stood atop the ship's wheelhouse where he commanded a panoramic view of his ship's operations. An hour earlier Christy had cautioned the watch officer to keep his lookouts especially vigilant—these waters were considered dangerous.

At 11:05 A.M. the helmsman was preparing to execute the next turn in the ship's zig-zag pattern—in one minute he would turn the ship 22.5 degrees to starboard. Just then a dull, heavy thud jarred the cruiser. The *San Diego*'s hull shook roughly fore and aft while her stern lifted slightly; a fountain of water erupted high into the air aft of midships, on the port side. Almost immediately, the *San Diego* began listing to port. The ship's alarm system blared out as submarine defense quarters were sounded; the fire control officer ordered the ship's batteries to open fire on anything that remotely resembled a submarine. Captain Christy rang for both engines full ahead while ordering the helm over to starboard, hoping to head his ship into shallow water in case of the worst. Down below, in the *San Diego*'s bowels, chaos broke loose.

Lieutenant J.P. Millon had been standing in the open doorway connecting the port and starboard engine rooms when he was suddenly thrust into the starboard engine room by a violent explosion, knocking him against Machinist's Mate George Stockton, who was operating the starboard engine throttle. Machinist's Mate Robert Hawthorne, stationed at the port engine throttle, was blown clear across the room and into a steel bulkhead by the blast. A broken steam line billowed scalding clouds of steam into the machinery spaces. Lieutenant Millon recovered from his initial shock and stepped back through the doorway and into the port engine room. A rolling wave of black, coal-streaked water was rushing toward him from behind the port engine, rapidly flooding the compartment. The main engine appeared to have been blown clear off its base, and the forward bulkhead, separating the engine room from the No. 8 fireroom, was twisted and distorted. Of the four men on duty in the port engine room, Lieutenant Millon could only find Hawthorne. Engineman James Rochet and Machinist's Mate Frazier Thomas were apparently killed instantly by the

The armored cruiser USS San Diego *was originally named* California, *but her name was changed when the Navy began using state names for battleships. The* San Diego *was the only major U.S. warship lost in World War I. Courtesy of the National Archives.*

explosion, while Engineman Thomas Davis had locked himself into the port shaft alley to lubricate the shaft bearings only seconds earlier. The water flooding the engine room quickly covered the only exit from the shaft alley, blocking the door to what would soon become his tomb. Millon ordered Stockton to close the water-tight door separating the two engine rooms, and made his way forward into the No. 7 fireroom. From there he tried opening the connecting doorway into the No. 8 fireroom, but was forced to slam it shut when he was greeted by a flood of water.

Up on the gun deck, the gunnery officers took to their task with the desperation of men at the losing end of a battle. Three-inch and six-inch shells began falling on any object floating in the sea. The forward starboard, three-inch gun banged off a shot at a barrel floating on the swells. On the port side aft, the crew of three-inch gun station No. 14 began lobbing shells at what looked to them to be a periscope some 200 yards away. Six-inch gun station No. 1, forward on the starboard side, fired at two objects very close together that also looked like a periscope. After two shots, their target disappeared and they began firing at other bits of floating wreckage. The port midships, three-inch

Descending the anchor chain of the charter boat Sea Hawk, *diver Frank Nardi lands atop the* San Diego*'s upside-down bow. The double tanks, dry suit and tool bag are typical of a northeast "wrecker," due to the cold, deep water and harsh conditions that enshroud many of these shipwrecks.*

gun crew brought their weapon to bear on an object that appeared about the size of a gallon can. All told, some 40 shells were fired at suspicious looking objects, real or imagined, before the ship's list forced the gun crews to abandon their posts.

Upstairs on the ship's bridge, Captain Christy received damage reports first-hand from his executive officer. Returning to the bridge after a hasty inspection below decks, Lieutenant Commander Gerard Bradford reported that frame No. 78 had been blown in below the waterline—the port engine room and No. 8 fire room were flooded. The surrounding bulkheads were strained and leaking, and the dynamo compartment was taking water. Meanwhile, the ship's list to

port was increasing by the minute, and it was soon apparent that the ship would capsize. Only ten minutes had passed since the explosion. Captain Christy gave the order to abandon ship.

The gun crews were ordered to keep firing until they could no longer operate their guns. Topside, the men found that there was no electric current to operate the boat cranes—the dynamos had been shut down by the rising water. Without the cranes, there was no way to launch the *San Diego*'s big cutters. Two whale boats, a dinghy and a wherry (a long, light, double-ended rowboat) were launched by hand, along with all the life rafts stored on the upper deck. In addition, some 50 mess tables and 100 kapok mattresses were thrown over the side by the escaping crew. Most of the men jumped into the calm sea, clinging to rafts and floating debris while struggling to swim clear of the vessel. Machinist's Mate Andrew Munson and Fireman Clyde Blaine were killed in the abandonment. Munson was struck in the head by a falling life raft after he had jumped into the sea; Blaine was last seen on the cruiser's upper deck, and was believed to have drowned trying to abandon ship. Seaman John Harris was the last lookout to leave the fore topmast, and never made it out of the *San Diego*'s cage mast—he was trapped and drowned as the ship capsized.

As the *San Diego*'s list reached 35 degrees, her port bridge wing dipped into the sea; Lieutenant Commander Bradford dove off the bridge to make his escape, leaving Captain Christy alone on board. After assuring himself that all hands had left his ship, he walked across two now horizontal ladders from the *San Diego*'s bridge to the boat deck, then up to the outside of her hull. Standing on her armor belt, he walked along the starboard side of the hull towards the ship's bottom, jumping first down to the bilge keel, then to her docking keel and finally into the sea. Just as Christy got clear of the ship, she rolled over onto her port side and then rolled completely upside down. Shortly afterward, the great cruiser disappeared from sight—she had sunk in less than twenty-five minutes.

Over a thousand men were now floating in the ocean ten miles off the beach, clinging to rafts, wreckage and the few boats they had managed to launch. The blast had destroyed the wireless—no distress signal had been sent and no one was aware of their plight. Captain Christy ordered two of the boats, under the command of Lieutenant C. Bright, to proceed toward shore and secure assistance. Later that afternoon the boats arrived at Point O' Woods on Fire Island, announcing the tragedy to the crew of Life-Saving Station Number 82. Soon the men were on the telephone with New York, and shortly thereafter shore stations began broadcasting the *San Diego*'s fate to coastal shipping. Meanwhile, Captain Christy had stepped a mast in his whaleboat and hoisted sail. Sighting two steamships to the southwest, he set out to intercept them and secure their assistance. The steamers turned out to be the *Malden* and the *Bussun*. Later, a third steamship, the *F.P. Jones*, came upon the scene and joined in the rescue operation. The three steamships remained in the area until about 3:00 P.M., searching for survivors before turning and heading for New York. The captains and crews of these vessels were later commended by the Navy for their bravery, risking their ships in submarine-infested waters to rescue the crew of the sunken cruiser. One thousand one hundred eighty-four persons were on board the *San Diego* that day; only six men were lost, and the remaining 1,178 were picked up by the three steamships or rowed ashore in the ship's boats.

The following morning six contact mines were discovered by minesweepers, floating some eight miles east of the Fire Island lightship. The mines were long, cylindrical objects, painted a light gray color with four deadly horns protruding from their upper side. The mines were unanchored, floating free and devoid of any marine growth, a sure sign that they had not been in the water long. Two weeks later, two more mines were found washed up on the eastern beaches of Long Island—trinkets left behind by the *U-156*.

The day after the sinking, as minesweepers were disposing of the *U-156*'s deadly cargo, a patrol plane reported sighting a submarine. With U-boat fever running high after the previous day's events, response was swift. The patrol plane attacked its quarry with depth charges, while the two minesweepers that had been rounding up the *U-156*'s mines turned and headed toward the scene at full speed. Two destroyers came racing down upon the interloper with guns blazing and depth charges rolling off their after decks. The attack brought air bubbles mixed with oil spouting to the surface. The sweepers snagged the target with cables so that it couldn't escape. Finally, a diver was sent down to examine the prisoner. Surfacing ten minutes later, the diver reported that the "submarine" was an old coal barge. Later it was learned that the "coal barge" was actually the upside-down hull of the armored cruiser USS *San Diego*.

More dives were made on the wreck over the course of the next several days, and one of the divers reported: "The wreck of the *San Diego* was lying in seventeen and a half or eighteen fathoms of water. Part of the vessel, the bow, is about seven and one half fathoms

from the surface and I should judge the stern is about fourteen fathoms. The wreck is lying completely upside-down and I landed on her bottom and inspected her whole bottom and it is in good condition, no abrasions or holes whatever. After I inspected the bottom I went over the side. I started forward and was hauled aft to about #4 smokestack on the port side. The first thing that I saw was a large hole about five feet in diameter twelve feet below the ship's waterline. Around the hole the side was bulging out. I was sure it was the *San Diego*."[3] After questioning by the court of inquiry, the diver later concluded that what he thought was hull plating "bulging out" was actually the ship's bilge keel. The significance of this detail is, of course, that the hull plating could not have been bulging *outward* if the hole were caused by an *external* explosion—i.e. a mine. After considering all the available evidence, a naval court of inquiry concluded that "the loss of the USS *San Diego* was due to an external explosion of a mine."[4]

Meanwhile, the *U-156* had headed north to undertake a more bizarre mission—the destruction of the North American fishing fleet. In what surely must have been intended to demoralize the American people, the *U-156* sank 21 fishing vessels in the Gulf of Maine region, from Cape Cod to the Bay of Fundy. Ranging in size from the tiny 72-ton fishing schooner *Nelson A.* to the 766-ton schooner *Dornfontein*, these helpless targets could have no material effect on the European war. But the spectacle of a poor fisherman's means of livelihood being destroyed surely brought the war home to the American public. The *U-156*'s commander, Kapitanleutnant von Oldenburg, at one point captured the fishing trawler *Triumph*, armed her and used her as a raiding vessel. The Oberleutnant, J. Knoeckel, bragged to a member of the *Triumph*'s crew that they had torpedoed the *San Diego* a month earlier, while von Oldenburg declared, "I have been sent here to annihilate the American fishing fleet and I am going to do it."[5] When the *U-156* finally left the American coast, its weapons had indeed sunk a total of 36 vessels for a combined tonnage of 34,220 gross tons. The loss of the *U-156* to a mine on her homebound voyage was a final irony that was undoubtedly sweet justice for the crew of the *San Diego*.

THE U-BOAT WAR CONTINUES

August of 1918 saw the arrival of two more of the German long-range raiders off the American coast. The *U-140*, commanded by Fregattenkapitan Waldemar

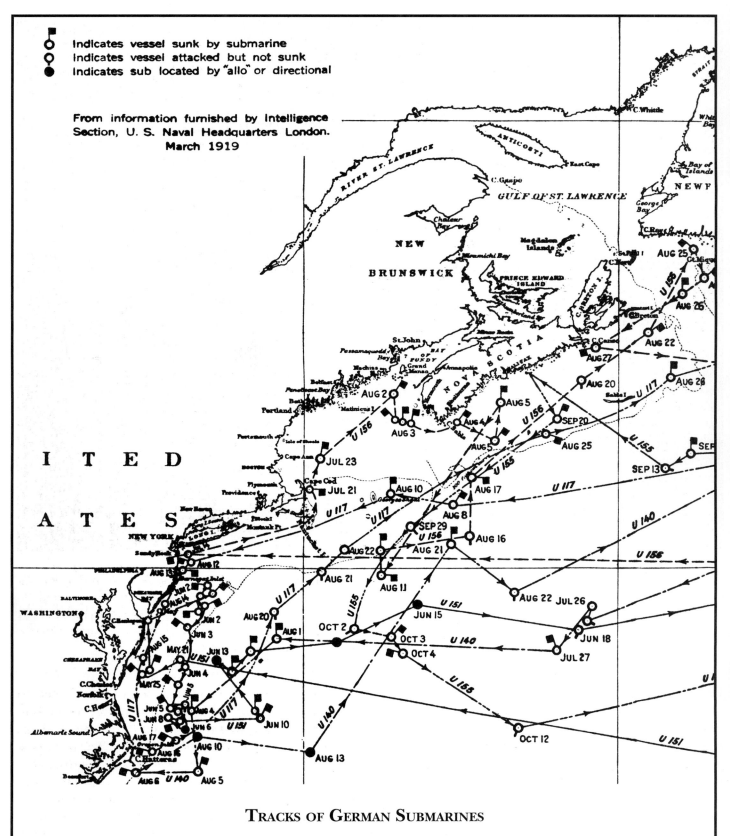

TRACKS OF GERMAN SUBMARINES

This portion of a U.S. intelligence chart shows the operation of German U-boats off the East Coast during the war. U-boat locations were established by direction finding of intercepted radio traffic, as well as U-boat sightings and vessels sunk. From "Publication Number 1, German Submarine Activities on the Atlantic Coast of the United States and Canada," Government Printing Office, 1920.

An interior view of the U-140 *after being turned over to the Allies at the war's conclusion. The photo was taken at the Portsmouth Navy Yard, New Hampshire about 1920. The sub was later sunk off the Virginia Capes by naval gunfire. Courtesy of the U.S. Naval Historical Center.*

Kophamel, announced her presence off the American coast by torpedoing the Japanese freighter *Tokuyama Maru* 200 miles southeast of New York on August 1st. The *U-117*, under command of Kapitan-leutnant Droesher, showed herself nine days later when she sank nine fishing vessels on the George's Bank, east of Nantucket and Cape Cod, only a few days after the *U-156*'s similar series of attacks to the north.

The *U-140* had not journeyed to the American coast under a cloak of secrecy—far from it. She had unsuccessfully pursued a number of vessels during her Atlantic crossing before encountering the Portuguese bark *Porto* 450 miles southeast of Cape Cod. Fleeing an enemy submarine was not possible for the crew of a three-masted bark, and her captain was forced to abandon her while the Germans sent her to the bottom with bombs planted on board, as well as shells fired from the submarine's deck guns. Before disposing of their first victim, however, the crew of the *U-140* spent five hours raiding the bark's food stores, showing particular interest in her cache of chickens and pork. The *Porto*'s crew of 18 were left afloat in the ship's boats, and were picked up by a passing steamship the following day. It was five days later when the *U-140* placed a single torpedo under the bridge of the freighter *Tokuyama Maru*. Two hours after the crew of 85 had abandoned the steamship, the U-boat surfaced and put two shells into her victim to finish the job.

After watching the *Tokuyama Maru* sink, the *U-140* headed southwest toward the coast of Virginia and North Carolina. On the morning of August 4th, she ran across the 10,300-ton American tanker *O.B. Jennings* some 100 miles off the Capes of Virginia. Noting a gun on her stern, Kophamel submerged and fired a single torpedo at his target. The shot missed after the captain of the steamer threw his ship's helm hard over to port in time to avoid the torpedo. Kophamel, in his log, claims that the ship was so large that its size deceived his estimate of her range and caused him to blow the shot. In any case, the *U-140* came to the surface and began pursuit with her deck gun blazing. The captain of the tanker, George Nordstrom, ordered more steam added to what was already his ship's rated full speed, and began zig-zagging away from the submarine while his gun crew fired back at the submarine. Smoke boxes were broken out on the tanker's stern in an attempt to form a screen to hide behind, and wireless calls for help were sent. Two and one-half hours after firing the torpedo at the tanker, the deck gun of the U-boat finally made a direct hit to the engine room, disabling the tanker. Another shell scored a direct hit in the magazine, and Captain Nordstrom was compelled to abandon ship.

The submarine proceeded to pull alongside the three lifeboats, asking who the ship's captain was. Before abandoning ship, however, Captain Nordstrom had taken the precaution of switching clothing with a man who had been killed in the gunfire exchange. Now completing the ruse, the men in the lifeboats told the German commander that their captain had been killed in the action. In response, the Germans took the second officer, Rene Henry Bastin, prisoner on board the U-boat before sinking the tanker with artillery fire.

THE STRANGE SAGA OF RENE HENRY BASTIN

Rene Henry Bastin, second officer of the tanker *O.B. Jennings,* was a mysterious character. He had joined the crew of the tanker in Southampton, England, before the transatlantic voyage. He was a Belgian and spoke both French and German fluently, which might have added to the suspicions both the crew and officers of the *Jennings* felt toward him. After being taken captive, Bastin remained on board the *U-140* until its return to Germany, and was later released after the armistice. Upon his return to the United States, he related his experiences aboard the German submarine to both the naval authorities and the press.

Bastin claimed to have been forcibly taken prisoner on board the submarine at the insistence of her commander. Yet the remainder of the tanker's crew told a different story, claiming that Bastin jumped on board the U-boat and spoke rapidly with her officers in fluent German. After a short conversation he shook hands with the submariners and disappeared below decks. Kophamel recorded in his war diary that the second officer "urgently requested to be taken prisoner on board." He provided the Germans with important information on shipping traffic and, significantly, provided help in crossing the Allies' northern barrage of mines stretching across the top of the North Sea on the return trip to Germany. Yet he was

This aerial view of the U-140 *while in American hands was probably taken when she was anchored off the Virginia Capes prior to her sinking. She was sent to the bottom by naval gunfire during Gen. Billy Mitchell's aerial bombardment demonstrations in June 1921. Courtesy of the U.S. Naval Historical Center.*

certainly not a spy, for he is referred to throughout the *U-140*'s logbook as "the prisoner."

Bastin, thanks to his apparently voluntary captivity aboard the U-boat, was able to experience firsthand both sides of the submarine war. Six days after being taken captive, on August 10th, the *U-140* was in hot pursuit of the Brazilian steamship *Uberaba*, and attempting to stop her with shellfire. The steamer's calls for help on the wireless were eventually answered and she was informed that four destroyers were racing toward her at full speed. Although the U-boat intercepted this news, she refused to break off the attack until the destroyers were almost upon her, when she finally submerged.

The first destroyer was the USS *Stringham*, and she came roaring down on the submerged U-boat with a fury, dropping a total of 15 depth charges (16 according to the *U-140*'s log). Kophamel thought he was doomed when the first series of charges were right on the mark. The depth charges continued, blowing in the U-boat's midships hatch and causing severe leaks throughout the boat. The submarine was in serious trouble, having shipped some 45 tons of water through the leaks in her pressure hull. The boat became difficult to hold on an even keel with all the loose water sloshing about, and it was only by using the boat's compressed air that Kophamel was able keep the water at bay and prevent the *U-140* from sinking. Eight and one-half hours after first sighting the *Uberaba*, the *U-140* came to the surface, relieved to find no one in sight. Surveying the damage to his submarine, Kophamel realized it was only the destroyer captain's inexperience that had prevented the U-boat from being sunk—a few more well-placed charges and she would have been finished. The *U-140* headed out into the Atlantic, away from coastal shipping, to spend the next several days making repairs.

There Kophamel realized that his exploits on the American coast were over. An oil slick stretched behind the submarine "all the way to the horizon,"[6] and the leak couldn't be stopped. The tell-tale slick would make her easy prey for American destroyers, and she was forced to head back toward Germany, though she did manage to send the 7,500-ton English steamship *Diomed* to the bottom while on her way home. Her adventures in the North Sea and the crossing of the northern barrage, as related by her prisoner, Rene Bastin, are fascinating, but apparently distorted.

Bastin's narrative relates the refueling operation between the *U-140* and the *U-117* north of England, near the Faeroe Islands, on September 9-13. The *U-117* had run seriously short of diesel oil, and via wire-

less arranged a rendezvous with Kophamel's boat. The two U-boats met on the 9th, but were unable to accomplish a fuel transfer due to the huge sea that was running. Not until September 12th, by which time the *U-117* was almost out of fuel, was the transfer accomplished. The submarines had been provided with no equipment to transfer fuel between boats at sea, and were forced to improvise. They managed to string a manila line between the two U-boats and, using empty shell cases as buckets, hauled the precious fuel oil from the *U-140* to the *U-117*. (Bastin's narrative is flawed, for he has the *U-140* receiving fuel from the *U-117*.)

Perhaps Bastin's most fascinating tale, however, is of the death of the *U-156*, destroyer of the *San Diego*. Bastin claimed to have been on the bridge of the *U-140* while she was running through the northern barrage in company with the *U-100*, *U-102*, *U-117* and *U-156*. He claimed to have known they were within the barrage because he recognized net buoys from when he was in the British transport service. Then he "suddenly saw a submarine blown up—it was the German *U-156*. She was on our port quarter and steaming in line with the *100*, which was a small sub. She must have struck a mine and was blown 500 feet in the air. A few seconds and everything had disappeared. All the other submarines kept on their courses and took no notice of it."[7] The date given by Bastin for this event is October 22nd, almost a month after both the sinking of the *U-156* and the return of the *U-140*, aboard which Bastin was captive, to Germany!

In fact, the *U-140* never met up with the *U-156*, and crossed the northern barrage in company with only the *U-117* on September 17th. According to the *U-140*'s log, Bastin provided important information to the Germans on the construction of the barrage, including an explanation of the cork buoys that marked a safe channel through the field. This enabled the two submarines to pass through the field unharmed, after which they separated. The *U-140* arrived in Kiel on September 20th, while on the same day the *U-117* finally ran out of fuel and had to be towed in by a German torpedo boat. The actual fate of the *U-156* can only be pieced together by German radio traffic intercepted by the Allies. On September 20th, the *U-156* answered a call from the *U-139*, giving her position and asking for information on the barrage. She also related to the *U-139* information on the traffic patterns off the American coast, where the *U-139* was headed. The submarines met that evening. On the 23rd, she radioed the *U-161* for information on the barrage—it was obvious that she was nervous about the crossing. On the morning of the 24th, the *U-156* reported her position to headquarters along with her intention to cross the barrage the following day, and the position she intended to cross. After this radio traffic was intercepted and decoded by the British, the destroyer *Marksman* and the submarine *L-8* were dispatched to intercept her. At 7:40 A.M. on September 25th, the *L-8* sighted a "vessel, nature undistinguishable"[8] in exactly the location the *U-156* had given. The *L-8* dived immediately, but could not relocate the other vessel; she surfaced an hour later, but never regained contact. The *U-156* was under orders to report her position after crossing the barrage, but no signal was ever sent. On the 26th and 27th, German headquarters called to the U-cruiser, but received no reply. The British submarine *L-8* was apparently the last vessel to catch sight of the *U-156* before she perished in the northern barrage.

This bow view is of the U-117 while in drydock at the Philadelphia Navy Yard in January 1920. The line of saw teeth on the bow is a net cutter. A number of German U-cruisers were brought back to the United States for study after the war's conclusion. Courtesy of the National Archives.

EXPLOITS OF THE *U-117*

The *U-117*'s primary mission was to lay minefields along the Atlantic coast, from New Jersey to Cape Hatteras. After disposing of the nine fishing vessels who crossed her path east of Nantucket on August 10th, she continued westward toward a landfall on the New Jersey coast, where she was to begin her mine-laying campaign. Unlike the *U-151* and *U-156* that had preceded her, the *U-117* was specifically designed to carry mines, housing up to 42 of the deadly devices inside her pressure hull. Equipped with two mine-launching tubes in her stern, the submarine could plant her mines while submerged, allowing her to approach the coastal shipping lanes unobserved. Her armament also included four bow torpedo tubes and a six-inch deck gun.

The U-117 *was put on display in Washington, D.C. in the spring of 1919. The submarine was used as part of the Victory loan campaign following the war. Courtesy of the National Archives.*

On August 12th, cruising south of Long Island toward the New Jersey coast, the *U-117* encountered the Norwegian steamship *Sommerstad*, heading toward New York in ballast. In a bizarre submerged attack on the steamship, in which a single torpedo fired by the submarine first circled its victim before sinking her, Kapitanleutnant Droescher added another vessel to his scorecard. Although there is no irrefutable evidence proving the identity of the "Virginia Wreck," lying 40 miles south of Long Island, this is generally considered to be the wreck of the *Sommerstad*.[9]

The following day Droescher attacked and sank the American tanker *Frederick R. Kellogg*, again with the use of a single torpedo, about 30 miles south of the Ambrose lightship and 11 miles off the New Jersey

coast. Left for dead by the German submarine, the *Kellogg's* stern sat on the bottom with her bow awash, refusing to go down. On August 15th, salvage operations were begun, and within two weeks she was refloated and towed into New York. The *U-117*, meanwhile, continued south where she laid a field of nine mines off Barnegat Light, seven mines south of Fenwick lightship off Cape Henlopen, eight mines south of Winter Quarter Shoals lightship off the coast of Virginia, and finally a field of nine mines off Wimble Shoals along the North Carolina coast.

In between planting her mines, the *U-117* managed to find time to sink several vessels using both torpedo and gunfire. On the 14th, she halted the five-masted American schooner *Dorothy B. Barrett* off the mouth of

This interior view of the U-117 *was taken in the midst of dissection by American authorities. German submarines were generally considered more advanced than the Allied equivalents, and were the subject of much study after the war. Courtesy of the National Archives.*

Delaware Bay, forced the crew to abandon ship and then sent her to the bottom with shellfire. The following day the submarine sank the four-masted motor-schooner *Madrugada* southeast of Assateague Island, Virginia. On the 16th, while submerged and laying mines off Wimble Shoals, North Carolina, she was interrupted by a steady stream of steamship traffic. A laden tanker was cause enough for Kapitanleutnant Droescher to put his mine-laying on hold while he put a single torpedo into the tanker *Mirlo*, setting it im-

mediately ablaze.[10] A second steamship was spared by the German commander because she was displaying Dutch colors, indicating her neutrality. As Droescher headed north, the burning oil and debris from the *Mirlo* was spread over such a wide area that he concluded a second ship must have collided with one of his mines and caught fire. Although severely short on fuel, the *U-117* managed to sink several more vessels while heading north toward Nova Scotia and Newfoundland on her way home. On the 17th she sent

Two victims of the U-117*: The SS* Sommerstad *(left) was sunk south of Long Island on August 12, 1918. Courtesy of the Peabody Essex Museum, Salem, Mass. The SS* Frederick R. Kellog *(above) was sunk off Ambrose Channel the following day. Courtesy of the U.S. Naval Historical Center.*

the Norwegian bark *Nordhav* to the bottom off Cape Hatteras with explosive charges planted on board her. On August 24th, she sank the Canadian schooner *Bianca* southeast of Halifax, again using explosive charges. The American trawler *Rush* followed on the 26th by the same method. On the 27th the *U-117* expended another torpedo on the Norwegian steamer *Bergsdalen* south of Newfoundland, and finally she sank the Canadian fishing vessels *Elsie Porter* and *Potentate* on the 30th east of St. Johns, Newfoundland. In the

months to follow, three more vessels would be credited to the *U-117*'s mines: the *San Saba, Chapparo,* and the *Saetia.* The *U-117* headed home to Germany after sinking 23 vessels off the U.S. coast. Two, the *Frederick R. Kellogg* and the *Bianca,* were later salvaged.

THE WAR DRAWS TO A CLOSE

For all the daring and bravado of the U-boat captains

off the American coast, the effort was too late to affect the outcome of the war. Back on the continent of Europe, new Allied offensives in late July and early August 1918 forced the German Army to pull back their western front. By mid-August, the supreme command of the German Army declared that the war was being lost. In October, Germany offered an armistice to President Wilson of the United States. Throughout the month of October letters passed back and forth between the two powers discussing terms. Wilson insisted that the terms of the armistice comply with the "14 Points" he had outlined back in January. One of the 14 points was guaranteed freedom of the seas—the U-boat war against merchant shipping must end. On October 21st the German government complied, signaling all U-boats to cease hostilities against merchant vessels. Those U-boats still at sea were ordered to form groups in preparation for a major naval action between the German High Seas Fleet and Britain's Grand Fleet. On the night of October 29th, the order was given for the High Seas Fleet to raise steam and set sail into the North Sea in search of the British Fleet. The long-awaited clash of the Dreadnoughts never occurred, however, as mutiny broke out in the German Navy and the fleet never left port. Revolution spread to Munich and Berlin.

While events in Europe were proceeding on a path toward peace, the U.S. East Coast was still recovering from the recent flurry of U-boat activity. And Allied radio intercepts were tracking the progress of two more U-cruisers: the *U-152* still over 1,000 miles to the east, and the *U-155*, which had deposited mines off Nova Scotia and was within 350 miles of the Virginia Capes. Sinkings continued during the month of October as the mines left behind by the *U-117* did their job. On October 4th, the American steamer *San Saba* struck a mine near Barnegat Inlet, New Jersey; on October 27th, the Cuban steamship *Chapparo* also struck a mine and went down in only two and a half minutes within a few miles from where the *San Saba* was sunk.

A DANCE IN THE FOG: USS *TARANTULA*

The 116-foot-long submarine patrol boat *Tarantula* was fairly fast for her size, and her 14-knot speed was nearly an equal match for the large U-cruisers. She was acquired by the U.S. Navy on April 25, 1917, less than three weeks after the declaration of war on Germany. Her millionaire owner, W.K. Vanderbilt, had given up his personal motor yacht for the war effort. Built in 1912 at Lawley and Sons shipyard in Massachusetts,

the Navy's newly acquired patrol boat was outfitted with a single six-pounder and two machine guns in preparation for coastal patrol duty. After conversion, she was assigned to the Third Naval District, covering the waters from Connecticut to New Jersey.

On the evening of October 28, 1918, the coast was blanketed with a fog so thick that steamship navigation in New York Harbor had come to a virtual standstill. The port's pilots, who had seen many a pea soup fog, claimed it was the worst they had seen in years. Nevertheless, the nation was at war and submarines had been operating off the coast. In fact, the previous day the Cuban steamer *Chapparo* had gone down off Barnegat Inlet. Shipping needed protection, and the *Tarantula* was patrolling her assigned sector southwest of the Fire Island lightship, headed toward New York at half speed. Lookouts were posted fore and aft.

At 8:45 P.M., a steamer's fog signal was heard reverberating over the ocean. The *Tarantula* responded with her own signal. Again the fog signal was heard by the crew of the naval patrol craft, and again they answered with their own blast. Back and forth the signals went, dueling organ pipes lost in a white blanket of nothingness. Unnerved by his inability to ascertain the position or course of the other ship, the patrol boat's commander altered course two points to the north. For 25 minutes a frightening game of hide-and-seek was played out upon a calm ocean, 30 miles southeast of New York Harbor.

Suddenly, a masthead light loomed out of the white-shrouded darkness, quickly followed by the side lights of a steamship. Full speed astern was rung up on the *Tarantula*'s engine telegraph, but it was too late. Only seconds after materializing out of the fog the 421-foot-long Dutch steamship *Frisia* plowed into the port side of the patrol boat, just forward of the bridge wing. The two vessels remained in a deadly embrace for several minutes before the *Frisia* drifted clear. Water poured into the tiny gunboat through the wound in her side, while the big Dutch steamer had hardly a scratch to show for the encounter. Two trips of the *Tarantula*'s lifeboat were all that was required to evacuate her entire crew to the *Frisia*, which was standing by in the fog. As the boat left the *Tarantula* for the second time, she was seen sinking rapidly by the bow before the fog obscured her. The *Tarantula*'s crew was transferred to the USS *Montgomery* later that night, and the *Frisia*, uninjured, proceeded on her way toward Halifax.

Exactly two weeks later, on November 11, 1918, an armistice agreement was reached ending the First World War.

6

BETWEEN THE WARS:
COLLISIONS AND RUMRUNNERS

World War I's submarine menace inflicted such devastation on merchant shipping that a massive shipbuilding program was required to combat it. English and European shipyards couldn't keep up with the demand for ships, and soon turned to America for help. In the early years of the war, ships were being sunk faster than they could be built. After the United States entered the conflict, the transport of American troops and war materiel overseas increased the need for ships even further.

So great and so immediate was the need for tonnage that even American shipyards had trouble keeping up with the demand. But innovation resides deeply in the heart and soul of Americans, and a number of ingenious solutions were put forth to ease the shortage of ships. Two rather remarkable answers to the problem were the wooden shipbuilding program and the use of "Lakers"—ships taken from the Great Lakes region and put into saltwater service.

At the outbreak of the European war, the general use of wood as a shipbuilding material had been displaced by iron and steel for nearly half a century. But the enormous demands placed on shipyards and steel mills by the war soon led to the revival of man's oldest shipbuilding material. Huge timber reserves in the Pacific northwest, along the Southern Atlantic and Gulf coasts and in New England provided ample material for building large wooden ships. A large-scale wooden shipbuilding program was soon implemented, and by the end of 1917 the United States Emergency Fleet Corporation had contracted for the building of 379 wooden cargo ships for war service. The vessels ranged upwards of 4,000 tons displacement and were powered variously by steam engine and the relatively new oil burning (i.e. diesel) engine. While some of these vessels saw overseas service, many were put into the coastal trade in order to free up steel ships for transatlantic duty.

Over the course of more than a century the inland sea formed by the five Great Lakes had developed its own shipping industry. Largely isolated from the world's saltwater oceans by the narrow canal and lock system connecting the Lakes to the Atlantic Ocean, ship designs were driven by the unique conditions on the Lakes. But when war broke out, the Great Lakes shipyards represented a large and untapped resource for supplying ships to the war effort. The size of any ship built in these yards and intended for ocean service was limited by the size of the locks in the Welland Canal, connecting Lake Erie with Lake Ontario. After the locks were enlarged in 1884, they permitted the passage of ships about 260 feet long and 43° feet wide. In 1901, the canals of the St. Lawrence River were enlarged to the same dimensions, permitting the free passage of appropriately sized vessels from the Great Lakes all the way to the Atlantic Ocean.

Even before the war, ships were sometimes built for ocean service in Lakes shipyards. Usually these vessels were designed so that they would fit through the locks of the Welland Canal, and were dubbed "canal-size" vessels. When the United States entered the war in 1917, there were 99 ocean-type freighters being built in Great Lakes shipyards—all of these ships were requisitioned for war duty by the United States Shipping Board. Most of the vessels were medium-sized freight carriers of a design developed by the Norwegians and known as the Fredrickstad type. The design was characterized by a three-island layout (that is with a fo'c'sle, center island bridge and stern superstructure) and a length between perpendiculars of 253 feet and a beam

The passenger steamer Argentina *was built in 1907 for the recently formed Austrian Shipping Union. Following The Great War, her home port of Trieste became part of Italy, and the shipping line became known as the Cosulich Line, named after its founders, the Cosulich brothers. Courtesy of The Steamship Historical Society of America.*

of 43° feet—a perfect fit for the Welland Canal.

Among the 99 ships being built in 1917 were two "oversize" freighters measuring 345 feet in length—too long to fit through the canals and make their way to the ocean. But ship builders had come up with an ingenious, if cumbersome, solution to this problem as early as 1891. The ships *Keweenaw* and *Mackinaw*, both too large for the canals, had been built for, and put into, ocean service in that year. The solution was termed "bulkheading," and amounted to cutting the completed ship in half, boarding up the resulting open ends, and taking the ship through the canals and locks in two pieces. Once through the canals, the ship's two halves were reassembled into a complete ship. The two "oversize" ships being built at the war's beginning were eventually bulkheaded through the canals and put into ocean service in support of the war effort.

The *Argentina* and the *Yankee*

The ability to cut a ship in half for transport through the canal system also left open the possibility of requisitioning ships already in service on the Lakes. The bulk ore carriers common to the Great Lakes were perfect for use in the Atlantic coastal coal trade. One such ship requisitioned by the United States Shipping Board in 1917 was the Pittsburgh Steamship Company's *German*. Measuring 296 feet in length and 40 feet wide, she couldn't make it through the canals in one piece, so she was cut in two and each section transported through separately. Reassembled on the other side of the locks, she was renamed *Yankee*, for obvious reasons in a war against Germany, and put into the coastal trade. After the war's conclusion the *Yankee* remained in service along the Atlantic seaboard rather than being returned to her native waters. Here she would soon meet up with another vessel that had been misplaced by the first global war.

The Austrian Shipping Union had been founded only a decade before the outbreak of The Great War by Fratelli Cosulich in 1903. Operating out of the city of Trieste, located at the base of the Istrian peninsula between Italy and Yugoslavia, the new shipping line established freight, and later passenger service, between Trieste and New York, New Orleans, Brazil and Argentina. It was perhaps fitting that the inaugural voyage of the new line's passenger service to South America was begun by the newly built and aptly named liner *Argentina* in 1907. The new ship was modest by passenger liner standards, for she measured only 390

feet long and was capable of a mere 15 knots. Despite her twin screws, she was no match for the fast Atlantic liners operating between Europe and America. But the ships of the Austro-Americana Line, as it was popularly known, were intended to make a profit by providing essential services on routes not served by the plush ships of the larger shipping companies. By 1913 the line had prospered, operating a fleet of 29 steamships with five more on order. One year later, however, disaster struck the upstart company and operations came crashing to a halt—World War I had begun. Several ships were lost to internment in foreign ports, while the remainder sat idly at dockside, waiting for the war to end.

When the war finally came to a close in 1918, the

The Great Lakes steamer German *was cut in half in order to fit her through the Welland Canal and transfer her to the coastal shipping trade. She served on the Atlantic Seaboard in support of the Allied war effort, and was appropriately renamed* Yankee. *Courtesy of the Great Lakes Historical Society.*

map of Europe had changed dramatically. Germany had been forced to cede the territory of Alsace-Lorraine to France, relinquish West Prussia and give up the Saar territory on the French-Belgian border; in addition, plebiscites were to be held in various other territories. Similarly, the Austro-Hungarian Empire was forced to recognize the independence of Hungary, Czechoslovakia, Poland and Yugoslavia. In addition, South Tirol, Trieste and Istria were handed over to the Italians, as well as parts of Carinthia and Carniola.

The city of Trieste, along with its inhabitants and businesses, now found itself part of the Italian nation. The principal owners of the former Austrian Shipping Union, the Cosulich brothers, reorganized their company and renamed it the Cosulich Line, beginning operations on May 5, 1919. After five years sitting idly in port, the same steamships that had once operated under the Austrian flag now flew the Italian flag from their mastheads. And only one month after beginning operations, the Cosulich brothers had the makings of a lawsuit on their hands.

Late on the evening of June 11, 1919, the Cosulich Line's passenger steamer *Argentina* was steaming eastward some 20 miles south of Long Island. She had left New York late that afternoon and was headed for her home port of Trieste. A dense fog hung over the ocean that evening, causing most vessels to reduce speed drastically—but the *Argentina*'s master was apparently eager to get to sea, and would later be accused of operating his ship at an excessive speed for the foggy conditions. While the *Argentina* would set no speed records during her career, the master of a passenger liner was always pressed to adhere closely to a set schedule. Keeping the ship's patrons happy was the first order of business. In essence, time was money, and speed was the order of the day, regardless of weather.

Freight steamers, however, operated under different rules—they had no particular schedule to meet, and if a ship's cargo didn't arrive in port tomorrow, it would surely get there the next day with little economic penalty. Hence the master of a cargo vessel was more likely to err on the side of caution when encountering adverse weather. On the same evening that the *Argentina* had departed New York, the 30-year-old former ore-carrier *Yankee* was slowly making her way up the coast toward Boston Harbor with a cargo of coal. Traveling through the same fog that engulfed the *Argentina*, the *Yankee*'s captain ordered his vessel slowed to a speed of only three knots. He also ordered fog signals to be sounded regularly at one minute intervals, as prescribed by international law.

At 10:05 P.M. the crew of the *Yankee* saw the massive hull of an ocean liner loom out of the fog, speeding directly toward them. As the *Argentina* closed upon the coal freighter, the *Yankee*'s engine telegraph was immediately swung to "all stop" in order to arrest her forward motion. But the collier was traveling so slowly that she barely had steerage way through the sea, and there was little she could do to avoid the impending collision. As precious seconds ticked by the oncoming liner refused to change course. In desperation, the *Yankee*'s captain ordered the ship ahead once again and the helm put hard over to port, attempting to turn out of the *Argentina*'s path. The maneuver almost worked, but the *Argentina* was moving too quickly and her starboard bow drove heavily into the forward port quarter of the smaller *Yankee*.

Meanwhile, the *Argentina*'s captain made a last ditch attempt at avoiding the titanic clash between ships. Taking advantage of his ship's twin screws, he tried to turn his vessel by throwing the starboard engine full ahead and the port full astern. The effort wasn't enough to turn the 5,526-ton liner in time, however, and instead caused her to shear off after the collision, throwing the *Argentina*'s stern into the *Yankee* and effectively dealing her two blows. It was this second impact that sealed the *Yankee*'s fate. The *Argentina*'s starboard propeller, driven by one of the ship's big triple expansion engines, gnashed deeply into the *Yankee*'s hull, allowing torrents of cold sea water to pour in. The pumps could not keep up with the flood of water and, despite valiant efforts to plug the hole in her hull, the ancient steamer sank five hours after the collision. Fortunately, there were no casualties and the captain and crew of the *Yankee* were taken on board the *Argentina*, which herself sustained very little damage. The rescued crew were dropped off at the Cardinal lightship, and later put aboard the tug *Marshal J. Sanford*, which brought them into New York.

The *Yankee* was a total loss. Sunk along with her cargo of coal some 20 miles offshore, she was reported as lying in 16 fathoms of water. There was little economic incentive for a salvage effort, and the *Yankee* was abandoned to the sea.

THE "NOBLE EXPERIMENT": PROHIBITION AND "RUMRUNNERS"

On January 14, 1919, the eighteenth amendment to the United States Constitution, prohibiting the manufacture, transportation and sale of liquor, was ratified by Nebraska, the 36th state to do so. Nebraska's vote ensured that this experiment in moral legislation

Jeff Pagano holds a liquor bottle found on an unidentified shipwreck lying 30 miles south of Jones Inlet, New York. Known locally as the "Catamount," she has tentatively been identified as a rumrunner due to the countless liquor bottles found at the site; in addition a welding torch was recovered that was dated to the mid 1920s. The steam engine is in the background.

would become the law of the land one year and two days later. Three previous attempts to pass a national prohibition amendment had been defeated in 1876, 1880 and 1887. It took the powerful and well-organized Anti-Saloon League of America, formed in 1895, until the end of the World War I to gain its great moral achievement.

In addition to the Constitutional amendment, Congress passed the Volstead Act in October 1919, giving the new law teeth by setting severe penalties for violators. The responsibility for enforcement of the new laws was placed under the auspices of the Treasury Department. These enforcement duties fell specifically under the jurisdiction of the Bureau of Internal Revenue. The United States Coast Guard would also become heavily involved with the repercussions of the

new law since its ancestor, the Revenue Cutter Service, had originally been charged with the prevention of smuggling at sea. The government estimated that enforcement costs might run as high as five million dollars per year; in truth the effort cost many times that amount, and at best only slowed the flow of smuggled liquor.

Despite a majority passage in both houses of Congress, the prohibition was extremely unpopular with the public. "Speakeasies," or illegal saloons, sprang up all over the country as the public simply refused to submit to the enforced morality of the Volstead Act. New York City became a hotbed of illegal smuggling as "bootleggers" supplied the black market with spirits imported from the West Indies, England, and the French Island of St. Pierre et Miquelon, off the coast of Newfoundland.

Supply ships heavily laden with thousands of cases of liquor anchored just outside the territorial waters of the United States, which were then internationally recognized as being three miles from shore. These depot ships were lined up in what came to be known as "rum row," and were so close to shore that they were easily visible from the beaches. Under cover of darkness, a legion of small craft would depart the small harbors and bays along the coast and venture the short distance offshore to rum row. Here they would make their purchases, load the liquor into their small boats and slip back into port. The large penalties for those caught smuggling liquor, including fines and prison terms, were balanced for many by the huge profits to be made supplying a thirsty public. The sprawling metropolis of New York attracted what was by far the largest rum row off the Long Island and New Jersey coastlines.

With myriad small craft making their nightly runs out to the waiting rum fleet, the Coast Guard had its hands full. Equipped with only a handful of cutters, enforcement proved nearly impossible. One of the biggest problems was the close proximity of the rum boats to shore, allowing nearly any type of craft to make the trip in decent weather. In addition, the short three-mile trip provided little, if any, opportunity for the Coast Guard to intercept the contact boats. Seizure of the ships themselves was foiled by the owners registering their vessels under the flags of foreign governments. Searching foreign vessels in international waters was outside the jurisdiction of the Coast Guard and drew protests from the relevant government. In order to make rum smuggling more difficult, the United States began international lobbying for an extension of territorial waters to (Continued on page 141)

A Transcription Error?

For many years a wreck lying some 18 miles south of Fire Island Inlet was known to divers and fishermen alike as the *Yankee*. Like many shipwrecks, her identity was accepted on faith, apparently determined by an earlier generation of explorers. However, in 1994 another shipwreck lying nearby,

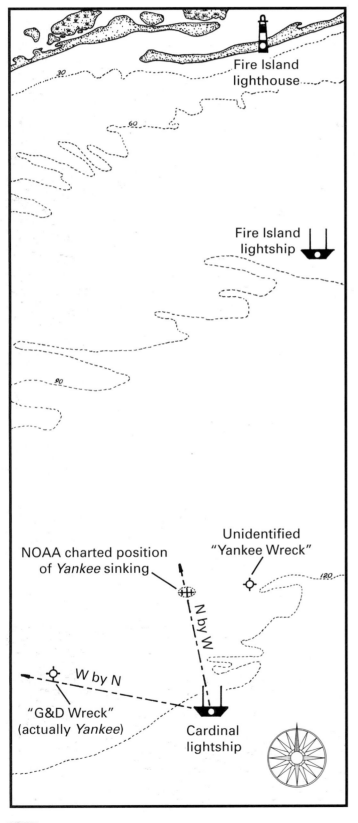

Fire Island
lighthouse

Fire Island
lightship

NOAA charted position
of *Yankee* sinking

Unidentified
"Yankee Wreck"

N by W

W by N

"G&D Wreck"
(actually *Yankee*)

Cardinal
lightship

the "G&D Wreck," was identified as being the *Yankee*, and researchers began scrutinizing the historical record. The *Yankee* sank quickly following a collision with the passenger liner *Argentina* on June 12, 1919. The wreck was recorded as lying "sunk in 16 fathoms of water about 4 miles N by W (true) of the Cardinal lightship." The Cardinal lightship was the naval minesweeper *Cardinal* (AM-6), which served as a temporary lightship after her launching in March 1918 until August 1919. Her station was located 22 miles south of Fire Island Inlet in position 40°16′ N, 73°15′30″ W. A wreck symbol marking the location of the *Yankee*'s sinking was added to subsequent NOAA charts of the area 4 miles N by W of the position of the temporary lightship. After the lightship was removed from its station, the source of the plotted position of the *Yankee* became somewhat obscure. The wreck that was incorrectly called the *Yankee* for many years (referred to here as the "Yankee Wreck") was apparently identified by its proximity to the recorded position of the sinking as marked on NOAA charts; the "Yankee Wreck" lies 2.1 miles east of the plotted position of the sinking—not very close considering that the wreck location was recorded as being 4 miles from the Cardinal lightship. The position was recorded using the old system of compass points, however, and the notation "N by W" (equivalent to 349°) could have easily been a mistakenly recorded "W by N" (equivalent to 281°). The effect of such a simple transcription error is apparent on the chart at left, showing the relative positions of the Cardinal lightship, the historically recorded position of the sinking, and the location of the "Yankee Wreck" and the "G&D Wreck." Note that a 281° (W by N) line-of-position drawn from the Cardinal lightship passes almost directly through the position of the "G&D Wreck"—at a distance of 5.3 miles! In locating the wreck in 1919, the visual bearing to the lightship would have been much more accurate than the distance, which would have been an estimate. It appears likely that a transcription error was responsible for the misidentification of the *Yankee*.

A GRAVEYARD FOR SHIPS

At two distinct locations on Staten Island, along the shores of the Arthur Kill, lies a veritable graveyard of old ships. Ancient vessels that had outlived their usefulness were abandoned here, and over the years have rusted, collapsed and even burned. One site, beneath and just north of the Outer Bridge Crossing, consists exclusively of wooden vessels, both ships and barges, abandoned on the edge of the channel. The second site, further up the Arthur Kill, is actually the marine equivalent of an automobile junkyard. Located on private property, ships of all types—steam tugs, freighters and barges, were abandoned and picked apart piece by piece for their salvagable parts.

IDENTIFIED AS THE *YANKEE*: THE "G&D WRECK"

Known for years as the "G&D Wreck," the steamship *Yankee* was only recently identified when John Lachenmeyer recovered a dish from the wreck site bearing the crest of the Pittsburgh Steamship Company. Built in Cleveland, Ohio in 1891 and originally named *German*, she was cut in half to get through the lock system of the Welland Canal and moved to the Atlantic coal trade in order to bolster Allied shipping against the German U-boat offensive during World War I.

Bergalls swarm around a deck winch on the bow.

Inside the fo'c'sle of the steamship's intact bow section, a fused block of anchor chain mirrors the shape of the square-walled chain locker that once contained it.

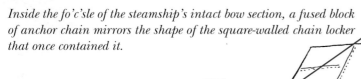

A deck capstan lying alongside the ship's port bow (left). Looking toward the surface along the side of the Yankee's *tall, plumb bow (right).*

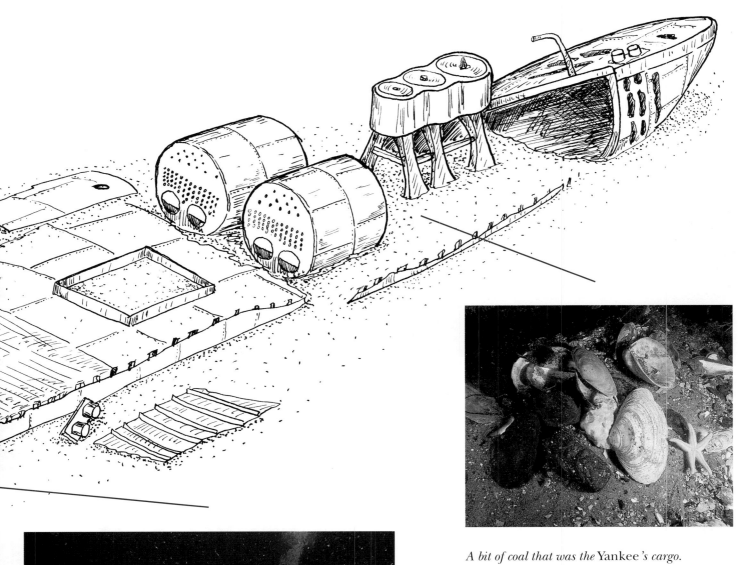

A bit of coal that was the Yankee's *cargo.*

Kevin Brennan explores wreckage in the "break" area between the ship's bow and her long midships cargo hold.

Dishes recovered bearing this crest, later identified as belonging to the Pittsburgh Steamship Company.

LONG LOST RUMRUNNER: THE *LIZZIE D.*

The 78-foot-long steam tug *Lizzie D.* disappeared mysteriously in October 1922. She was last reported adrift 50 miles east of Fire Island; the Coast Guard cutter *Acushnet* spent two days searching for the missing tug in the vicinity of the Nantucket lightship, but there was no sign of her and the search was abandoned. The *Lizzie D.* would not be heard from for 55 years, when she was discovered by Captain John Larsen, owner of the dive charter boat *Deep Adventures*. In 1977 he dropped a group of divers on a new wreck site in 80 feet of water south of Long Beach. Joan Fulmer recovered the tug's bell with *Lizzie D.* inscribed on it, while other divers brought up whisky bottles. The purpose of the *Lizzie D.*'s final voyage had suddenly become clear; her fate, however, still remains a mystery. Today the popular wreck site is explored regularly by divers, who still occasionally find bottles of prohibition bourbon, scotch and rye.

Jeff Pagano examines the intact bow of the rumrunner Lizzie D.

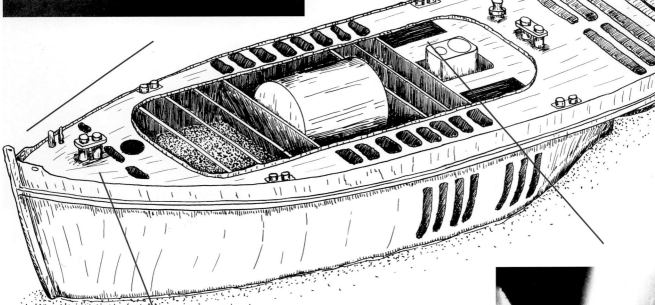

A large towing bit (left), typical of a working tugboat, graces the foredeck of the Lizzie D. *The wreck is fascinating for divers to explore, for her hull is intact and she still looks like a "ship" sitting on the ocean bottom. Her superstructure is now gone, leaving many openings in her deck that give access to the interior (right).*

Divers exploring this lost rumrunner can still find prohibition liquor bottles, sometimes unbroken and on rare occasions with their contents intact (left). The Lizzie D.'s interior is filled with broken glass, silt, shells and debris from the deteriorating wreck (middle, left). Mixed in amongst this potpourri can be found Old Bridgeport rye (bottom, left), Atherton bourbon (bottom, right) and Johnny Walker scotch bottles (middle, right), or at least pieces of bottles. Extreme caution is required when digging for bottles as more than one diver has cut his hands on shards of broken glass. (Photo at left courtesy of John Lachenmeyer. Bottle identification courtesy of Henry Keatts.)

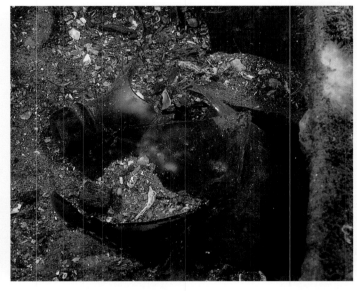

CONVERTED OIL BURNER: *LILLIAN*

Although the freighter *Lillian* was built after World War I, when oil was coming into widespread use for boiler fuel aboard ships, she was equipped with coal-fired boilers. Sometime later, however, she was converted to burn oil fuel in her existing boilers. Oil proved a more efficient fuel than coal, giving more heat per ton and requiring a smaller engine room staff to operate. Although converting boilers designed for coal to oil-burning was not especially difficult, installing fuel tanks in the coal bunker spaces did require fairly extensive rework.

This overgrown and tangled mass of copper tubing (left) near the Lillian*'s boilers may be part of an oil fuel pumping or pre-heating system. The* Lillian*'s boiler furnaces (right) were modified to burn oil after her building in 1920. The familiar coal furnace doors were removed and replaced (middle, right), and an oil burner with spray nozzles fitted. The cagelike object (bottom, right) is likely a part of this oil-firing apparatus. A porthole from the ship's superstructure lies amongst the wreckage (bottom, left).*

a distance of 12 miles. This would prevent smaller, less seaworthy craft from venturing offshore in all but the calmest conditions, as well as providing more opportunity for interception of the contact boats. After much negotiation, jurisdiction over the seas within 12 miles of shore was eventually achieved by international agreement, although the actual limit was then defined as approximately one-hour's steaming distance from shore for the vessel involved. Thus the limit was only approximately twelve miles, and actually varied for different vessels.

The development of rum row and the associated smuggling operations came about slowly, and the extent of the problem wasn't fully apparent until 1922. The beginning of the rum fleet is generally attributed to Captain Bill McCoy, whose reputation for supplying quality products has left us with the slang term "the real McCoy." The rise of bootlegging in the early twenties provided the impetus for a great expansion in the size of the United States Coast Guard. The Coast Guard's enforcement duty quickly took on the overtones of a war, pitting the Coast Guard against bootleggers in what became known as the "rum war at sea." Faced with the tough matter of enforcing an unpopular law with inadequate resources, the Coast Guard did an amazing job. Many rumrunners were captured and many arrests were made; the court system became overloaded with cases involving violations of the Volstead Act. Some of the captured vessels were requisitioned and put into service in the Coast Guard as anti-smuggling boats, and ironically, pursued their former comrades. Others were sunk by shellfire or collision, for the rumrunners displayed a remarkable propensity for refusing to halt when discovered by patrol craft until actually fired upon. Some of the contact boats simply disappeared at sea, never to be heard from again. Little could be done by their owners ashore in such cases, for few details of their real missions could be outlined to Coast Guard officials in reporting the disappearance. Typical was the case of the steam tug *Lizzie D*.

A small note in *The New York Times* on October 31, 1922, reported that the 78-foot-long, steel-hulled tugboat had been missing for ten days. She had left her dock in Brooklyn on October 19th and had apparently encountered some sort of trouble. She was last reported 50 miles east of Fire Island, drifting southwest. The Coast Guard cutter *Acushnet* was sent to search for her, but no trace was ever found—she had simply disappeared. Fifty-five years later at least part of the mystery was solved when Captain John Larsen, running his charter boat, *Deep Adventures*, discovered

the wreck of the vessel seven miles southwest of Jones Inlet.

Divers descending on the new, and as yet unidentified wreck, found a steel tugboat sitting upright on the ocean bottom in some 80 feet of water. Her identity was established by diver Joan Fulmer, who brought up the tugboat's bell with the name *Lizzie D*. inscribed on it. Entering the ship's hold divers discovered that she was filled with cases of liquor—apparently she had paid a visit to rum row on her final voyage! Nothing else is known of her fate. Just what transpired on her final voyage, how and why she was reported adrift 50 miles east of Fire Island, and what caused her to end up on the ocean bottom southwest of Jones Inlet, will probably never be known.

The "noble experiment" in enforced morality, as President Herbert Hoover once called it, was a failure. In actuality, it led to a lack of respect for the law, a huge increase in organized crime, and little positive effect on public morality. The federal government was forced to face the failure of the Volstead Act, and it came to realize the huge potential revenue base of taxing liquor. On December 5, 1933, the twenty-first amendment to the United States Constitution went into effect, repealing the eighteenth amendment and the national prohibition.

COLLISION IN REVERSE:
GRECIAN AND *CITY OF CHATTANOOGA*

How can two steamships, both running with their engines in reverse, end up in a collision leaving the bow of one vessel stuck in the port side of the other? This was the question that faced an inquiry board convened by the Steamboat Inspection Service during the summer of 1932. The two vessels involved were the Merchants & Miners Transportation Company's *Grecian* and the Savannah Line's *City of Chattanooga*.

The steamship *Grecian* was built as a combination passenger and freight carrier at the turn of the century. The 265-foot-long vessel began life with a difficult birth in 1899, when she stuck on the ways at her launching ceremony. Built at the Harlan & Hollingsworth shipyard in Wilmington, Delaware for the Winsor Line, it took a day or two of coaxing before she finally slid down the launching ramp and was set afloat. A steel-hulled screw steamer, she was powered by a triple-expansion engine driven by the steam from four large boilers. In the enduring tradition of early steamships, however, she was also provided with a two-masted schooner rig for emergency propulsion. She

The steamship Grecian *was sent to the bottom in 1932 after a collision with the* City of Chattanooga. *She has since become a popular dive site off the coast of Block Island, providing both interesting exploration and relatively clear water. Courtesy of The Steamship Historical Society of America.*

had accommodations for up to 100 passengers, as well as a freight capacity of 2,500 tons in four cargo holds. Years later, no longer profitable as a passenger vessel, she was bought by the Merchants & Miners Transportation Company. Her new role was to carry general cargo between the ports of Baltimore, where she was registered, Norfolk and Boston. It was on one of these coastal freight runs, her holds filled with a potpourri of general cargo, that she met up with the passenger liner *City of Chattanooga*. Built in Norfolk in 1923, the *City of Chattanooga* was more than 100 feet longer than the *Grecian*, measuring 381 feet in length and displacing 4,348 tons.

The *Grecian* and her crew of 40 had left Boston Harbor on the night of May 26th, bound for Baltimore. Sometime after midnight Captain H.E. Callis found his vessel enveloped in a fog so thick "one could not see the length of the ship."[1] As the *Grecian* entered the dense fog bank, Captain Callis reduced speed from

12° knots to 9, and then finally to 7° knots. Shortly before 3:00 A.M., the *Grecian*'s captain heard the fog whistle of another vessel nearby. He immediately brought the *Grecian* to a halt and tried to ascertain the location of the whistle. After listening, he put his ship's helm over to port and started slowly ahead, only to hear the mysterious vessel's whistle resonating through the fog once again, this time just off his port bow. Captain Callis ordered the *Grecian*'s engines full speed astern, trying desperately to back his command out of danger. Looming out of the fog off the port beam came a set of steamer lanterns.

The lights proved to be the *City of Chattanooga*, carrying 85 passengers to the same Boston port that the *Grecian* had so recently left. The *Chattanooga*'s Captain L.P. Borum later stated to the press: "We were almost stopped at the time of the crash. The *Grecian* was going across our bow. She loomed up out of the fog about two minutes before the collision. We put our engines

The steamship City of Chattanooga *was the* Grecian*'s destroyer. Launched in 1923, the* City of Chattanooga *collided with the* Grecian *in a dense fog south of Block Island. The* Grecian *did not survive the collision. Courtesy of The Steamship Historical Society of America.*

in reverse, but it was too late."[2] Despite the fact that both ships reportedly had their engines running full speed astern, the *City of Chattanooga* crashed headfirst into the *Grecian*'s port side with enough force to cut a three-foot-deep gash in the freighter's hull. Fortunately for the *Grecian*'s crew, Captain Borum of the *Chattanooga* deliberately kept his engines running slowly ahead after the collision. This action kept the two vessels together, effectively plugging the hole in the *Grecian*'s side and slowing her sinking. Even so, "She was shipping water like Niagara Falls,"[3] according to Tom Nottage, one of the *Grecian*'s lookouts.

In a few minutes following the crash, "twenty-eight officers and seamen, stumbling up from the fireroom, fo'castle and cabins, made their way across lurching, wet decks to the upper deck of the *Grecian* and swarmed up ropes thrown down from the *Chattanooga* to safety."[4] Four men never made it to the *Chattanooga* and were lost, drowning in the darkened sea. Captain

Borum of the *Chattanooga* kept the bow of his ship stuck in the *Grecian*'s side as long as he could, only ordering his engines into reverse when the *Grecian* threatened to pull the *Chattanooga*'s bow under. The *Grecian* disappeared in only 13 minutes.

The *City of Chattanooga* sent out a signal reporting the accident: "At about 1:50 A.M. we struck the steamer *Grecian* and she sank in a few minutes off Block Island. We anchored. Passengers and crew o.k."[5] A few minutes later another message: "We are blowing three blasts at intervals and searching for members of crew who are not yet rescued with lights and boats."[6] These messages were picked up by nearby Coast Guard vessels, who sped to the scene. There they found the *Grecian*'s two masts sticking ten feet out of the water some five miles south of Southeast Light on Block Island's southern flank. The *Chattanooga* stood by about one-half mile away, her lights burning brightly. The Coast Guard destroyers *Upshur* and *Porter* searched to leeward of the *Grecian*'s wreck for the four missing men. Amidst a sea covered with floating wreckage and ladies' shoes from the *Grecian*'s cargo, the destroyers discovered two bodies and a capsized lifeboat. In a final irony, while the *Upshur*'s crew deployed a navigational buoy to mark the *Grecian*'s grave, the steamer's guilt-lettered name board came floating to the surface along with crates, barrels and other articles of the ship's cargo.

Although Captain Callis of the *Grecian* would not directly blame the captain of the *Chattanooga*, he couldn't understand her actions prior to the crash. Speaking to the press he stated: "I don't consider that I am at fault. I did all I could and the *Chattanooga* did all it could do. The only thing I see is that if Captain Borum had only ported his wheel the collision would not have happened. I can't understand why he gave the starboard signals."[7] The board of inquiry summoned by the Steamboat Inspection Service, however, recommended that charges of reckless navigation be brought against Captain Callis of the *Grecian*.

CONVERTED STEAMSHIP: *LILLIAN*

Competition, both economic and military, drove the evolution of steamships to ever-greater efficiencies. While any fuel that would burn hot enough to convert water to steam could theoretically be used in a ship's boilers, coal had been the fuel of choice for steamships until the First World War. Coal produced more heat per ton than wood, which was the only other practical fuel available for marine boilers during the nineteenth century. But in the early years of the twentieth century two major innovations in marine power plants made their way into newly built ships: steam-driven turbine engines to replace reciprocating engines, and the use of oil fuel to produce steam.

The steam turbine promised to revolutionize marine propulsion by providing a more efficient engine in a smaller and lighter package that required less maintenance, and was less prone to vibration at high speeds. This new wonder machine came at a much higher installation cost, however, than its simpler and well-proven reciprocating predecessor. While it was particularly well suited for fast vessels such as passenger liners and warships, its relatively small increase in fuel efficiency did not generally justify its increased up-front cost for the owners of slower cargo ships. The use of oil fuel, on the other hand, found widespread acceptance in commercial vessels of all types after the First World War. While the use of oil had been pro-

posed years earlier during the nineteenth century, lack of an adequate supply had prevented it from coming into widespread use. But when the British Admiralty made a commitment to oil power for its warships in 1913, a supply system was brought into being that became available for commercial purposes at the war's close.

Oil provided a number of economic advantages over coal. Just as coal was a more efficient fuel than wood, oil produced more heat per ton than coal. This meant less fuel was needed for a given voyage, leaving more room aboard freighters for paying cargo. An additional advantage was that fewer men were required to operate the power plant as the backbreaking job of the stoker, shoveling coal into the furnace and ash out, was eliminated. Oil produced no ash to be removed as coal did, and the job of supplying the furnace with oil was performed by pumps rather than shovels. The Cunard Line steamer *Mauretania*, as originally built, was powered by coal and required an engine room staff of 366 men while burning more than 1,000 tons of the dirty substance per day. In 1921-22 she was converted to oil power and the engine room staff was reduced to 79 men, while fuel consumption fell to 620 tons per day![8] Even with all these economic advantages, ship owners were slow to convert to oil. But with an increasing supply available after the First World War, more and more ships were built with oil-fired boilers, and older vessels were often converted.

The American steamship *Lillian* was built in 1920 by the Bethlehem Shipbuilding Corporation in Wilmington, Delaware. Despite the fact that oil fuel was becoming more and more common, the *Lillian* was built with two big coal-fired boilers supplying steam to her three-cylinder, triple-expansion engine. Sometime later, however, her owners apparently opted for better fuel economy and converted her six furnaces to burn oil. Owned and operated by the A.H. Bull Steamship Company, the 19-year-old steamer was running a cargo of sugar from Puerto Rico to New York in 1939 when a collision ended her career.

In early 1939, although tensions in Europe were running high, the world was still at peace. German merchant ships plied the world's oceans freely and were welcome in ports across the globe. Thus there was no ill-will wished upon her when the steamship *Wiegand* of the North German Lloyd Line departed New York for Japan on the morning of February 27th, her cargo holds filled with scrap iron. Captain Leopold Ranitz's steamer had left Pier 5 in Brooklyn at 11:00 A.M., expecting a routine voyage that would take him halfway around the globe before delivering his cargo.

But seven hours after leaving the safety of port, a dense fog fell across the ocean, and Captain Ranitz was forced to reduce speed from a comfortable nine knots to five.

The American freighter *Lillian*, meanwhile, was making her way north along the Jersey shore through the same fog bank. Her commander, Captain Frank Boyer, had also been forced to reduce his ship's speed. Shortly before 7:00 P.M., Captain Boyer heard the faint sound of a fog whistle drifting across the surface of the misty ocean. He ordered the *Lillian*'s engines "all stop," attempting to ascertain the other vessel's location, but heard nothing. After three minutes of silence, he ordered his ship ahead once again, proceeding toward New York at 6 knots. The *Lillian*'s own fog whistle was blaring out its monotonous tone every 60 to 90 seconds.

At just past 7:00 P.M. a set of lights materialized out of the soupy darkness only 300 feet ahead—the mystery vessel he had heard earlier had appeared. He immediately ordered the wheel hard over and the engines "all stop"; a moment later he ordered the engines "full astern," trying in vain to slow the momentum of the 328-foot-long, 3,482-ton freighter. Less than a minute later the two ships came together, the *Lillian* crashing headlong into the starboard side of the *Wiegand* just behind the forecastle. Although the *Wiegand*'s hull plates were badly twisted and she had a 12-foot-long gash in her bow, she was in no danger of sinking.

The *Lillian*, however, was not so lucky. Her collision bulkhead had collapsed under the impact and she immediately began to settle by the bow. When Captain Boyer sent his third officer forward to survey the damage, he returned to report that the entire bow was gone. While Captain Boyer gathered his officers to discuss the best course of action, the *Lillian*'s radioman, William Helmbold, began pounding out an SOS signal on the ship's wireless. It appeared to Captain Boyer that his ship would not last long, but he held off abandoning ship and asked the *Wiegand* to stand by. The Coast Guard had picked up the SOS call and dispatched the cutters *Campbell*, *Galatea* and *Icarus* to the scene; a nearby steamship, *Munmotor*, also responded to the distress call.

About one hour after the collision Captain Boyer decided that he could wait no longer and gave the order to abandon ship. Helmbold gallantly stood by his station and continued to send distress signals until the ocean was literally lapping at his ankles before he, too, was forced to take to the lifeboats. Even then the ingenious sailor tied the key of his radio down so that it would send a continuous, whining signal over the airwaves that rescue craft could home in on through the dense fog.

The entire crew of the *Lillian* put off safely in two boats and was picked up by the *Wiegand*. Captain Boyer and 16 of his crew were transferred first to the cutter *Icarus* and then to the Bull Line freighter *Emilia*. There they stood by in case it became necessary to reboard the *Lillian*, which was not sinking nearly as rapidly as was first believed. For more than 17 hours the *Lillian* stubbornly remained afloat, and all that time her wireless screamed out its continuous, now annoying, tone. The Coast Guard cutter *Campbell* tried to put a man aboard her to silence the infernal noise, but rough seas made it impossible. Finally, at 4:00 A.M., the whining beacon was silenced by shooting off the offending ship's wireless aerial.

The Merritt-Chapman & Scott Towing Company had dispatched the tug *Relief* to the scene in the hope of making a salvage attempt. She arrived just past noon the following day, but as she approached to within 100 yards of the ship the *Lillian* finally slipped beneath the waves. The *Wiegand* returned to port alongside an armada of tugs, where she underwent $50,000 in reconstructive surgery before resuming her career. But her career as a merchant ship freely plying the seas would not last long, for soon German submarines would prowl the oceans, destroying Allied shipping and making German merchant ships unwelcome in most ports around the world. And the little *Icarus*, which had played such a brief part in the rescue of the *Lillian*'s crew, would soon make an important contribution to the war effort by sinking the German submarine *U-352* off the North Carolina coast.

7

WORLD WAR II:
THE U-BOATS RETURN

One of the conditions of the Treaty of Versailles concluding the First World War was that Germany was forbidden to possess any submarines. This demand by the victorious powers was hardly surprising, for the unrestricted submarine campaigns during the war had very nearly crippled England's supply lines and decided the war in Germany's favor. At the war's end, 176 German U-boats were handed over to the Allied powers, while those remaining in Germany were destroyed or dismantled. The famous treaty signed in the Palace of Versailles' Hall of Mirrors unambivalently stated: "The construction and acquisition of any kind of submarine, even for trade purposes, is forbidden to Germany."[1] The great power that had built a naval fleet rivaling England's, and who had unlocked the military potential of the *unterseeboot,* now found herself without a single submarine.

But technology has always been a valuable commodity. Germany's knowledge and experience in designing, building and operating a fleet of submarines, a fleet that had opened the world's eyes to the value of this relatively new weapon, would soon draw the nation back into the business of building U-boats. Many of the submarines turned over to the Allied powers after the war were studied, dissected, copied and imitated. Much was learned through these studies, since Germany's submarine technology was far more advanced than that of foreign navies at the time. By 1920, construction plans for the large U-cruisers *U-142* and *U-117* had been sold to Japan. German engineers began working as consultants, through a foreign intermediary to avoid treaty violations, on submarine programs for both the Argentine and Italian navies. In 1925, the German Navy established a secret U-boat department, ironically entitled "Anti-U-Boat Defense

Questions," with the purpose of clandestinely furthering submarine development. Secret funding was provided by the Navy in preparation for the day when Germany could once again build U-boats. During the 1920s, both Turkey and Finland contracted with the German Navy for the design and construction of several submarines. These submarines were built in foreign yards with German personnel as consultants. Later, similar arrangements were made with the Spanish Navy. The contracts cleverly stipulated that German officers and engineers were to be involved in the boat's operational trials, bringing Germany one step closer to her own reunion with the *unterseeboot.*

Meanwhile, deep within a secret branch of the German Navy, debates raged over the most suitable type of U-boat for the inevitable German rearmament. In 1932, plans were put into motion for the birth of a new German fleet—naturally it included submarines. Vital parts such as periscopes and torpedo tubes were secretly built and put into storage. Rolled steel was shipped into Germany and construction sheds erected. On June 18, 1935, the long-negotiated Anglo-German Naval Agreement was concluded—Germany was once again legally permitted to build and operate a fleet of submarines. To the amazement of a watching world, Germany launched her first U-boat only four months later.

U-BOAT DEVELOPMENT: TYPES I THROUGH IX

The first U-boats to slide down the launching ways were tiny, 250-ton submarines designated Type I boats, and were intended for coastal defense operations only. Measuring 134 feet in length, they carried a crew of

25 men and were armed with six torpedoes and a single antiaircraft gun. Two larger, 800-ton boats were also built, and were delivered the following year. The larger boats, designated Type II, measured 238 feet in length, carried 14 torpedoes and an antiaircraft gun, as well as a 10.5 cm (4-inch) deck gun. The Type II boat was manned by a crew of 43 and had a surface range of 6,700 nautical miles at 12 knots—much more formidable than the 1,050 nautical mile range of the Type I boats.

Early negotiations preceding the final Anglo-German Naval Agreement had led Germany to believe that its total tonnage of submarines would be restricted to a fixed percentage—likely 33 percent—of Britain's total submarine tonnage. This expected treaty limitation led to the development of a medium size U-boat suitable for open ocean operations, designated Type VII. (Types III through VI existed on paper only, and were never built.) This submarine type was intended to maximize the size of Germany's U-boat fleet while still complying with the impending treaty. As it turned out, the final naval agreement allowed Germany parity with Britain's submarine fleet. The Type VII could also be built faster than the Type II boats, allowing a quicker rebuilding of the fleet once the naval agreement went into effect. The Type VII was a 500-ton boat measuring 212 feet in length and had a range of 4,300 nautical miles. Manned by a crew of 44, the submarine was armed with eleven torpedoes, an antiaircraft gun and an 8.8 cm (3.46-inch) deck gun. This medium size U-boat, along with its numerous variations, would later become Germany's workhorse in the Battle of the Atlantic.

Still another U-boat type was desired by the German naval command. There was a requirement for a submarine with both increased range and speed in order to allow a "lengthy stay in the Western Mediterranean."[2] This led to the development of the Type IX submarine. Based on the earlier Type II boats, the new design displaced approximately 1,000 tons, measured 250 feet in length and carried a crew of 48. Armed with 22 torpedoes, two antiaircraft guns and a 10.5 cm deck gun, the new type had a surface range of 8,100 nautical miles at 12 knots, as well as a maximum surface speed of over 18 knots. It was these long range U-boats that would first bring the submarine war to American shores.

THE FLAMES OF WAR RETURN TO EUROPE

The German populace was bitterly resentful of its de-

feat at the end of the First World War, as well as of the terms of the peace treaty. The treaty had stripped Germany of large regions of its frontier territories and forced the Empire's disarmament. Militarily defeated, Germany had little choice but to accept the terms of a treaty it claimed were "intolerable for any nation."[3]

This resentment, combined with economic hardships brought about by the burden of war reparations and the rebuilding of a war-torn Germany, agitated the German people. During the 1920's, political and economic unrest saw the rise of the National Socialist German Workers' Party (N.S.D.A.P.), known more commonly by its abbreviated name, the Nazi Party. In January 1933, a dark cloud formed over the European continent as Adolf Hitler and the Nazi Party came into power.

After consolidating power, Hitler quickly moved to rearm Germany. In 1938, he sent troops into Austria, proclaiming an *Anschluss*, or reunification, of Austria and Germany; later that year the German areas of the Sudetenland, on the Czechoslovakian border, were ceded to Germany at the Munich Conference. In March 1939, German troops invaded Czechoslovakia and established the German Protectorate of Bohemia and Moravia. Germany next turned to Poland, demanding incorporation of the Polish corridor city of Danzig into German territory, as well as a German corridor connecting East Prussia with Germany; Poland refused. Both Britain and France finally responded to the rapidly escalating German expansion by pledging to guarantee the territorial integrity of Poland. On September 1, 1939, German troops invaded Poland. Two days later Europe was once again at war—it was the second time in a still-young century.

THE RETURN OF SUBMARINE WARFARE

At the beginning of hostilities Germany possessed only 57 operational submarines, 32 of which were small, 250-ton boats suitable only for coastal defense patrols. This was hardly an adequate fleet for conducting an unrestricted submarine campaign against enemy shipping. Nearly one year earlier Admiral Karl Donitz, commander in chief of Germany's U-boat arm, had insisted that a fleet of 300 boats was necessary for the proper conduct of a convoy war against Britain. His plan for 300 U-boats was based on the belief that at any given time, 100 boats would be on their way to, or returning from, the operational theater; a second 100 boats would be in their bunkers being overhauled; and a third 100 boats would actually (Continued on page 150)

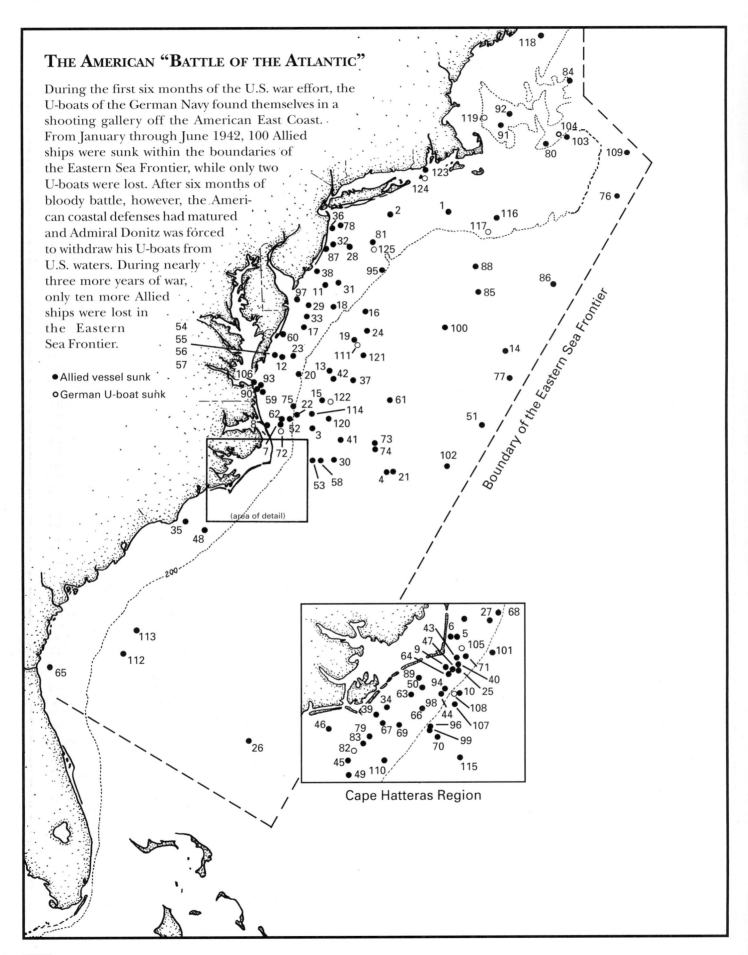

THE AMERICAN "BATTLE OF THE ATLANTIC"

During the first six months of the U.S. war effort, the U-boats of the German Navy found themselves in a shooting gallery off the American East Coast. From January through June 1942, 100 Allied ships were sunk within the boundaries of the Eastern Sea Frontier, while only two U-boats were lost. After six months of bloody battle, however, the American coastal defenses had matured and Admiral Donitz was forced to withdraw his U-boats from U.S. waters. During nearly three more years of war, only ten more Allied ships were lost in the Eastern Sea Frontier.

• Allied vessel sunk

○ German U-boat sunk

Boundary of the Eastern Sea Frontier

(area of detail)

Cape Hatteras Region

VESSEL LOSSES WITHIN THE EASTERN SEA FRONTIER

Key	Vessel	Date Sunk	Sunk By	Key	Vessel	Date Sunk	Sunk By
1	Norness	1/14/42	U-123	65	Esparta	4/9/42	U-123
2	Coimbra	1/15/42	U-123	66	Malchace	4/9/42	U-160
3	Allan Jackson	1/18/42	U-66	67	Atlas	4/9/42	U-552
4	Lady Hawkins	1/19/42	U-66	68	San Delfino	4/10/42	U-203
5	City of Atlanta	1/19/42	U-123	69	Tamaulipas	4/10/42	U-552
6	Ciltvaira	1/19/42	U-123	70	Ulysses	4/11/42	U-160
7	Norvana	1/22/42	U-66	71	Empire Thrush	4/14/42	U-203
8	Olympic	1/22/42	U-130	72	U-85 (type VII)	4/14/42	USS Roper
9	Empire Gem	1/23/42	U-66	73	Desert Light	4/16/42	U-572
10	Venore	1/23/42	U-66	74	Alcoa Guide	4/16/42	U-123
11	Varanger	I/25/42	U-130	75	Chenango	4/20/42	U-84
12	Francis E. Powell	1/27/42	U-130	76	West Imboden	4/20/42	U-752
13	Rochester	1/30/42	U-106	77	EmpireDrum	4/24/42	U-136
14	Tacoma Star	1/31/42	U-109	78	Arundo	4/28/42	U-136
15	Amerikaland	2/1/42	U-106	79	Ashkhabad	4/29/42	U-402
16	WL Steed	2/2/42	U-103	80	Taborfjell	4/30/42	U-576
17	San Gil	2/3/42	U-103	81	Bidevind	4/30/42	U-752
18	India Arrow	2/5/42	U-103	82	U-352 (type VII)	5/9/42	USS Icarus
19	China Arrow	2/5/42	U-103	83	HMS Bedfordshire	5/12/42	U-558
20	Ocean Venture	2/8/42	U-108	84	Skottland	5/17/42	U-588
21	Blink	2/11/42	U-108	85	Plow City	5/21/42	U-588
22	Buarque	2/15/42	U-432	86	Margot	5/22/42	U-588
23	Olinda	2/18/42	U-432	87	Persephone	5/25/42	U-593
24	Azalea City	2/21/42	U-432	88	Berganger	6/2/42	U-578
25	Norlavore	2/24/42	U-432	89	FW Abrams	6/11/42	US mine
26	Mamura	2/26/42	U-504	90	HMS Kingston Ceylonite	6/15/42	U-701
27	Marore	2/26/42	U-432	91	Port Nicholson	6/15/42	U-87
28	RP Resor	2/27/42	U-578	92	Cherokee	6/15/42	U-87
29	USS Jacob Jones	2/28/42	U-578	93	Santore	6/17/42	U-701
30	Arbutan	3/7/42	U-155	94	USS YP-389	6/19/42	U-701
31	Cayru	3/8/42	U-94	95	Rio Tercero	6/22/42	U-202
32	Gulftrade	3/10/42	U-588	96	Ljubica Matkovic	6/24/42	U-404
33	Hvoslef	3/10/42	U-94	97	John R Williams	6/24/42	U-373
34	Caribsea	3/11/42	U-158	98	Manuela	6/24/42	U-404
35	John D Gill	3/13/42	U-158	99	Nordal	6/24/42	U-404
36	Tolten	3/13/42	U-404	100	Moldanger	6/27/42	U-404
37	Trepca	3/13/42	U-332	101	William Rockefeller	6/28/42	U-701
38	Lemuel Burrows	3/14/42	U-404	102	City of Birmingham	6/30/42	U-202
39	Ario	3/15/42	U-158	103	Alexander Macomb	7/3/42	U-215
40	Australia	3/16/42	U-332	104	U-215 (type VII)	7/3/42	HMS Le Tigre
41	Ceiba	3/16/42	U-124	105	U-701 (type VII)	7/7/42	Army bomber
42	San Demetrio	3/17/42	U-404	106	Chilore	7/15/42	U-576
43	Kassandra Louloudis	3/17/42	U-124	107	Bluefields	7/15/42	U-576
44	EM Clark	3/18/42	U-124	108	U-576 (type Vll)	7/15/42	Navy planes
45	Papoose	3/19/42	U-124	109	Lucille M	7/25/42	U-89
46	WE Hutton	3/19/42	U-124	110	Panam	5/5/43	U-129
47	Liberator	3/19/42	U-332	111	U-521 (type IX)	6/2/43	PC-565
48	Esso Nashville	3/21/42	U-124	112	Esso Gettysburg	6/10/43	U-66
49	Naeco	3/23/42	U-124	113	Bloody Marsh	7/2/43	U-66
50	Dixie Arrow	3/26/42	U-71	114	Plymouth	8/5/43	U-566
51	USS Atik	3/27/42	U-123	115	Libertad	12/4/43	U-129
52	Equipoise	3/27/42	U-160	116	Pan Pennsylvania	4/16/44	U-550
53	City of New York	3/29/42	U-160	117	U-550 (type IX)	4/16/44	USS Gandy, Joyce, & Peterson
54	Allegheny	3/31/42	U-754				
55	Barnegat	3/31/42	U-754	118	Cornwallis	12/3/44	U-1230
56	Menominee	3/31/42	U-754	119	U-857 (type IX)	4/7/45	USS Gustafson (1)
57	Ontario	3/31/42	U-754	120	Belgian Airman	4/14/45	U-879
58	Rio Blanco	4/1/42	U-160	121	Swiftscout	4/18/45	U-548
59	Tiger	4/1/42	U-754	122	U-548 (type IX)	4/30/45	USS Natchez, Coffman (2)
60	David H Atwater	4/3/42	U-552				
61	Otho	4/3/42	U-754	123	Blackpoint	5/5/45	U-853
62	Byron D. Benson	4/5/42	U-552	124	U-853 (type IX)	5/6/45	USS Atherton, Moberly
63	British Splendour	4/7/42	U-552				
64	Lancing	4/7/42	U-552	125	U-869 (type IX)	unknown	

(1) Post war analysis of the USS *Gustafson*'s attack records indicate that this was probably not a sinking.

(2) Post war research indicates that the *U-548* was sunk off Nova Scotia, where the *U-879* was previously believed to have been sunk; this sinking is likely *U-879* or *U-857*.

The last remaining Type VIIC U-boat can be found on display at the German Navy Memorial in Laboe, Germany. The Type VIIC was the workhorse of the German submarine campaign during World War II. Photo by Henry Keatts.

be on station. This was the fleet he felt was required to bring England to her knees, yet he had only 57 submarines at his disposal.

Between the wars technological developments had led Britain to believe that the U-boat threat was obsolete. In particular, the famous ASDIC (known as SONAR in the United States) underwater detection system promised to make the submarine obsolete by robbing the U-boat of its chief advantage—invisibility. The Germans had not been idle during the years of peace, however, and in addition to improved U-boats, had developed new tactics to combat the battle-proven system of convoys employed during the First World War. Admiral Donitz's long dreamed-of employment of the *rudeltaktik*, or "wolf-pack" attack, was soon brought to reality with resounding success. Rather than a series of lone wolves hunting haphazardly throughout the world's shipping lanes, the available submarines were deployed in long lines stretching across the ocean, waiting to ambush Allied merchant convoys. Once a convoy was sighted, U-boat headquarters was informed of the convoy's position by radio. All available U-boats were then ordered to intercept the convoy and attack in unison at night and on the surface. Explosion after explosion split the night as the massed German sub-

marines proved more than the convoy's escorts could handle.

Donitz's wolfpack tactic, originally conceived during his internment in a British prison camp during the First World War, quickly proved itself. But the U-boat campaign was still handicapped by a lack of submarines. More interested in the conquest of France, Hitler had given the Army priority in steel allocations at the expense of the Navy; the size of Germany's U-boat fleet did not see an increase until nearly the end of 1940. In June of that year, France fell to the Axis powers. The German Army reached the Atlantic coast on June 19th; three days later an armistice was signed partitioning France into occupied and unoccupied zones. The German Army was now in possession of the entire northern and western French coastlines, and the German Navy had submarine bases on England's doorstep.

The new bases eliminated the long journey around the British Isles (or the shorter but much more hazardous one through the English Channel), that the U-boats had been forced to traverse to reach the Atlantic. Able to spend more time on station sinking ships, U-boat successes increased dramatically. In June alone merchant sinkings amounted to 284,000 tons—

up from a monthly average of 95,000 tons since the war's beginning. Merchant ship sinkings for the remainder of 1940 averaged 250,000 tons per month. The Germans were seemingly sinking ships at will and strangling England's seaborne supply lines; the men in the U-boat fleet would later call it "the happy time."[4]

In 1941, however, despite a trebling of the number of available submarines, merchant ship losses dropped to 180,000 tons per month. Defensive convoy tactics had begun to improve and more escorts were available, thanks to a massive building program and the transfer of 50 World War I mothballed destroyers to Britain in the Anglo-American Lend-Lease Act. The first German "happy time" had drawn to a close.

OPERATION *PAUKENSCHLAG*

The United States entered the war in early December 1941. Only five weeks later an onslaught of German U-boats began a bloodbath off the American coast that would ultimately claim nearly one-half million tons of shipping, and some 2,000 lives, during the first six months of 1942. During the First World War, a total of six long-range U-cruisers were sent across the Atlantic to the North American coast; these six submarines managed to sink a total of 99 vessels with an aggregate tonnage of 166,907 gross tons. During World War II, the *first wave* of U-boats sent to the East Coast consisted of five submarines with many more to follow.

Shortly after the U.S. entry into the war, Donitz requested 12 Type IX boats for Operation *Paukenschlag*, the code name for his surprise attack on North American shipping. The superior range and armament of the Type IX made it the perfect choice for this transatlantic mission. Due to ongoing operations in the Gibraltar area, however, releasing 12 of the long range U-boats was out of the question—Donitz was given only six boats and one of those boats, the *U-128*, required repairs that delayed her departure. The attacking squadron had been reduced to only five submarines.

In mid-January 1942, the five German U-boats fanned out along the North American East Coast, intent on delivering a punishing first strike to merchant

The Latvian freighter Ciltvaira *fell victim to Hardegen's U-123 on January 19, 1942 off North Carolina. Her back broken, she drifted for several days before going down. Courtesy of the National Archives.*

shipping. Kapitanleutnant Reinhard Hardegen in *U-123* struck the first blow on January 11th (a day earlier than the operation was ordered to begin) by sinking the British steamer *Cyclops* 160 miles south of Halifax, Nova Scotia; 100 lives were lost. Hardegen then sped southwest toward his assigned target area—the approaches to New York Harbor. Meanwhile, Fregattenkapitan Ernst Kals, commanding *U-130*, made landfall off Nova Scotia, and before heading south, sank the ships *Frisco* and *Friar Rocks* on the night of January 12th. The first victim off the American coast came one day later, during the early morning hours of January 14th. It was Hardegen again, this time expending five torpedoes in a fiery attack on the huge 9,577-ton tanker *Norness*, 60 miles southeast of Montauk Point, Long Island. The following day, headlines in *The New York Times* brought the frightening news to the American public: "Tanker Torpedoed 60 Miles Off Long Island; Navy Picks Up Survivors, Warns All Shipping."[5] But before these dramatic headlines were even printed, Hardegen had struck again. This time the recipient of Hardegen's torpedoes was the 6,768-ton British tanker *Coimbra*, sunk early on the morning of January 15th, 30 miles south of Shinnecock, Long Island. The frigid, North Atlantic water would claim 36 lives before rescue came. Death had arrived on America's doorstep.

The next of the U-boats to score was the *U-66*, commanded by Fregattenkapitan Richard Zapp, who sent the tanker *Allan Jackson* to the bottom off the coast of North Carolina on January 17th, causing the death of another 22 men. On the 19th, Zapp struck again, sinking the passenger steamer *Lady Hawkins*, with 200 men, women and children perishing in the attack and its aftermath. That same day, Hardegen conducted a blazing finale to his East Coast marauding by sending both the *City of Atlanta* and the *Ciltvaira* to the bottom and damaging the *Malay*. The attacks were carried out with both gunfire and his last remaining torpedo. Forty-four men went down with the *City of Atlanta*.

January 20th was a day of reprieve for East Coast shipping—not a single vessel was attacked along the entire American coast. But the following day saw a resumption of enemy action when Kals torpedoed the tanker *Alexandra Hoegh* several hundred miles east of Cape Cod. On the 22nd, Kals moved inshore and sank the tanker *Olympic* off the Virginia Capes, while Zapp torpedoed the freighter *Norvana* off North Carolina; 60 men were lost in the two sinkings. On the 23rd, Kapitanleutnant Heinrich Bleichrodt, commanding *U-109*, was finally heard from when he sank the *Thirlby* south of Nova Scotia. Zapp went into action again on

Kapitanleutnant Reinhard Hardegen, commander of the U-123, *struck the first blow of Operation* Paukenschlag. *Hardegen sent nine ships to the bottom before heading home to Germany. Courtesy of the National Archives.*

the 24th, torpedoing the *Empire Gem* and the *Venore*, both off the North Carolina coast; 76 men were added to the growing death toll. On January 25th, Kals torpedoed the Norwegian tanker *Varanger* off the New Jersey coast; the *U-123* disposed of the *Culebra* with gunfire far out to sea, on her way home to Germany; Kapitanleutnant Ulrich Folkers finally appeared off the coast, attacking but failing to sink the tanker *Olney*. The following day, however, Folkers scored, when he sent the freighter *West Iris* to the bottom off the Virginia Capes—35 more lives lost. That same day Hardegen sent yet another ship, the huge tanker *Pan Norway*, to the bottom in mid-Atlantic with shellfire. Kals attacked two tankers on January 27th, sending the *Francis E. Powell* to the bottom off Delaware and damaging the *Halo* with gunfire near Diamond Shoals.

The tanker F.W. Abrams *was a victim of "friendly fire" off the coast of North Carolina on June 11, 1942. Departing Diamond Shoals during a heavy rainstorm, she ran into an Allied minefield and sent herself to the bottom. Courtesy of the National Archives.*

In 15 days, 5 U-boats had killed 20 ships and damaged three others. Over 600 lives had been lost, yet the battle had just begun.

THE BEGINNING: *NORNESS* AND *COIMBRA*

The loss of the tankers *Norness* and *Coimbra* marked the beginning of the American "Battle of the Atlantic"—the return of the U-boats that had plagued east coast shipping during World War I. Front page headlines spread news of the sinkings across the country; it

could no longer be considered just a European war. The bows of both ships protruded above the stormy winter sea for days—a ghostly reminder to those who passed of the ever-present U-boat menace. Long oil slicks slowly bled across the surface of the ocean, forming a convenient trail for those seeking evidence of the enemy's presence. The seeping of oil from these two sunken hulks continues even to this day.

The survivors of both wrecks owed their lives to chance rescues by passing ships and patrol planes, for neither got off distress signals that were received by friendly ears. The *Norness*'s radio officer did manage to send a distress signal: "SOS. Have been torpedoed or struck mine, 40 nm west of Nantucket lightship. Norness.";[6] unfortunately, the only receiver of this call for help was the very German U-boat that had sunk her! Hardegen used five of his valuable torpedoes in the destruction of the *Norness*, a necessity that must have exasperated him. As he turned his back on the *Norness* and headed west in search of new targets, Hardegen left two lifeboats and a raft in his wake, filled with the tanker's survivors. The orphaned sailors bobbed about on the ocean swells for half a day before being discovered. One boat was sighted by the fishing trawler *Malvina D.* out of New Bedford, while the other boat and the raft were spotted near the stricken tanker's protruding bow by an Army patrol plane. Sixteen days later a naval plane flying out of Quonset Point Naval Air Station, Rhode Island, sighted a large oil slick leading to the bow of the ship still protruding above the ocean.

The sinking of the *Coimbra* produced a similar monument. Only nine men survived the attack on the British tanker and the subsequent drift in the icy Atlantic. An assortment of rafts and open lifeboats held the initial survivors as they drifted helplessly in the rough winter sea. One by one the men slipped away, succumbing to the cold. Finally a patrol plane sighted one of the lifeboats and radioed a nearby destroyer which picked up those left alive. The plane returned with photographs of the tanker's bow jutting gruesomely from the sea—photographs that later appeared in *The New York Times* with the caption "Final Plunge of Torpedoed Tanker".[7] A similar photograph appeared in *Life* magazine ten days later. Such images did much to bring the proximity of the war to the public's attention.

In both cases, U.S. Army patrol planes were directly involved in the sighting and rescue of survivors. The Army Air Force had been flying daily patrols over the coastal ocean since December 8th. While the Navy was responsible for the protection of the coast and had at its disposal 103 aircraft, almost none were suitable for maritime patrol duty. Nor were adequate numbers of Navy ships available to protect East Coast shipping. A hodgepodge fleet of only 20 vessels was assigned to the Eastern Sea Frontier, a 1,500-mile stretch of coastline extending from the Canadian border to Jacksonville, Florida. This shortage of suitable patrol and escort craft, combined with the disorganization inherent to a new and unprepared combatant, made inevitable the devastation of East Coast shipping that began with the sinking of *Norness* and *Coimbra*.

A Dangerous Cargo: *R.P. Resor* and *Gulftrade*

Throughout the month of February ships continued to fall to the prowling U-boats. Tankers and freighters alike were attacked with impunity, their crews left to their own devices at the mercy of the winter sea. Dumped in the ocean, often far from shore, the men of the merchant marine were forced to fight for their very survival and the rough, frigid ocean often swamped lifeboats and soaked cold, exhausted men. The sea is a hostile bedmate in the depths of winter. But a tanker's crew lived in fear of an even greater danger, for the very cargo their ships carried was in essence a huge bomb, whose explosive power was measured in thousands of tons of the one essential ingredient powering the industrialized world—oil.

The 7,451-ton tanker *R.P. Resor* had left Houston, Texas on February 19th, bound for Fall River, Massachusetts, loaded with 78,729 barrels of bunker C fuel oil. By the evening of February 26th, she had reached the New Jersey coastline. The sea was nearly calm with only a slight ripple to mar the surface of a long, gentle ground swell. The air was crisp and cold, with the sky taking on that endless clarity found only in the depths of a cold winter night; a brilliant moon cast a ghostly illumination across the surface of the sea. Able Seaman John J. Forsdal, one of only two men on board the tanker who would live to see the light of dawn, later told authorities that he "could easily distinguish the individual lights on the New Jersey shore,"[8] even though they were some 20 miles away. It was a perfect night to be a U-boat captain—Korvettenkapitan Ernst-August Rehwinkel, in command of *U-578*, undoubtedly agreed.

At about 11:30 P.M., a firestorm erupted in the cold, clear night as a single torpedo ripped into the port side of the *R.P. Resor*. Oil and debris were blown skyward and the tanker was instantly engulfed in flames from stem to stern. Seaman Forsdal, standing watch alone on the *Resor*'s bow, found himself isolated from his crewmates by the rapidly spreading fire. He had to choose between the frigid, winter Atlantic and the white hot blaze of the tanker; his fortune was in having a choice. Unable to make his way aft, he dropped a life raft over the side and slid down a line into the cold Atlantic. Swimming through the icy sea, whose surface was now covered with a thick layer of heavy oil, became a frantic struggle for survival. Flames spread across the sea behind him, chasing him from his burning ship. As he desperately swam to escape the spreading flames, a second explosion wracked the tanker, sealing its fate. A Coast Guard picket patrol boat later found Forsdal clinging to a life raft and covered in thick, coagulated oil. The Chief Boatswain's Mate on board the picket boat later stated that "Forsdal was so coated with thick congealed oil that we had to cut his clothes and his life jacket off with knives. They were so weighted with oil we couldn't get him aboard. Even his mouth was filled with a blob of oil."[9] This same picket boat picked up the *Resor*'s only other survivor, a member of the U.S. Navy Armed Guard, Daniel L. Hey. The remainder of the *Resor*'s complement, 48 men, did not survive the fiery cauldron that their ship had become.

The flames engulfing the tanker were so bright they were easily visible from the New Jersey shore. The fire served as the *Resor*'s distress signal, summoning the rescue vessel that saved the two survivors while dooming the rest of the crew. The *Resor* continued to burn throughout the following day. Crowds of onlookers on the New Jersey shore were treated to a glimpse of war as a huge, billowing cloud of oily smoke rose high into the sky. On February 28th, the tanker finally burned itself out and the Navy tug USS *Sagamore* took it under tow. That evening the stern struck bottom, 31 miles east of Barnegat Light, and the *Resor* rolled over and sank.

Just over one week later, residents of Barnegat, New Jersey, who were still awake at a quarter-to-one on the morning of March 10th would have gasped in horror as a huge pillar of flame suddenly leapt skyward. The Gulf Oil tanker *Gulftrade*, steaming north only three and one-half miles off the beach, received a single torpedo from Kapitanleutnant Viktor Vogel's *U-588*. The sea was rough with a fresh breeze blowing from the southwest; visibility was good. The *Gulftrade*'s Captain, Torger Olsen, had switched on his navigation lights two hours earlier in order to avert a possible collision with several large ships in his vicinity. Failing to black out his ship again after those encounters was a mistake he later freely admitted. The torpedo struck the *Gulftrade* between the main mast and the bridge, splitting the tanker in two and sending a column of fire skyward and igniting the *Gulftrade*'s cargo. Although the *Gulftrade* was carrying bunker C fuel oil just like the *R.P. Resor* before her, she was saved from a similar fate by the rough sea. Captain Olsen later told authorities that the flames from the burning oil were "shooting up to the top of the mast"[10]—the *Gulftrade*'s mast towered 96 feet above her main deck. But less than one minute after the torpedo explosion, a big sea swept over the *Gulftrade*'s deck and extinguished the flames.

The men on board the *Gulftrade* were spared the *Resor*'s inferno, but after the flames were doused they found their ship in two pieces, drifting apart. From the crew of 34, including Captain Olsen, nine men escaped from the ship's bow section in the undamaged port lifeboat; the starboard boat had been destroyed by the blast. The remaining 25 men were on the tanker's stern, where there were two undamaged boats. Eighteen men made their escape from the foundering stern in those two boats, while seven elected to stay on board their ship, hoping that she would remain afloat. Those men chose wisely for shortly after launching, the two boats from the stern section were swamped by the rough seas and none of the 18 occupants survived.

The nine men from *Gulftrade*'s bow section were picked up by the U.S. Coast Guard cutter *Antietam*. The cutter then attempted to reach the men still on board the tanker's stern, but her propeller became fouled in a floating mooring line. She stood by as USS *Larch* came upon the scene two hours later and took the seven men off. The two halves of the tanker settled to the bottom ten miles apart.

FREIGHTERS TOO: SS *ARUNDO* AND MV *BIDEVIND*

While fat tankers and their vital cargoes were highly prized targets for U-boat captains, it was a fair bet that any freighter found leaving the American coast was also loaded with war materiel. The Dutch freighter *Arundo* left New York Harbor on the morning of April 28th, bound for Alexandria, Egypt via the southern tip of Africa. In her hold, and lashed to her decks, were 123 trucks and two locomotives, along with an assortment of other war materiel. The trucks were being shipped to the Allied Middle East Command in North Africa, to combat the German Afrikakorps under General Erwin Rommel.

It was a clear morning with just a trace of a breeze. After clearing the harbor entrance and leaving the Ambrose lightship 15 miles astern, the *Arundo* turned from her southeast course and headed nearly due east, steaming at ten knots across a calm sea. Two tankers and a naval destroyer were nearby while two other merchant vessels could be seen in the distance. This close to New York Harbor, Captain A.C. Trdelman must have thought a torpedo attack impossible, but at 9:30 A.M. Chief Officer Akkerman, along with the ship's Third Officer, watched in horror as a white swath of water a yard wide, came streaking toward their ship. Seconds later the white arrow intersected the Dutch freighter's course directly under her bridge. The ship shook vigorously "from stem to stern"[11] as a towering pillar of water shot skyward. The torpedo's explosion was strangely muffled, but powerful enough to blow a huge hole in the freighter's side, as well as blowing the hatch covers clean off the No. 2 cargo hold. The *Arundo* quickly listed almost 90 degrees to starboard and, only five minutes after being struck, slipped bow first to the bottom of the New York shipping lanes. At least 41 of the 43 crew managed to escape in three lifeboats and two rafts, but two boats were damaged in launching and the third was pulled under when the ship sank. Only 37 were rescued by the destroyer USS *Lea* several hours later. Four men were apparently killed by one of the locomotives as it slipped off the *Arundo*'s listing decks and tumbled into the sea, directly on top of some men left swimming in the water; two other men were missing and unaccounted for.

The bold U-boat captain who had crept so close to the harbor entrance in broad daylight, and torpedoed a ship within sight of a U.S. Navy destroyer was Kapitanleutnant Heinrich Zimmermann, in command of the Type VIIC boat *U-136*. The German commander must have spooked himself in the shallow coastal waters, however, for he fled the scene of the sinking rather than pursue the other targets clearly in sight. But Zimmermann wasn't the only German captain in the area; not far away was Kapitanleutnant Karl-Ernst Schroeter in *U-752*.

While Zimmerman had been probing the entrance to the coast's busiest shipping port, Schroeter was patrolling further offshore where the operation of a U-boat was far less dangerous. Seventy miles southeast of New York the water is considerably deeper, giving a submarine more maneuvering room. Prowling in the dark of night held the advantage of allowing surface attacks, much preferred by most commanders. Just before 11:00 P.M. on April 30th, the lookouts on board the Norwegian freighter *Bidevind* sighted the dark silhouette of a submarine's conning tower 500 yards off the starboard beam. Seconds later the sea erupted just aft of the *Bidevind*'s engine room—Schroeter had hit his mark.

The *Bidevind* slowly flooded through the hole blown in her stern and began listing to starboard. A distress signal was sent on the emergency transmitter; the regular radio aerial had been damaged by the blast and the generators had stopped. The *Bidevind*'s crew, 36 men in all, abandoned their listing vessel within five minutes using three of the ship's boats, one of them a power boat. Shortly after the crew had taken to the boats, a second torpedo shattered the vessel's stern, throwing debris over 100 yards; she quickly flooded and settled to the bottom. The debris thrown by the

second blast damaged one of the lifeboats, forcing its occupants to transfer to one of the undamaged boats. Fortunately, the power boat was undamaged and was used to tow the second lifeboat to shore, where all 36 of the crew landed safely at Tom's River, New Jersey. The *Bidevind* had been inbound for New York from Bombay, India, carrying a cargo of spices, wool and goat skins.

The month of May was fairly quiet along the Long Island and New Jersey coasts as far as U-boats were concerned. The Greek freighter *Stavros* was torpedoed by the *U-593* on May 14th, but she did not sink and managed to limp into New York under her own power. Eleven days later, on the evening of May 25th, Kapitanleutnant Gerd Kelbling's *U-593* sent the tanker *Persephone* to the bottom only 2° miles outside Barnegat Inlet on the New Jersey coast. Despite that bold attack, sinkings along the entire coast during the month of May had amounted to only five ships—down from 26 in April.

SPIES AND A TORPEDOED FREIGHTER

June brought a resurgence of U-boat activity as ship sinkings rose to 17 for the month. In addition to merchant sinkings, the German submarines added a new twist to their contribution to the war effort. Likely intended as a propaganda effort aimed at unsettling the American populace, much as the attacks on the coastal fishing fleet during World War I, the Germans landed two groups of saboteurs on American soil. Eight men who had previously spent time in the United States and who spoke fluent English were selected for the operation, dubbed *Pastorious*. They were landed in two groups of four men each.

Just past midnight on June 13th, the *U-202*, commanded by Kapitanleutnant Hans-Heinz Linder, slipped through a dense fog to within a few hundred yards of the beach at Amagansett on Long Island's east end. Four men left the relative safety of the U-boat in a collapsible rubber boat and rowed to the beach.

Coast Guardsman John Cullen had left the Amagansett Coast Guard Station just after midnight and headed east on a routine beach patrol. He was to patrol six miles east of the station on foot, much as his forebearers in the United States Life-Saving Service had done before him. Halfway to his destination, however, a group of shadows materialized out of the foggy blackness near the water's edge. As he drew closer his flashlight illuminated the face of a sinister-looking man with a streak of gray hair. There (Continued on page 169)

Sunken Battleground of World War II

January 14, 1942: *Norness*

The *Norness* was the first American victim of "Operation *Paukenschlag*," Donitz's coordinated surprise attack against East Coast shipping. A victim of Reinhard Hardegen's *U-123*, the *Norness* was torn apart by three torpedoes on a dark January night 60 miles southeast of Montauk Point. Two sailors lost their lives while abandoning the sinking hulk. Hardegen was able to identify his victim by a distress signal sent by the tanker, and marked his war prize with the misspelled notation "Nornes" on his course track.

During the summer of 1993 a group of ten divers made the first ever dives on the wreck of the *Norness* from the dive charter boat *Seeker.* Lying in 286 feet of water, the dive was made using a special gas mix of helium, nitrogen and oxygen. The stern section of the wreck was found lying on its starboard side in a remarkable state of preservation (left). The hull was broken off midway between the stern and bridge superstructures, with the forward section apparently missing. Swimming about the *Norness*'s stern was an eerie yet fascinating experience, made even more spectacular by the appearance of a huge ocean sunfish who swam the decks of this historic sunken tanker with us for a full ten minutes.

The decks of the Norness *are still complete with ladders (below, right), boat davits, skylights and defensive gun tubs, much as the day she went down. The wreck makes for hazardous exploration, however, for she is wrapped in abandoned fishing nets, and her crazily canted decks add to the confusion of navigating her interior (below, left).*

Sunken Battleground of World War II

January 15, 1942: *Coimbra*

The sinking of the tanker *Coimbra* followed that of the *Norness* by a day, when two torpedoes split the dark night and sent the *Coimbra* to the bottom in three pieces. Her bow remained awash for several days, refusing to sink. Forced to take to the ship's life boats and rafts on a cold January night, only nine of the *Coimbra*'s 46 crew members survived an icy ordeal before they were finally rescued. Today the *Coimbra* lies beneath 180 feet of water 30 miles south of Shinnecock, Long Island. She is a popular fishing destination, particularly for shark. She is less frequently visited by scuba divers who are attracted by the clear water often found here. On a calm day the wreck site is marked by a thin slick of oil that can be seen stretching down current—oil that still leaks from her hull.

A diver explores the stern section of the Coimbra, *which lies listing to starboard and broken into three large sections (above).*

The ship's name can still be found spelled out in rusted steel letters on her bow (right).

Shipwrecks serve as outstanding artificial reef sites due to the myriad hiding places they offer marine creatures such as this ocean pout (below, left).

This skylight leads into the stern crew quarters of the ship, which is now largely an empty steel skeleton (below, right).

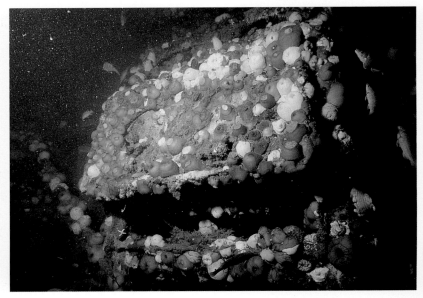

FEBRUARY 26, 1942:
R.P. RESOR

Fires were an additional hazard faced by tanker crews during the war. Carrying a volatile cargo of bunker fuel oil, the *R.P. Resor* was struck by a single torpedo launched by the *U-578*. The tanker immediately caught fire and burned so brightly that the smoke and flames were visible from the New Jersey shoreline, more than 20 miles away. There were 50 men on board the *Resor*; only two survived the fiery inferno.

The fires burned for almost two days before finally running out of fuel (left). Courtesy of the National Archives.

A doorway in the stern superstructure invites exploration, but is obstructed with overgrown debris (below, left).

A diver swims over the Resor*'s canted stern deck (below, right).*

Sunken Battleground of World War II

March 10, 1942: *Gulftrade*

Only a week after the torpedoing of the *R.P. Resor*, the spectacle was repeated when the tanker *Gulftrade* was torpedoed 3° miles off the New Jersey coast. The attacker was the *U-588*. The *Gulftrade* was carrying bunker fuel oil and, like the *Resor*, she caught fire immediately. Fortunately for most of the *Gulftrade*'s crew, the rough sea quickly extinguished the flames. Those rough seas were to blame for the death of 18 crewmen, however, swamping the boat they had abandoned their ship in. The *Gulftrade* broke in two and her two halves settled to the bottom ten miles apart.

The Gulftrade*'s bow remained awash for some time after it grounded in 60 feet of water off the New Jersey coast (right). Courtesy of the National Archives.*

The Gulftrade*'s stern sits in 90 feet of water 13 miles northeast of Barnegat Inlet, New Jersey. It is remarkably intact for such a relatively shallow wreck, inviting exploration of the interior of her tank compartments (above, left).*

Her partly collapsed boilers reveal tubing that gives the appearance of a bank of organ pipes (above, right).

The red rust of her hull, combined with a profusion of marine life particularly of mussels, gives her a colorful appearance to the visiting diver (right).

APRIL 28, 1942: *ARUNDO*

At 9:30 A.M., practically just outside the entrance to New York Harbor, the Dutch freighter *Arundo* was blasted by a single torpedo launched by Kapitanleutnant Heinrich Zimmermann's *U-136*. The Chief Mate and 3rd Officer saw the torpedo track just before it hit—there was no time for reaction. Although the resulting explosion was not loud, a violent concussion blew the hatch covers off the No. 2 cargo hold and the ship began listing sharply to starboard. Within five minutes she went down, bow first. Today she lies in 130 feet of water 15 miles east of Asbury Park, New Jersey. Her hull is a twisted and collapsed jumble of hull plates and beams, while a cargo of truck parts (lower, left and right) and soda bottles (right) lies scattered throughout the *Arundo*'s wreckage, part of a cargo destined for the Allied campaign in North Africa.

APRIL 30, 1942: *BIDEVIND*

Under a moonlit sky one hour before midnight, a torpedo explosion blew a hole in the side of the Norwegian freighter *Bidevind*. Losing all power and listing slowly to starboard, the *Bidevind* was quickly abandoned by her crew, who took to the ship's lifeboats. Shortly thereafter, a second torpedo shattered the ship's stern, sending her quickly to the bottom. The responsibility for this attack lay with Kapitanleutnant Karl-Ernst Schroeter and the *U-752*. The freighter's crew landed at Toms River, New Jersey the following afternoon. The *Bidevind*'s hull landed upside down on the ocean bottom, 200 feet beneath the surface. Today she is occasionally explored by divers (left), braving the deep depths.

SUNKEN BATTLEGROUND OF WORLD WAR II

MAY 25, 1942: *PERSEPHONE*

About 3:00 in the afternoon, the Panamanian tanker *Persephone* was torpedoed while part of a coastal convoy. She was only 2° miles off the New Jersey coast, just outside of Barnegat Inlet! The bold U-boat commander responsible was Kapitanleutnant Gerd Kelbing, who used two of the *U-593*'s torpedoes to sink the tanker—but he only sank her part way. The shallow water this close to shore permitted the tanker's stern to rest on the bottom while her bow and superstructure remained awash. The tanker's forward half was eventually salvaged and partly utilized to repair another damaged vessel. The ship's stern was left on the bottom and later destroyed as a hazard to navigation; today she is little more than a pile of steel rubble on the ocean bottom

COURTESY OF THE NATIONAL ARCHIVES

COURTESY OF THE NATIONAL ARCHIVES

JUNE 13, 1942: SPIES ON THE BEACH

Just past midnight Coast Guardsman John Cullen stumbled across four Germans on the beach near Amagansett, beginning a two-week odyssey fit for a spy novel. Landed on the Long Island coastline by the German submarine *U-202*, the men were part of a secret mission, code named *Pastorious*, to sabotage American industrial plants; four more saboteurs were landed almost simultaneously on the Florida coast. At least two of the Germans must have lost their nerve, however, for they quickly turned themselves in and led authorities to the other six men. Tried by a military court as spies, the two men who turned themselves in were sentenced to prison terms—the remaining six were swiftly executed. From left to right: Herbert Haupt, Lt. Meakin (USA) and George Dasch, who turned the group in.

JUNE 22, 1942: *RIO TERCERO*

The Argentine freighter *Rio Tercero* was torpedoed without warning at 6:45 A.M., 90 miles southeast of Fire Island by the *U-202*, under Kapitanleutnant Hans-Heinz Linder. The freighter's captain, Luis Pedro Scalese, was outraged by the act as Argentina was a neutral nation in the conflict. He was detained on board the German submarine for a short time and told that his ship was sunk because it was not on the U-boat commander's list of Argentine vessels. It is difficult to believe that Kapitanleutnant Linder was unaware of the *Rio Tercero*'s nationality—she had *thirteen* Argentine flags painted on the sides of her hull, hatch covers and superstructure; her name was similarly painted *nine* times. The ship settled to the bottom 90 miles east of Atlantic City, New Jersey, in deep water near the edge of the continental shelf.

COURTESY OF THE U.S. COAST GUARD

162

April 16, 1944:
Pan Pennsylvania and *U-550*

At 8:05 A.M. the American tanker *Pan Pennsylvania* was struck by a single torpedo on the port side. The tanker's deck cracked and heaved up; the crew quickly grew panicky and men began jumping overboard before order was restored and the ship could be safely abandoned by lifeboat.

The crew's initial panic was understandable in light of the tanker's cargo—gasoline. In all, 81 men were on board the ship: 50 crewmen and 31 armed guardsmen. Just after the last survivors were picked up by the U.S. Naval destroyer escorts *Joyce* and *Peterson*, *Joyce* picked up a solid sound contact. A pattern of 13 depth charges was dropped by *Joyce*. The destroyer escort *Gandy* was also nearby and as she moved in to follow up the attack with one of her own, the offending U-boat surfaced (above)—*Gandy* turned and came in at high speed to ram. All three naval vessels opened fire on the now helpless submarine *U-550*.

The U-boat's crew manned their own guns and returned fire while the *Gandy* closed in and rammed the submarine just astern of the conning tower. The Germans continued fire but were forced to abandon the sub as it began to sink by the stern. The *Peterson* closed in for the kill, firing two depth charges set to explode shallow. Following these last detonations the submarine disappeared from view, headed straight for the bottom. Thirteen German survivors were picked up, including the *U-550*'s commanding officer

COURTESY OF HENRY KEATTS

Kapitanleutnant Klaus Hanert.

With guns blazing aboard the three destroyer escorts and the German submarine, it is not surprising that some stray tracer shells hit the still floating *Pan Pennsylvania*, igniting her cargo of gasoline. The ship later capsized and refused to sink, requiring significant effort by surface gunfire and air bombardment to finally send her to the bottom. Of the 81 men on board the tanker, 25 perished. The crew of the U-boat fared worse, however, for only 12 of the Germans ultimately survived. This battle took place some 100 miles southeast of Montauk Point. The U-boat went down in 300 feet of water; the tanker drifted for two days before being sunk in 250 feet of water.

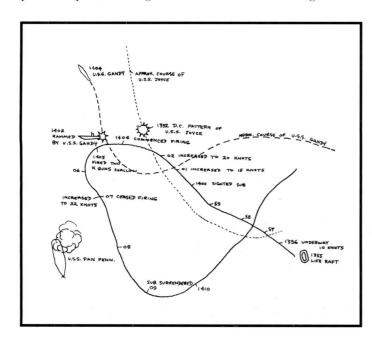

Attack plot from the USS Peterson *(left). Courtesy of the National Archives.*

Gary Gentile exploring the cavernous interior of the Pan Pennsylvania*'s bow (right).*

Sunken Battleground of World War II

May 5-6, 1945:
Blackpoint and *U-853*

By the war's close the U.S. Navy had become more than adept at answering the U-boat challenge. One day after Admiral Donitz radioed all U-boats to cease hostilities, the *U-853* torpedoed the collier *Blackpoint* in Rhode Island Sound. The now battle-proven U.S. Navy rose swiftly to the occasion, quickly locating the intruding U-boat and mounting an attack. For 16 hours, 3 destroyers intermittently pounded the bottomed submarine with hedgehogs and depth charges. In the shallow waters of Block Island Sound, the crew of the U-boat had no chance. There were no survivors.

A pattern of hedgehogs is dropped on the now-immobile U-853; *note the USS* Atherton *in the distance waiting her turn to attack (above, left). Courtesy of the National Archives.*

This open hatchway, surrounded by periscope stalks, leads into the interior of the U-853's *conning tower (left).*

The U-boat *was depth charged so extensively that her pressure hull was breached, bringing debris from the submarine's interior to the surface (below). Courtesy of the National Archives.*

Today the interior of the U-853's crew quarters are still strewn with reminders of the U-boat's human occupants (above, left).

The conning tower and periscope shears form the highest part of the wreck, attracting swarms of fish (above, right).

Farther forward, the U-853's knife-edged bow still stands defiantly above the ocean floor (below, right).

Human remains inside the U-853 remind us that these sunken submarines are all war graves (below).

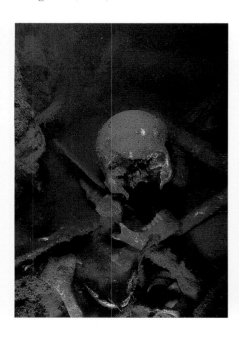

LEGACY OF THE U-BOATS

The Type VII U-352 lies on her starboard side in clear Gulf Stream waters 22 miles south of Cape Lookout, North Carolina (above).

The hull of the U-352 is intact except for the forward section of the bow, which is broken and twisted slightly to starboard, exposing her torpedo tubes (left).

John Chatterton on the charter boat Seeker, hunts for the elusive U-550 (below). Chatterton and Dan Crowell have led several searches for the submarine.

The German submarine offensive against the American East Coast left a total of 114 merchant ships on the ocean bottom within the boundaries of the Eastern Sea Frontier. The cost to the German Navy was 11 U-boats lost in these same waters. While casualties were often high among the crews of torpedoed merchant ships, sunken U-boats usually had few, if any, survivors—there were a combined total of 49 survivors from the 11 U-boats sunk in the Eastern Sea Frontier during the war.

Of the 11 U-boats sunk in these waters, only five have been located and positively identified since the war's end. Those whose positions are known include the *U-85, U-352, U-701, U-853* and the *U-869*. The *U-215*, sunk on Georges Bank east of Cape Cod, may have been located in 1987 during a side scan sonar search for one of her victims, the *Alexander Macomb*, but there has been no confirmation of this by divers and the position was apparently not recorded. The *U-550* is believed sunk some 60 miles south of Nantucket in approximately 300 feet of water, but several searches for her remains have proved unsuccessful. The *U-576* was sunk off Cape Hatteras in approximately 600 feet of water; at least one attempt to visit her remains by Ken Clayton was not successful. The remaining three, *U-521, U-857* and *U-548* have never been located.

The five U-boats that have been positively identified remain a lasting legacy of the American "Battle of the Atlantic." With the exception of the *U-701*, whose location is carefully guarded by her discoverer, Uwe Lovas, these sunken submarines are regularly visited by scuba divers.

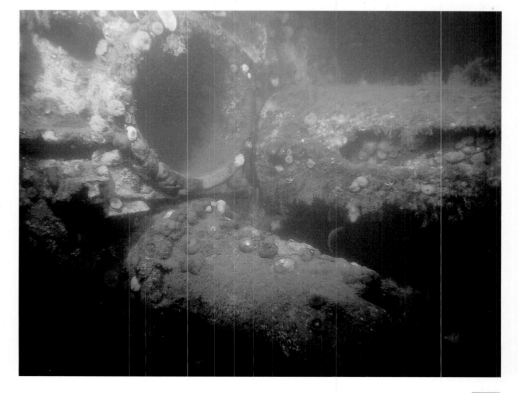

Off Nags Head, North Carolina are the remains of the U-85, *the first U-boat sunk in U.S. waters in World War II. Her open conning tower hatch is an alluring temptation to visiting scuba divers (above).*

The conning tower of the recently identified, but still mysterious U-869 *has been torn from the main hull and lies alongside (right).*

THE U-BOAT THAT SHOULDN'T BE: U-869

In September 1991, a sunken German U-boat was discovered off the New Jersey coast that, according to official American and German records, shouldn't be there. Extensive research, along with exploration of the wreck site, has established that she is the *U-869*; the attack or disaster that sent her to the bottom remains a mystery. Clockwise from upper right: Pat Rooney with a life raft stored in a canister outside the U-boat's pressure hull; In November 1991, John Chatterton recovered a knife from the wreckage with the name "Horenburg" scratched into the handle—it would prove a key clue to the submarine's identification; Rooney alongside the torn pressure hull of the control room; diver peers out of the conning tower hatch; a china plate bearing the date 1942.

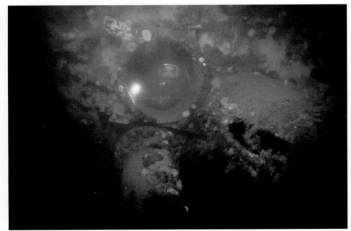

were three other men with him, all claiming to be fishermen who had run aground. Two of the men were dragging a heavy object up the beach and someone made an exclamation in a foreign tongue which sounded like German to Cullen. Asking what was in the heavy bag, the Coast Guardsman was told it contained clams. The stranger moved closer and shoved a wad of bills into Cullen's hand, suggesting, "Forget about this. Forget you ever saw us."[12] The stranger pulled the young man even closer, glaring into his eyes and asking, "Look at me. Would you recognize me again? Maybe we'll meet sometime in Southampton."[13] Cullen answered correctly: "No."

A badly frightened John Cullen backed slowly away until the strange men disappeared in the fog. Then he turned and ran three miles back to the Coast Guard Station, where he blurted out his fantastic story. Soon six Coast Guardsmen armed with rifles were making their way down the beach in search of the intruders. They found nothing but fog and darkness cloaking the beach; there seemed to be no sign of Cullen's mysterious German invaders. Cullen and one of the other men, however, felt the beach shaking and heard the low rumble of diesels out on the bar somewhere. Straining their eyes to see through the shifting fog and darkness, for an instant they thought they saw the shadowy silhouette of a U-boat just off the beach, aground on the bar. Hardly equipped to deal with armed German soldiers in the darkness, and unable to find any concrete evidence of the intruders, the men returned to their station. At dawn, however, they once again made their way down the beach to the spot where John Cullen claimed to have met the four strangers. It was Cullen who uncovered the first clue—a discarded pack of German cigarettes half buried in the sand. A trail in the sandy beach spoke of a heavy object being dragged up from the water. They followed the trail to a wet spot of sand that had recently been disturbed. Nearby lay a rolled-up pair of bathing trunks. Excavating the wet area of sand, the men found four tin-covered wooden boxes and a canvas bag containing clothing and a military cap—the cap bore a swastika. Back at the station the boxes were pried open—they were filled with explosives and detonators.

The Coast Guardsmen called Washington and the FBI quickly became involved. But the German who had confronted Cullen on the beach made it easy for the authorities; he decided to give himself up and betray his comrades. Two days after the landing, George Dasch phoned the FBI office in New York. Dasch had apparently convinced one of his fellow saboteurs, Ernest Burger, to accompany him to Washing-

ton, where he again telephoned the FBI offices. The two men were soon in Federal custody and revealed the plans for a second landing of four more men at Ponte Vedra Beach in Florida by the *U-584*. Investigating agents found that the Florida landing had already taken place, but with Dasch and Burger's help they were able to round up all of the German spies only two weeks after they had landed. The German mission to blow up bridges, railroads and aluminum plants had ended in dismal failure. Afraid that the saboteurs might get off with light sentences in civilian courts, since they had not actually committed any violent acts of espionage, President Roosevelt ordered a military trial. All were found guilty and, with the exception of Dasch and Burger, were executed on August 8th in the nation's capital by electric chair. The two men who had turned themselves in were given long prison sentences, but they were later paroled by President Truman in 1948 and returned to Germany.

While the American authorities were busy chasing down saboteurs, the *U-202* was busy offshore. Patrolling some 90 miles east of Atlantic City, New Jersey, Kapitanleutnant Linder encountered the Argentine cargo-passenger steamer *Rio Tercero*, outward bound from New York to Buenos Aires with a general cargo. Argentina had painstakingly maintained a neutral status in the war that was engulfing much of the world, yet two of her ships had already been sunk by U-boats. Whether or not these vessels were sunk out of arrogance or by mistake, the Argentineans were taking no chances—13 Argentine flags were painted on the *Rio Tercero*'s hull and superstructure, while her name was painted on the ship no less than nine times! Despite these elaborate precautions to clearly indicate her neutrality, at 6:45 A.M. on June 22nd, without warning, a single torpedo exploded adjacent to the ship's boiler room and triggered a boiler explosion. Four men were killed instantly by the combined explosion and the *Rio Tercero* began to fill rapidly with seawater.

Although 36 of those still alive abandoned the sinking vessel, one seaman slipped on the ship's deck and was sucked into the depths as the *Rio Tercero* sank stern first, only 11 minutes after she had been torpedoed. The men had managed to get off a quick SOS, and received a reply from New York before abandoning ship. Twenty minutes after their ship went down, the crew was startled as the *U-202* boldly came alongside their lifeboats and took the ship's captain, Luis Pedro Scalese, on board. Below decks, the Argentine captain was questioned by Kapitanleutnant Linder while protesting that his ship was neutral and should not have been torpedoed. Linder offered the Argentine

The Dixie Arrow *was torpedoed by the U-71 off the coast of North Carolina on March 26, 1942. Three torpedoes broke the tanker's back and turned her cargo of crude oil into a fiery inferno that billowed black smoke for miles. Eleven of 33 men on board perished in the attack, while the remainder were rescued by the destroyer* Tarbell. *The ship burned and drifted for hours before finally succumbing to her wounds and sinking in 90 feet of water. Her masts could still be seen protruding from the sea for months, and were later used for target practice by pilots. Today her hulk is a popular dive site for scuba divers visiting Cape Hatteras on North Carolina's Outer Banks. Both courtesy of the National Archives.*

captain three glasses of cognac and a pair of shoes for his bare feet, while confiscating the *Rio Tercero*'s logbook. After Captain Scalese rejoined his men in the lifeboat, four Germans appeared on the U-boat's deck—they were armed with two machine guns. The captain and crew of the *Rio Tercero* looked on helplessly—it appeared that they were about to become innocent victims in a war they wanted no part of. Perhaps Linder intended to erase the only witnesses to his torpedoing of the neutral freighter. Linder's intentions will never be known, however, for at that instant a U.S. Army patrol plane miraculously appeared on the scene, forcing the U-boat to quickly crash dive amidst a rain of depth charges from the aircraft and make its escape. The crew of the *Rio Tercero* expressed their gratitude to the U.S. forces, whom they were sure had saved their lives.

A Feeble Response Grows Stronger

The First World War had decisively proved that con-voys were the most effective measure available for the protection of merchant shipping against U-boats. But the success of convoys was dependent upon the use of armed escort vessels. Without escorts, convoys were nothing more than a flock of sheep set up for the slaughter. The severe shortage of suitable escort vessels along the Eastern Seaboard delayed implementation of a convoy system early in the war. Rather, ships were routed as close to shore as possible and took their chances. The result of this haphazard approach to coastal shipping was disastrous; by the end of March, 59 ships had been lost to enemy action in the Eastern Sea Frontier.

At the beginning of April a system of coastal convoys that came to be called the "bucket brigade" was instituted along the East Coast. Since there were still insufficient escort vessels for a proper convoy, ships were instructed to travel only during daylight hours, while at night they were corralled into protected anchorages set up along the coast. The designated anchorages and harbors were spaced approximately 120 miles apart, allowing even the slowest merchant ships

The long-range Type IXC/40 U-185, similar to those used in Operation Paukenschlag *was sunk in mid-Atlantic on August 24, 1943 by aerial attack. Courtesy of the National Archives.*

to move along the coast from anchorage to anchorage in a single day. U-boats were most dangerous during the hours of darkness when their low silhouettes allowed them to operate undetected on the surface. During daylight they were more vulnerable to the few patrol craft operating off the coast, as well as to patrolling aircraft, a mortal enemy of the submarine. Proper convoys with escort vessels were finally introduced in mid-May 1942.

Although the Army Air Force had made its planes available to the Navy for coastal patrol duty, there were still not enough planes to adequately cover the coastal shipping lanes, particularly in the early months of the war when U-boats were taking a deadly toll on coastal shipping. The Civil Air Patrol, a self-organized group of amateur fliers and plane owners, offered to patrol the sea lanes off the Atlantic Coast. Reluctantly, the Navy accepted and beginning in March 1942, an armada of tiny, privately owned airplanes began patrolling the coastal shipping lanes. A very few were armed with a single depth charge or several aerial bombs, but most were unarmed and served as observation plat-

forms only, relaying the positions of torpedoed ships and their survivors so that they might be rescued. They also reported suspicious-looking surface craft and submarine sightings to the military.

Civilian patrols along the coast, however, were not limited to aircraft. The Coastal Picket Patrol, often known by the informal name of the "Hooligan Navy," eventually conducted similar patrols of the coastal shipping routes. Consisting largely of auxiliary sailing yachts, fishing boats and motor yachts requisitioned for patrol duty, these small vessels conducted offshore patrols in search of German U-boats beginning in July 1942. A few were armed with depth charges and machine guns, but most had only rifles and handguns with which to defend themselves. All, however, were equipped with radios to report sightings. On a few occasions these patrol boats actually sighted surfaced U-boats, although there was little they could do other than report their encounters. Greenport, Long Island was home port for some 350 men of the Picket Patrol, whose fleet of 33 vessels sailed up to 200 miles offshore in search of the enemy. By late 1943 the Picket

The tanker Acme *took a single torpedo from the* U-124 *on the night of March 17, 1942. The* Acme *didn't sink, however, and is shown here under tow on her way to Newport News. Courtesy of the National Archives.*

Tankers, with their valuable cargoes of oil and gasoline, were especially juicy targets for German U-boats. The Tiger *was hit by one of* U-754*'s torpedoes off the coast of Virginia on April 1, 1942. She remained afloat for more than ten hours before finally sinking. Courtesy of the National Archives.*

Patrol had served out its usefulness, and as more Naval patrol craft became available the civilian patrols were discontinued.

The combined patrols of the U.S. Navy, Army Air Force, Civil Air Patrol and the hodgepodge fleet of the Hooligan Navy largely forced the German submarines to remain submerged during the day and conduct surface attacks at night. But endless advancing technology soon produced a new weapon—radar—which robbed the U-boat of its protective cloak of darkness. Radar was the above-water equivalent of asdic and sonar, using radio waves to locate targets, effec-

tively giving its user "eyes" with which to see ships, including surfaced submarines in the dark. There were not enough radar sets to go around early in the war, but as the units became available, Navy vessels and eventually aircraft were equipped with the new device.

It was radar that was responsible for the first U-boat sinking off the American coast, early on the morning of April 14, 1942. The destroyer USS *Roper* was patrolling off Nags Head, North Carolina, just past midnight when she picked up a blip on her radar scope. The *Roper* turned to investigate and soon picked up the sound of screws. A single torpedo came streaking by, narrowly missing the destroyer's thin, needle-sharp bow. The *Roper*'s huge searchlight played out over the darkness, illuminating the stark silhouette of the *U-85*'s conning tower. Caught in shallow water, the U-boat had no choice but to stand and fight. A well-placed 3-inch shell from the destroyer's deck gun damaged the *U-85*'s conning tower and she rapidly sank by the stern. German sailors scrambled overboard as their boat settled beneath them in its final dive. The *Roper* circled and dropped depth charges on the spot where the U-boat had disappeared, ensuring her kill. No effort was made to pick up the surviving Germans floating in the Atlantic; the concussion of the exploding depth charges killed the submariners to a man. War has tragedies on both sides.

Three and one-half weeks later, the U.S. Navy claimed another U-boat kill, also off the coast of North Carolina. The Type VIIC boat *U-352* had made the mistake of firing a lone torpedo at the U.S. Coast Guard cutter *Icarus* late on the afternoon of May 9th. The torpedo exploded 200 yards short of its target, confirming the cutter's earlier sonar reading which indicated the presence of a U-boat. The submarine tried to hide under the turbulence of the torpedo explosion, but the cutter's commander anticipated the tactic and dropped a pattern of depth charges on the spot. As more charges were dropped, the partly flooded *U-352* was forced to the surface some 40 minutes after the initial attack. The Germans abandoned ship into a firestorm of machine gun fire as soon as she hit the surface. Three-inch shells from the *Icarus*'s deck gun pummeled the U-boat's conning tower and hull, and she slowly slipped beneath the sea for the last time. The *Icarus*'s commander fired a single depth charge over the sinking submarine while ignoring the German survivors in the water. Unsure of what to do about the Germans, the American commander radioed for instructions before finally picking up the 33 men who had escaped from the sinking *U-352*. One of the Germans succumbed to wounds suffered during the gun battle, while the remainder of the crew became prisoners of war.

Nearly two months passed before another U-boat was sunk off the Eastern Seaboard. On July 3rd, the British anti-submarine trawlers HMS *Le Tigre* and HMS *Veteran* sent the *U-215* to the bottom east of Cape Cod. The *Le Tigre* picked up a sound contact while moving in to assist the torpedoed freighter *Alexander Macomb*, which was part of a convoy the British escorts were assigned to protect. After several depth charge attacks the contact stopped moving and survivors of the *Macomb*, drifting nearby in a life raft, reported seeing

the submarine come briefly to the surface before sinking.

Four days later an aircraft scored off Cape Hatteras when 2nd Lieutenant Harry Kane caught the *U-701* on the surface. Swooping out of the clouds, Kane's Army Lockheed-Hudson bomber dropped three bombs on the diving U-boat, two of which scored direct hits, breaching the submarine's pressure hull. An attempt to blow the U-boat's ballast tanks and bring her to the surface proved futile, and the men began pouring out of the conning tower hatch as the U-boat hit bottom, using their escape lungs. A second group of survivors had managed to seal themselves into the forward torpedo room; they also used their escape lungs to reach the surface one-half hour after the submarine sank. Lieutenant Kane dropped life preservers and a raft to the men in the water, but they drifted away in the strong Gulf Stream current before the Germans could reach them. The Germans would spend 50 hours drifting north in the Gulf Stream before they were rescued. Thirty-five men had escaped the sinking U-boat in two groups; only seven men survived their ordeal in the ocean. The fate of these German sailors was hauntingly familiar to that suffered by the crews of many sunken tankers and freighters on the other side of the conflict.

One week later, on July 15th, still another U-boat was sent to the bottom off the Carolina coast. After working his way into the midst of a convoy and torpedoing the freighters *Chilore* and *Bluefields*, along with the tanker *J.A. Mowinckel*, the *U-576* shot to the surface, either out of control or to view the destruction it had caused. Two Navy patrol planes dove in to attack with depth bombs while an armed merchant ship brought her deck gun to bear. The bombs straddled the submarine and apparently shattered her hull before she went down spewing oil and debris across the ocean surface. A destroyer moved in on the now stationary sound contact and delivered the final blow with a depth charge attack.

Over the course of a two-week period, three U-boats had been sunk in the Eastern Sea Frontier; only four merchant ships were lost in these same waters during the entire month of July. It was apparent that the tide had turned—the American defenses had matured and the siege was over. Germany's prowling gray sharks withdrew in search of easier prey.

LAST DANCE: *BLACKPOINT* AND *U-853*

So complete was the withdrawal of U-boats from the

Shown here during commissioning, the U-853 *was the last victim of the American "Battle of the Atlantic," receiving swift retribution for sinking the collier* Blackpoint *off Rhode Island. Kapitanleutnant Helmut Sommer is fifth from the right in the front row, while Oberleutnant Helmut Fromsdorf, who commanded the* U-853 *during her final action is on his left. Courtesy of Henry Keatts.*

Both petty officer Helmut Fehrs (left) and radio operator Erich Schoadt (center) went down with the U-853. *W. Dechen (right) had been transferred before the U-boat's fateful final cruise. Courtesy of Henry Keatts.*

Eastern Seaboard that not a single ship was sunk by enemy action during the remainder of 1942. The year 1943 was equally quiet for merchant shipping in the Eastern Sea Frontier. Five ships were sunk by a handful of submarines over the course of the entire year, while a single U-boat was sent to the bottom, Kapitanleutnant Klaus Bargsten's *U-521*, off the coast of Virginia. Nineteen-forty-four proved no better for Germany, with two merchant ships sunk at the cost of one more U-boat. It was obvious that the "happy time" off the American coast was long gone.

By 1945, U-boat losses had reached staggering proportions: 153 U-boats were lost between January and May 1945 world-wide, while only 282,000 tons of merchant shipping was sunk. Germany found herself being crushed in a vise as British and American troops advanced on the western front while the Russian Army closed in from the east—the end was inevitable. On April 30th, after appointing Grand Admiral Karl Donitz president of the Reich and Commander in Chief of the armed forces, Adolf Hitler committed suicide.

Donitz's job was now to end the war. On the night of May 4th, the new President of the Reich halted the war at sea by broadcasting the following message to his beloved submarines: "All U-boats. Attention all U-boats. Cease fire at once. Stop all hostile action against Allied shipping. Donitz."[14] This directive was soon followed by Donitz's famous message: "My U-boat men! Six years of war lie behind us. You have fought like lions. An overwhelming material superiority had driven us into a tight corner from which it is no longer possible to continue the war. Unbeaten and unblemished you lay down your arms after a heroic fight without parallel."[15]

Somewhere to the east of Long Island, however, a lone U-boat failed to receive, or accept, this final order. Moving into the shallow coastal waters of Rhode Island Sound, the *U-853*'s commander, Oberleutnant zur See Helmut Fromsdorf, claimed the final Allied victim of the American "Battle of the Atlantic." At 5:40 P.M. on May 5th, a single torpedo fired by the *U-853* blew away the stern of the 5,353-ton collier *Blackpoint*. Fifteen minutes later the ancient collier capsized, later sinking to the bottom four miles southeast of Point Judith, Rhode Island, taking 12 of the 46 men on board with her.

Although the *Blackpoint* was unable to broadcast a distress signal, a nearby merchant vessel sent out the signal. Thirty miles to the south the message was picked up by the Coast Guard frigate *Moberly*, traveling in company with the U.S. Navy destroyer escorts *Amick* and *Atherton*. The end of the war was at hand, and the crew of the destroyer escorts had been stowing ammunition in preparation for entering port—the men were heading home. Suddenly called into action, the three vessels sped to the scene of the sinking and began sweeping south along the U-boat's anticipated route of escape. Two-and-one-half hours after the *Blackpoint* had been struck, the *Atherton* picked up a sonar contact east of Block Island. Soon the sonar operator picked up the faint sound of the submarine's screws; the target appeared to be moving east very slowly. The *Atherton* moved in to attack, firing 13 magnetic depth charges. One apparently hit home on the sub's metallic hull and exploded. Meanwhile, the destroyer escort *Amick* was ordered away from the scene, leaving *Moberly* and *Atherton* to conduct the attack alone. *Atherton* moved in to make a second and then a third attack, this time firing hedgehogs at the enemy. Each attack produced several explosions, but their source was uncertain: were they the result of direct hits on the submarine's hull, or had the hedgehogs detonated unexploded depth charges remaining from the first attack? Or were the hedgehogs simply detonating after hitting the bottom?

The attack was temporarily discontinued when sonar contact was lost in the turbulent water created by the explosions. It was several hours before contact was regained and the attacks continued, bringing air bubbles, oil and pieces of wood to the surface. The U-boat appeared dead on the bottom. Working in such shallow water proved difficult for the destroyer escorts, however. As round after round of depth charges were dropped on the target, the attackers found that their explosives detonated before they could clear the blast area, damaging their own craft in the process. As dawn came the attackers found ample evidence that they were successful—air bubbles and oil slicks appeared over the target, along with an assortment of floating debris, including escape lungs, life jackets, life rafts and an officer's cap. Dawn also brought the arrival of two blimps to assist in the continuing attacks. The destroyer *Ericsson* had arrived during the night and assumed command of the operation, bringing the attacking force back to three vessels. A strange procession took place east of Block Island on the morning of May 6th: one of the three ships would move in and make a depth charge attack, then drift off and repair the damage sustained by her own explosives. While repairs were being carried out, the next ship moved in to make her attack. On and on the pounding continued, bringing more and more wreckage to the surface—bits of cork, a life raft, foul weather gear and even a chart desk floated up from the depths. One of the blimps dropped a sonobuoy, and the sonar operators listened in on a "rhythmic hammering on a metal surface."[16] Was it a last, desperate plea for help from the doomed Germans? The depth charging continued.

That afternoon and again the following day, divers were sent down to examine the enemy. They found dead bodies strewn about the inside of the control room and managed to identify the kill as the *U-853*. There were no German survivors from this final battle off the American coast—a battle that ended only nine hours before an unconditional surrender was signed by the Germans in Reims, France. The war had finally come to a close.

EPILOGUE: THE U-BOAT THAT SHOULDN'T BE

Both German and American records indicate that a total of ten U-boats were sunk in the Eastern Sea Frontier during the war. All were sunk by U.S. and British military forces, using both surface ships and aircraft, and the approximate location of each is recorded in official documentation. There were, of course, many claimed sinkings that were dismissed by military authorities during the war. According to claims made by the Civil Air Patrol, the pilots in their organization sighted 173 U-boats, dropped bombs and depth charges on 57 of them, and sent two to the bottom. When a mysterious sunken U-boat was discovered 60 miles off the New Jersey coast in 1991, the veterans of the Civil Air Patrol quickly claimed that the discovery substantiated their efforts during the war.

On July 11, 1942, a Civil Air Patrol (CAP) plane patrolling off the New Jersey coast sighted a surfaced U-boat 40 miles east of Atlantic City, New Jersey. Nearly out of fuel, the pilot was unable to take any action other than reporting the sighting by radio. A Grumman Widgeon armed with two depth charges was dispatched to the scene and managed to locate a dark, submerged silhouette, trailing an oil slick, some 40 miles off the coast. It was exactly where the CAP crew had reported it. The Widgeon pilots later reported that they followed the slowly moving shadow for six hours, hoping that it would rise to the surface and give them a better shot with the two depth bombs their plane carried. Finally, the submarine rose to periscope depth and the plane dove in to attack, dropping one depth charge directly atop the submarine. The pilot quickly circled and dropped his remaining weapon in the middle of the spreading oil slick, hoping to deliver the coup-de-grace. The aircraft's navigator later claimed he had seen the U-boat's bow rear up from the ocean and then slip back beneath the waves, leaving behind a slick of oil and debris.

Although the pilot and navigator were both sure that they had sunk an enemy submarine, the U.S. Navy never credited the Civil Air Patrol with a U-boat kill. Veterans of the CAP claim that throughout the war the Navy was reluctant to give their civilian organization credit for sinkings when their own response to the German onslaught of 1942 was so pitiful. But the Civil Air Patrol's claim became more plausible in September 1991.

Forty-nine years after a Grumman Widgeon reportedly dropped two depth charges on an enemy submarine somewhere off the New Jersey coast, a group of scuba divers aboard the dive boat *Seeker* discovered the submerged remains of a German U-boat some 60 miles off that same coast. The story told by the CAP quickly became the leading theory in the search for the submarine's identity. Exploration of the wreck site determined that she was a Type IX German U-boat, and human remains established that she was a war loss. But claims that she was the victim of the July 1942 CAP depth charge attack were put to rest when an escape lung air flask was recovered. Stamped with a hydrostatic test date of April 15, 1944, this piece of evidence showed that the submarine was sunk late in the war, and couldn't be the victim of the claimed CAP sinking.

The closest of the ten official U-boat sinkings in the Eastern Sea Frontier lies some 120 miles away. Could

this be an unknown victim of the American "Battle of the Atlantic," or was she one of the known victims whose position was mislocated? The two closest recorded U-boat sinkings, neither of whose positions have been confirmed, are the *U-521*, believed to have been sunk 100 miles off the coast of Virginia, and the *U-550*, believed sunk over 100 miles southeast of Montauk Point, Long Island. While the wreckage of neither of these submarines has been located or identified, it seems highly unlikely that the forces that sank these boats could have erred that badly in their navigation. Indeed, if they had, they might never have returned to port!

Extensive archival research, combined with evidence recovered from the wreck site, narrowed the probable identity of the U-boat to one leading candidate. The trail of evidence leading to this conclusion is twisted and partly circumstantial, but represents a fascinating tale of detective work.

On November 6, 1991, John Chatterton recovered a knife from the submarine's galley with the name "Horenburg" inscribed on the handle. This would later prove a valuable piece of evidence, but locating service records for individuals in the German Kriegsmarine proved difficult. Continued work on the wreck site determined definitively that the submarine was a type IXC/40. Further, recovery of a portion of an electrical diagram from the submarine established that she was built in the Deschimag yard in Bremen. This known, a list of all Type IXC/40 boats built at Deschimag Bremen was compiled by the research team—the mystery U-boat must be one of those on the list. Work proceeded to eliminate the boats on the list one-by-one, hoping to leave the identification of the sought-after boat by default.

Meanwhile, research in Germany finally located the apparent owner of the knife recovered from the wreck site, a *funkmeister* (radio officer) named Horenburg, who was assigned to the *U-869* in 1944. This seemed definitive, except that the *U-869* was reported sunk off the coast of Gibraltar on February 28, 1945, in a depth charge attack by the USS *Fowler* and French frigate *l'Indiscret*. Other than the U-boat's location on the wrong side of the Atlantic, this submarine seemed to fit all the evidence. She was a Type IXC/40 boat built at the Deschimag Bremen yard and was lost late in the war. Since the *U-869* was apparently never anywhere near the American coast, however, the focus of the research shifted to other possible U-boats.

Further research in Germany indicated that the *U-548*, previously believed to have been sunk 100 miles east of Cape Henry, Virginia, was actually the likely victim of an attack 180 miles southeast of Halifax, Nova Scotia, on April 19, 1945. That a U-boat was sunk at that location was not new information, but the victim had previously been identified as *U-879*. This discovery left the fate of the *U-879* a mystery. An obvious possibility was that she was sunk where the *U-548* was previously believed to have gone down, off Cape Henry. If that were the case, the two U-boat sinkings had simply been interchanged in the historical record.

The matter was further complicated, however, by an examination of the attack record of the destroyer USS *Gustafson*. The *Gustafson* was credited with sinking another U-boat, the *U-857*, approximately 25 miles northeast of Cape Cod on April 7, 1945. It appears likely, however, that the *Gustafson* was incorrectly credited with a U-boat kill in that action. The destroyer made a total of six hedgehog attacks on a sonar contact, with the second attack resulting in one explosion and the appearance of an oil slick. Contact was maintained for approximately three hours, but subsequent attacks yielded no further hits. Contact was later lost and a thorough search of the area failed to locate the submarine or any wreckage on the bottom. The conclusion of the review committee was that the attack only slightly damaged the submarine, if indeed there was even one present. This left both *U-879* and *U-857* as candidates for the boat discovered off New Jersey. Both *U-857* and *U-879* were Type IXC/40 boats, were sunk late in the war, and were headed for operations off the American coast. About the time it appeared likely that the New Jersey U-boat was either the *U-857* or *U-879*, however, the *U-869* made a reappearance.

Research in England provided crucial new evidence as to the fate of the *U-869*. Earlier in the war British intelligence had broken the German enigma code, allowing them to read all German radio traffic between operational U-boats and headquarters. Records indicated that the *U-869* had left Kristiansand on the southern Norwegian coast on December 8, 1944. Her assigned patrol area was grid square CA 53, which is directly southeast of New York! On January 8, however, *U-869* was directed by headquarters to change her patrol area and head for grid square CG 9592, which is west of Gibraltar. *U-869* reported her fuel status the following day, and this was the last recorded signal transmitted from the submarine. No acknowledgment of her change in patrol area was ever transmitted to headquarters by *U-869*. If *U-869* never received the transmitted orders to change her destination, she would have continued across the Atlantic and operated off the New Jersey coast, as originally assigned.

That the *U-869*'s original patrol area was almost exactly where the mysterious sunken U-boat was found fit quite neatly with Funkmeister Horenburg's knife being recovered from the wreck. All other data discerned from the wreck also fit this identification, and it now appeared almost certain that the wreck was that of the *U-869*.

The theory now needed proof from the wreck site. Working in difficult conditions in 230 feet of water, John Chatterton's persistence finally paid off in August 1997. A team of Chatterton, John Yurga, Pat Rooney and Richie Kohler set up a "bucket brigade" to get Chatterton into the tight confines of the U-boat's electric motor room with a single tank, leaving his doubles and stage bottles outside the wreck. Sifting through mountains of silt and boxes of spare parts, he found tags with the U-boat's identification number on them: *U-869*.

Although now identified, the sub's sinking remains a mystery. Whatever did send her to the bottom badly damaged her. The conning tower is torn off and lies amidst a debris field on the submarine's port side, alongside the completely demolished control room. Another large hole was blown in the stern. Whether the conning tower was blown off in a depth charge attack, was torn off many years after her sinking by a fishing trawler, or is attributable to some other cause is uncertain. When she was discovered, all her hatches were found open and there was reportedly an escape lung lying on the deck outside the pressure hull, fueling speculation that her crew attempted to escape while she lay on the bottom.

Both the beginning and the end of the American "Battle of the Atlantic" took place in the waters surrounding Long Island. The beginning came with the sinking of the *Norness* and *Coimbra* in January 1942, only weeks after the United States' entry into the war; helpless tankers torpedoed in the dark of night, along the coast of a neophyte combatant in a raging war for control of the seas. This challenge to the U.S. Navy, a provocation thrust upon her very doorstep, went largely unanswered for six long months. Although the sleeping giant was slow in awakening, once aroused she rose admirably to the occasion. The end of this great battle off the American coast was marked by the sinking of the collier *Blackpoint* by *U-853* in early May 1945, enraging the swift and vengeful wrath of the U.S. Navy one last time. The massive conflict that had engulfed the entire globe began a transformation that would propel the United States to world domination, establishing her as one of the world's only two "super powers."

The Era of Modern Navigation

Navigation on the open ocean has always been a tricky affair. The featureless surface of the sea provides travelers with no landmarks, few clues to direction and no safe havens from storm or calamity. Still, man has persisted in venturing forth upon the world's oceans. Over the course of centuries, he has accumulated enough knowledge and developed sufficient navigational tools to serve his purposes. Compasses were invented to tell direction; knotted ropes and taffrail logs evolved to determine a vessel's speed through the water. Together, these basic instruments allowed a navigator to keep track of his ship's course and speed, and thus his approximate position relative to a known starting point—a method of navigation known as dead reckoning. Later, man invented cross-staffs, astrolabes, octants and sextants to determine his latitude by observing the heavenly bodies. With the addition of accurate chronometers, he was able to determine his longitude as well. By keeping records of his explorations, man developed detailed charts of the world's oceans and coastlines; combined with his cleverly conceived armada of navigational instruments, he managed to traverse the world's oceans for centuries. But his navigational methods were far from perfect, and there were many accidents and mishaps.

With the dawn of the electronic age came a host of new instruments that revolutionized navigation, promising to make seafaring virtually foolproof and accident-free. The discovery and harnessing of radio waves led to the widespread use of the wireless telegraph at the turn of the century, providing both ship-to-ship and ship-to-shore communications. The new communication device was put to good use some ten years after its introduction when the cryptic dots and dashes of Morse code stabbed out the urgent calling "CQ CQ CQ" on the morning of January 23, 1909. What followed was the frightening announcement that the White Star liner *Republic* had been rammed by an unknown vessel and was sinking, 26 miles south of Nantucket Island—she needed immediate assistance. The offending vessel turned out to be the small Italian liner *Florida,* whose collision bulkhead kept her afloat while the *Republic* slowly settled beneath a fog-shrouded ocean. The relatively new wireless telegraph had provided the stricken ship with a revolutionary capability—she was able to summon help from both land stations and ships located miles away. No longer would ships in distress find themselves isolated and alone on the vast expanse of the ocean.

Not long after the introduction of the wireless, radio direction finders were invented and a system of radio beacons were installed along heavily traveled coastlines. Since radio waves easily penetrate both fog and the dark of night, ships were able to utilize the new beacons to accurately establish their position regardless of visibility. But it was the technology developed during World War II that brought a plethora of new instruments into being that truly revolutionized the science of navigation. Position finding was aided by the introduction of Loran A (later refined into present day Loran C), Decca and Omega; all three systems utilize a series of shore-based radio transmitters that put out precise and carefully timed signals. Sophisticated shipboard receivers are used to interpret the signals and determine a ship's position amongst a grid of invisible hyperbolas stretching across the earth's surface. These new instruments enabled a ship to easily establish its position in any weather and with previously unheard of accuracy—so long as the transmitters were operating.

Collision avoidance entered a new era with the widespread introduction of radar aboard merchant ships after the war. Carefully honed during the conflict to detect enemy ships and submarines, radar was now applied to peacetime use. By bouncing radio waves off distant and unseen objects, their range and location could be determined and displayed on an oscilloscope-type screen. This effectively provided a ship's commander with "eyes" that could see in both darkness and fog, and would prove *(Continued on page 182)*

MODERN ELECTRONIC NAVIGATION INSTRUMENTS ▬

RADIO POSITION FINDING SYSTEMS

Radio direction finding was developed as a means of finding a ship's position shortly after the practical introduction of radio waves early in the twentieth century. Fixed radio beacons were established at regular intervals along the shoreline specifically for this purpose. By using a special receiver, an operator can determine the compass bearing to each beacon, although not the range. Plotted on a chart, the bearing to each beacon becomes a line-of-position that the radio operator must lie upon. The intersection of two or more lines-of-position provides a fix of the ship's location.

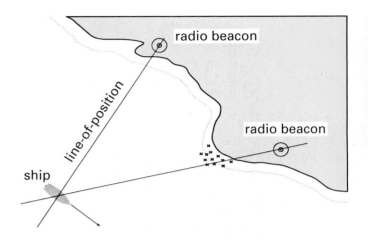

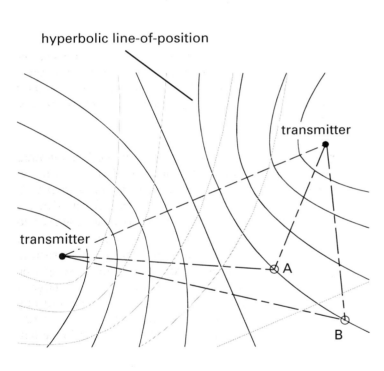

Loran is a "hyperbolic" navigation system—so called because it is based on the mathematical definition of the hyperbola. A series of radio stations have been established at various locations on shore that transmit carefully timed radio pulses in unison. To determine a vessel's position, a receiver with a highly accurate clock measures the difference in time between the arrival of the two pulses; the time difference is measured in micro-seconds and represents what we commonly know as loran "numbers." This time difference defines a hyperbolic line-of-position on which the operator must lie. Mathematically, a hyperbola is a set of points (a curve) such that the difference of their distances from the two focus points (the radio transmitters in this case) is a constant; since travel time is proportional to distance for radio waves, each hyperbolic line-of-position corresponds to a constant time difference between the receipt of the two radio pulses. In the accompanying diagram, a receiver at points A and B would display the same time difference since they both lie on the same hyperbola. Thus one time difference tells the loran operator that he lies somewhere on a particular hyperbolic line-of-position. A series of transmitters allows vessels to monitor two or more stations at once, allowing the determination of several lines-of-position and a complete fix.

THE WONDER OF RADAR

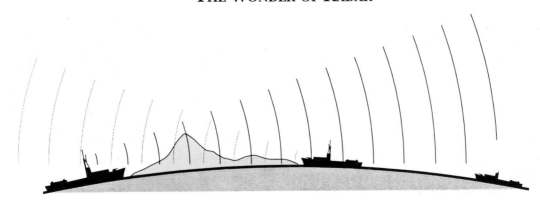

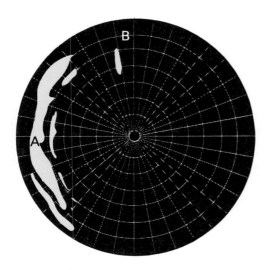

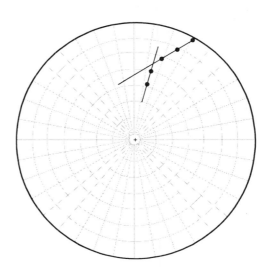

A radar display of the scene on the opposite page (bottom) as seen from the ship on the left. The land mass to port is shown at A (above), and the second ship within detection range is at B. Targets created by returning radar reflections are represented by luminescent green "blobs" on a darkened background.

While the display on a radar scope is fairly simple to "read," the interpretation is complicated by the fact that on a ship the observer is moving as well as the target The only sure way to understand the relative motions of the observer and target is to plot their relative positions over time.

Radar, an acronym that stands for RAdio Detection And Ranging, was developed during World War II as a means of finding enemy ships, submarines and aircraft. In operation, a transmitter sends out a beam of microwave radio energy; any objects encountered by the radio waves generally produce reflections that can be picked up by a receiver, and displayed on a cathode ray tube. The radio wave reflections can be used to determine both distance and bearing to the target, making the instrument very useful for navigation and collision avoidance, particularly under conditions of limited visibility. Since radio waves generally travel in straight lines, a radar set's range is limited by the distance to the horizon—thus the higher the transmitter/receiver antenna, the greater the set's range. Despite the obvious advantage radar provides ship operators, it takes training and experience to correctly interpret a radar screen's display. Objects appear as luminous "blobs" on the scope, with the user always at the screen's center. Range rings and bearing lines allow the determination of a target's range and bearing. Only by constantly plotting a target's range and bearing over time, however, can the user obtain a clear picture of a target's course and speed relative to the user's vessel, including any course changes made by the target. Failure to plot radar bearings has been at fault in more than one collision at sea.

GLOBAL POSITIONING SYSTEM (GPS)

The long-awaited Global Positioning System is now on line, and promises to eventually phase out the older loran system. Developed for military use, the system is available to civilian users as well, although in a less accurate form than used by the military. The system consists of 18 satellites, each orbiting the earth twice per day. Each satellite continuously transmits extremely precise time and position signals; a receiver interprets these signals and provides direct latitude and longitude data to the user. The receiver must be able to access signals from three satellites to provide a two-dimensional position fix (latitude and longitude), while sig-

nals from four satellites can also provide vertical position information. The military version of the system uses specially coded signals not available to civilian users and reportedly provides position accuracy to within 8 meters. Uncoded signals are provided by the same satellites for non-military users that produce position fixes that are somewhat less accurate. The system has been devised so that the uncoded signals can be turned of during times of war or national crisis, so that this information can be denied to hostile forces.

The White Star liner Republic *was one of the first ships to use the wireless telegraph to summon assistance at sea. A large canvas patch can be seen covering the gaping wound in her side, but the ship sank despite efforts to save her. Courtesy of The Steamship Historical Society of America.*

The Italian liner Florida, *shown here with her bow stove in, rammed the* Republic *south of Nantucket and sent her to the bottom; the* Florida *remained afloat. Courtesy of The Steamship Historical Society of America.*

invaluable in preventing collision between ships at sea.

A few short years after the war this fantastic collection of new instruments put a wealth of information at a ship commander's fingertips. The modern ship captain could accurately determine his position in any weather. He could "see" in the dark and through fog. He could speak directly to the commander of another vessel or to authorities ashore. And he could receive accurate and up-to-date weather forecasts continuously by radio.

But despite these incredible technological advances, accidents still occurred, and ships continued to go down.

COLLISION IN THE FOG:
ANDREA DORIA AND *STOCKHOLM*

Forty-seven years after the *Florida* rammed and sank the *Republic* in the fog south of Nantucket Island, the scene was replayed in virtually the same location; de-

spite the technological wizardry developed over half a century, the outcome was the same.

The 697-foot-long luxury liner *Andrea Doria* was the pride of the Italia Line. Named after a 16th-century Italian Admiral who was a contemporary of Christopher Columbus, the great ship was considered by many to be the most beautiful vessel afloat. She was literally a floating art gallery, and her decks were graced with great works specially created for her by renowned artists. Her passenger accommodations were divided into three classes, each having its own dining saloon, bars, cocktail lounge and swimming pool. Her sleek black hull and raked white superstructure gave her the look of a speedy ship; her normal cruising speed of 23 knots lived up to her appearance. Constructed in Italy between 1950 and 1953, the *Andrea Doria* was equipped with all the latest navigation instruments. Her captain, Pierro Calamai, had at his disposal both magnetic and gyrocompasses, an automatic pilot, radio direction finders, a loran receiver, two radar scopes and even a complete meteorological station; she was as well

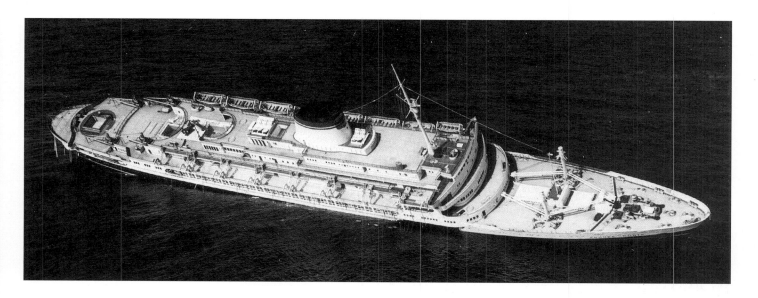

The story of the Italian liner Andrea Doria *is one of the most famous of sea tragedies. The hole caused by the collision with the Swedish-American Line's* Stockholm *can be seen just below the ship's starboard bridge wing. Courtesy of the U.S. Coast Guard.*

equipped as any liner on the ocean. Pierro Calamai had commanded her since her maiden voyage in January 1953, and when she left Genoa, Italy on July 17, 1956, heading for New York Harbor, it was the beginning of her 101st Atlantic crossing.

Not all passenger liners in the transatlantic service were as large as the *Andrea Doria*, which was the thirteenth-largest liner in the world. The Swedish-American Line's *Stockholm* measured only 524 feet in length, and had the distinction of being the smallest ship in the transatlantic service. Somewhat more austere than the extravagant *Andrea Doria*, the *Stockholm*'s interior was simple and comfortable. Her designers had chosen the quiet elegance of rich wood paneling rather than the plush works of art found aboard the *Doria*. Both her hull and superstructure were painted a glistening white, a reminder that her native land lay in the cold northern waters of Scandinavia. To that end she was equipped with a specially reinforced bow of heavy steel plate, giving her the ability to break through sea ice in the cold winter harbors of her homeland. Built in Gothenburg, Sweden shortly after the war she was launched in 1948, and like the *Andrea Doria*, was equipped with a large range of modern navigation instruments. Her bridge equipment included magnetic and gyrocompasses, radio direction finders and two radar scopes, although she lacked a loran navigation system.

On July 25, 1956, the *Andrea Doria*, inbound for New York Harbor, found herself passing through intermittent fog as she headed directly toward the Nantucket lightship. The *Stockholm* was outbound from New York, and traveling on an eastward course that would bring her one mile south of the Nantucket lightship. This was against the advice of the 1948 Convention for the Safety of Life at Sea, which recommended that eastbound ships travel a lane 20 miles south of the lightship; the northern lane was reserved for westbound ships. But the recommendations of the convention were not rules, and ships often ignored the traffic lanes in the interest of saving time. The *Stockholm* had chosen to ignore the Convention's recommendations.

The waters south of Nantucket Island are often shrouded in heavy fog, and as the *Andrea Doria* passed through these drifting white blankets of mist her captain ordered a token reduction in speed, from 23 to 21.8 knots. The radar sets were switched on and her foghorn began blasting its intermittent warning to nearby shipping. A careful course plot was kept on the *Doria*'s bridge, using both time-honored dead reckoning and the ship's accurate loran receiver. Desiring to adhere to her scheduled arrival the next morning, the *Doria* sped west toward New York, her electronic "eyes" peering through the dense fog.

Despite warnings of fog ahead, the slower *Stockholm* found herself in clear weather and continued to speed eastward at her full 18 knots. Lacking the convenience

A lone lifeboat sits on a calm, misty ocean as the Andrea Doria *clings desperately to life. All but 51 persons were rescued in the tragedy. Courtesy of The Mariners' Museum, Newport News, Virginia.*

of the modern loran navigation system, her dead reckoning plot was constantly updated with the older, but well proven, method of radio direction finding. These electronic fixes placed the *Stockholm* several miles to the north of her intended course track. In order to bring the ship back onto the intended course, her Third Officer, Johan-Ernst Bogislaus August Carstens-Johannsen, altered course slightly to the south.

At 10:20 P.M., the *Andrea Doria* passed one mile south of the Nantucket lightship. The crew's only indication that they had passed the navigational aid was a small blip on the *Doria*'s radar scope and the sound of a foghorn somewhere to starboard. At 10:45 P.M., the *Andrea Doria*'s radar scope displayed another greenish blip, 17 miles ahead and only four degrees off her starboard bow—almost directly in her path. A few minutes later, a similar blip appeared on the radar scope aboard the *Stockholm*, slightly off her port bow. The two ships were racing through the night, closing on each other at a combined rate of nearly 40 knots; two small, greenish blips on a cathode-ray screen were all they could see of each other. There was no time for indecision.

To the officers aboard the *Andrea Doria*, the ship ahead appeared to lie slightly to starboard; to those on board the *Stockholm*, the approaching vessel appeared to lie slightly to port; both interpretations could not be correct. As the two vessels approached each other, their respective commanders both believed that the ships would pass safely in the night; Captain Calamai aboard the *Doria* believed the ships would pass starboard-to-starboard, while Third Officer Carstens aboard the *Stockholm* believed the ships would pass port-to-port. At 11:05 P.M., Captain Calamai ordered his ship's course altered four degrees to port to give the approaching ship, now only three and one-half miles ahead, more room. Two minutes later, Carstens ordered the *Stockholm* turned sharply to starboard with the same intention.

At the very instant the *Stockholm* began its turn, the dim glow of her navigation lights broke through the fog bank and appeared as a nightmarish vision to the *Andrea Doria*'s captain. The *Doria*'s officers watched in horror as the *Stockholm* turned rapidly toward their ship. Big ships do not turn or stop quickly, and when traveling at very near full speed, their response is positively sluggish. The two ships were only one mile apart and traveling directly toward one another at breakneck speed. In a futile attempt to avoid the inevitable, Captain Calamai ordered the *Doria* turned hard to port.

At 11:10 P.M., the reinforced bow of the *Stockholm* crashed into the *Andrea Doria*'s starboard side at full speed, just below the bridge. When two ships whose weight is measured in thousands-of-tons crash into one another at full speed, the destructive power unleashed is difficult to imagine. A huge, gaping hole was ripped into the side of the *Doria*'s hull, *(Continued on page 194)*

ELEGANT TREASURES FROM THE *ANDREA DORIA*

Sunk in a dramatic collision in July 1956, the *Andrea Doria* now echos a siren call to adventurous divers around the globe. Considered by many to be the ultimate wreck dive, explorers come in quest of the vast "treasures" the once-elegant liner still holds. Designed to carry transatlantic passengers in comfort and style, divers now collect souvenirs from all over the ship that was once considered a floating art gallery. Beautiful ceramic panels created by Italian artist Romano Rui graced the 1st class cocktail lounge, and are treasured finds for divers (left, courtesy of Pat Rooney). A passenger liner, the *Andrea Doria* had no shortage of fine china on board. Much china still displays the Italia Line's logo, and is sought by explorers: silver-plated 2nd class service, restored to its former luster (above, left, courtesy of Pat Rooney); elegant hand-painted 1st class service (above, right) with delicate scenes in pastel colors; the ship's dining lounges had distinctive touches, such as colorfully painted flower vases on each table (below, left, courtesy of Pat Rooney); each dining lounge had its own china design, displayed on these 1st, 2nd and 3rd class cups and saucers (below, middle). All these treasures serve to lure enthusiastic divers into the labyrinth of her interior, such as Pat Rooney (below, right), pictured with dishes recovered from the wreck.

Andrea Doria: A Legend Among Shipwrecks

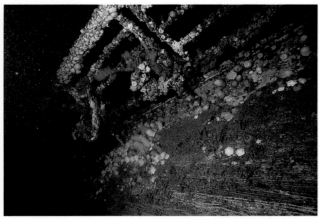

Teak-decked promenades were once trod upon by passengers crossing the Atlantic on perhaps the most elegant liner afloat (above); the massive port propeller hovers over the Doria's *prone hull, dwarfing diver Richie Kohler (above, middle); the port life boat davits are still in their retracted position— the* Doria's *list prevented their use (above, right).*

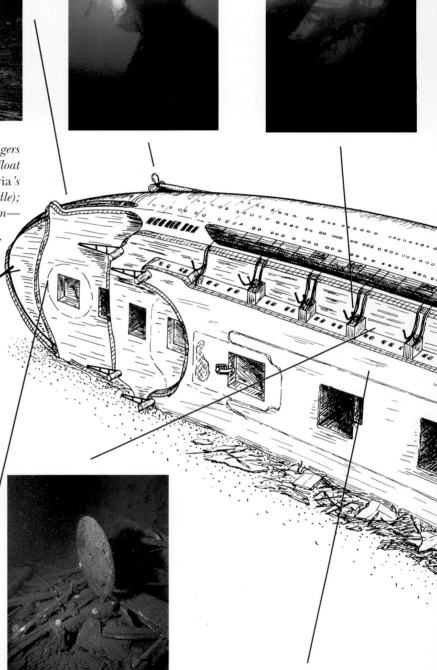

Jeff Pagano cleans a brass letter on the ship's stern spelling out ANDREA DORIA.

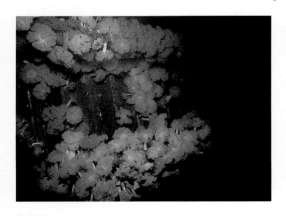

A plush veil of white sea anemones line the handrails of a stairwell deep in the stern (left); bar stools still stand erect from the now-vertical deck inside the 1st class bar (right); a glass-topped cocktail table stands above a jumbled pile of debris inside the 1st class cocktail lounge (above).

Little remains of the ship's interior appointments today; toilet fixtures stand strangely alone without their enclosing walls (right).

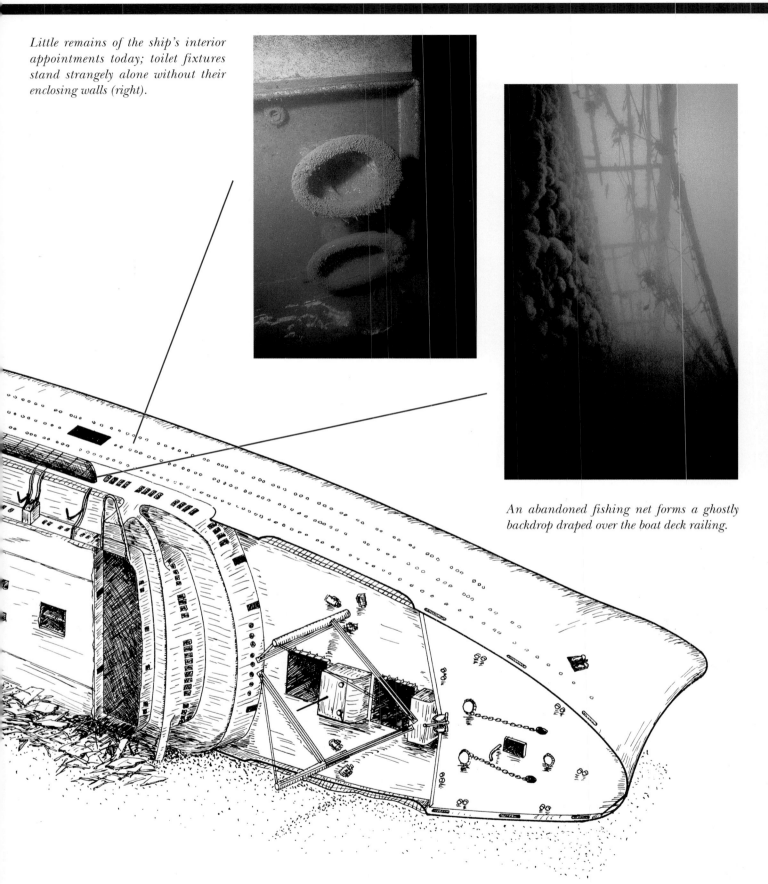

An abandoned fishing net forms a ghostly backdrop draped over the boat deck railing.

Strong currents, often poor visibility and deep depths make the *Andrea Doria* one of the most challenging wreck dives in the world, only adding to her allure. She lies on her starboard side beneath 250 feet of cold and often rough North Atlantic water. Abandoned fishing nets cling to her hull in a deadly embrace; inside, rotting interior walls and hanging electrical cables endanger divers who brave her dark interior in search of some of the treasures the wreck still holds.

The *Andrea Doria* Today

The 1st class swimming pool was equipped with a slide for passengers' enjoyment (left). Today, the slide's railing is carpeted with marine growth (right).

Clockwise from left: a mound of china dishes discovered by John Chatterton in a stairwell near the 2nd class dining room sent souvenir-hunting divers into a feeding frenzy; silver-plated bowls and goblets tumble out of a cabinet on the foyer deck, outside the 2nd class dining room; row upon row of windows and portholes, obscured by silt and marine growth, peer into the dark and cavernous interior of the ship; a brass inlaid shuffleboard court on the teak afterdeck—some of its numbers have been removed by divers seeking souvenirs.

STILL ON STATION: AMBROSE RELIEF LIGHTSHIP

Sunk in a collision in the fog—an event she was designed to prevent—the Relief lightship settled on an even keel on the ocean bottom at her station on June 24, 1960. Today this unfortunate aid-to-navigation still stands on station—110 feet beneath the ocean's surface. Nearby stands the four-legged light tower that now marks Ambrose station and the entrance to New York Harbor. The lightship's masts were knocked down by wire-drag, along with her two deck houses, not long after the sinking to eliminate any possible future hazard to navigation. One of the lights and mast were later recovered by divers, while the remaining light basket can still be seen sitting on her deck, although the lantern assembly is missing.

The high rising prow of the lightship looms out of the darkness of the ocean depths.

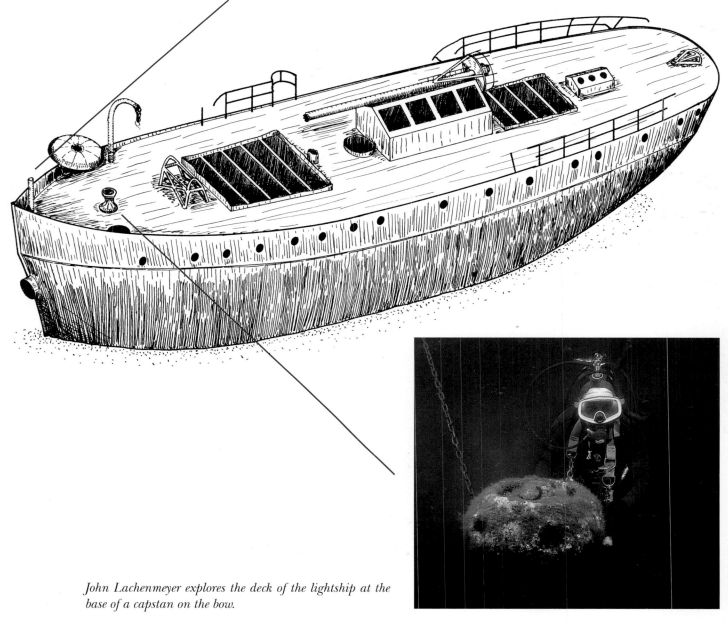

John Lachenmeyer explores the deck of the lightship at the base of a capstan on the bow.

Slain by a Giant: Motorship *Pinta*

There was little hope for the tiny motorship *Pinta* when the huge steamship *City of Perth* bore down on her on a clear evening in May 1963—the larger vessel outweighed the smaller by a margin of 15:1! The tiny *Pinta* quickly settled to the bottom in 80 feet of water seven miles east of Asbury Park, New Jersey. Only five months later a group of divers from the Oceanographic Historical Research Society visited the new shipwreck. The divers recovered her ship's bell, inscribed with her name, along with various other items. Today the ship lies on her port side in an area of rather murky visibility. Her hull is essentially intact, although her superstructure and smokestack have collapsed, and her propeller removed by salvors.

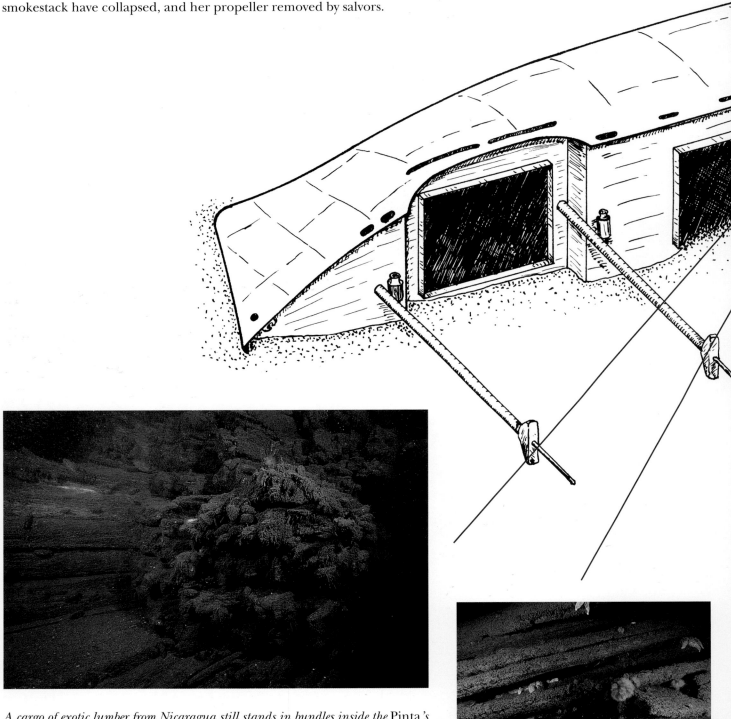

A cargo of exotic lumber from Nicaragua still stands in bundles inside the Pinta's *cargo holds (above). Some of the timbers were recovered by divers and found to be in usable condition; most remain on board the* Pinta, *however, where the tumbling stacks provide homes for marine creatures, such as the lobster (right).*

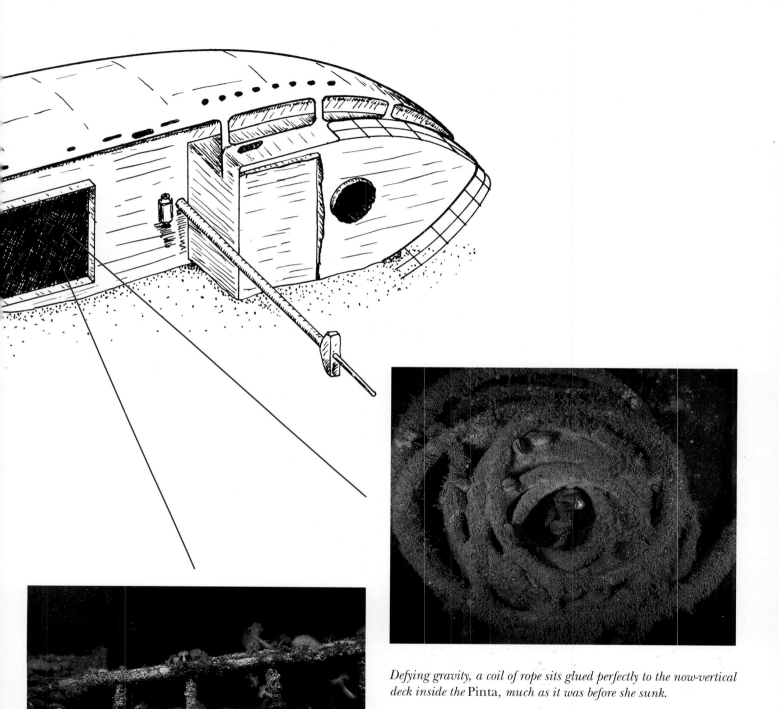

Defying gravity, a coil of rope sits glued perfectly to the now-vertical deck inside the Pinta, much as it was before she sunk.

Sea anemones and mussels camouflage a ladder inside one of the ship's cargo holds.

SLICED IN TWO BY A LINER: *STOLT DAGALI*

After the tanker *Stolt Dagali* was sliced in two by the passenger liner *Shalom* in November 1964, her stern section quickly settled to the bottom along with 19 of her crew. The stern section came to rest on its starboard side in 130 feet of water, where it lies today. It has become a popular dive site among recreational scuba divers who delight in exploring a relatively intact shipwreck in waters of good visibility. Her interior is easily accessible through many open doorways and the large engine room skylight. Explorers must exercise caution, however, as the ship is filled with silt and rotting debris, and swimming about her insides can be disorienting since she lies on her side—the walls are now floors and ceilings, while the floors and ceilings are now walls....

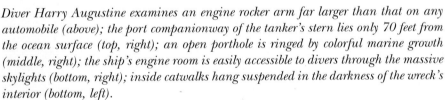

Diver Harry Augustine examines an engine rocker arm far larger than that on any automobile (above); the port companionway of the tanker's stern lies only 70 feet from the ocean surface (top, right); an open porthole is ringed by colorful marine growth (middle, right); the ship's engine room is easily accessible to divers through the massive skylights (bottom, right); inside catwalks hang suspended in the darkness of the wreck's interior (bottom, left).

The sinking of the Andrea Doria *was also one of the most photographed maritime tragedies in history. Shown here near the end, the* Doria's *stern begins the final plunge while leaving behind a trail of debris. Harry Trask photo courtesy Boston Herald.*

The Swedish-American Line's Stockholm *was built with a reinforced ice breaker bow, which may have helped her survive the accident, and help send the* Andrea Doria *to her grave. Courtesy of the U.S. Coast Guard.*

while the *Stockholm*'s bow was crumpled like an accordion. The two ships stuck together for several seconds, then as the *Andrea Doria*'s momentum carried her forward, the *Stockholm* pivoted about the impact point, ripping out more of the Italian liner's bowels as she pulled free. Despite the enormous damage done to her bow, the *Stockholm*'s collision bulkhead held. The *Andrea Doria*'s steel hull had been ripped clean open, however, and she began to flood rapidly.

The *Andrea Doria* quickly took on a list so severe that her port lifeboats could not be launched. The *Doria*'s starboard lifeboats, along with boats sent over from the nearby *Stockholm*, were put to work evacuating the passengers and crew. A fleet of rescue vessels, including the French liner *Isle de France*, had been summoned by radio and soon arrived on the scene. After

all had been accounted for there were 51 persons killed in the accident, while 1,660 persons were successfully rescued from the sinking *Andrea Doria*.

The ship herself was doomed, and despite staying afloat for 11 hours, she disappeared beneath the waves at 10:09 A.M. the following morning, July 26, 1956. Man's modern navigational wonders had failed.

SITTING DUCK: THE RELIEF LIGHTSHIP

For centuries lighthouses have been used to guide ships to port and harbor entrances, as well as to mark hazardous points of land and rocky outcroppings. Where navigational considerations required a lighthouse, but no spit of land was available to build one on, lightships were often employed. Essentially floating lighthouses, lightships were specially designed ships equipped with one or more masts that supported huge lamps high above the water's surface. A lightship was moored in place with a heavy anchor and chain at its designated station, where it displayed its lights and served as a stationary beacon for shipping. The ships were also equipped with foghorns and bells, and were manned by a permanent crew. Since 1939 these crews came from the Coast Guard, which absorbed the Bureau of Lighthouses in that year. The Coast Guard was itself a descendant of the Revenue Cutter and Life-Saving Services.

The waters surrounding Long Island have employed a number of lightships over the years. The most famous is undoubtedly the Nantucket lightship, moored approximately 100 miles east of Montauk Point and south of the Nantucket shoals where it served as a bea-con to ships arriving in the New World. Closer to Long Island shores was the Fire Island lightship, stationed south of Fire Island Inlet from 1896 until 1942, when it was removed for the duration of the war and never reestablished. The nation's very first lightship was established in 1823 off Sandy Hook at the entrance to New York Harbor. The Sandy Hook lightship was also the very first in the United States to be equipped with electric lights, which were fitted in 1894. Previous to the introduction of electricity, lightships employed oil lanterns for their beacons. In 1908, the Sandy Hook lightship was moved eight miles east to mark the entrance of the newly dredged Ambrose Channel. It was then that the station was renamed Ambrose, after John Wolfe Ambrose, an engineer credited with developing much of modern day New York Harbor. Another lightship, which marked the entrance to New York Harbor between 1868 and 1966, was originally estab-

The Relief lightship was used to substitute for lightships off-station for repair; she was sunk while on Ambrose station. Courtesy of the U.S. Coast Guard.

lished to mark the location of the wrecked steamship *Scotland*, and appropriately named the "Wreck of the Scotland lightship." This floating beacon was located two and one half miles east-southeast of Sandy Hook light, near the remains of the *Scotland*, herself a victim of collision in 1866. In 1870, the wreck of the *Scotland* was removed and the lightship was discontinued. After numerous complaints from mariners, however, who had come to rely on her beacon for entering New York Harbor, the lightship was reestablished in 1874.

Intended as aids to navigation, it is somewhat ironic that lightships were actually quite prone to direct involvement in maritime accidents. Anchored in the center of the shipping lanes through the worst weather nature had to offer, it was perhaps inevitable that these navigational aids were occasionally run down. The Fire Island lightship was a victim of collision on two separate occasions. On May 8, 1916, she was run into by the steamer *Philadelphian*, who left a two-foot gash in the side of her hull. The crew managed to effect emergency repairs and she was towed into port by the *Philadelphian*. Eight years later the steamer *Castillian* ran into the lightship during a heavy fog, and she again required repairs. The Sandy Hook lightship was also involved in several collisions. She was rammed in 1874 and then again in 1888, while the Scotland lightship was rammed no less than six times between 1892 and 1905. In 1934, the White Star liner *Olympic* ran down the Nantucket lightship, sending it to the bottom. Lightship duty obviously had its inherent dangers.

Despite the addition of radar to a lightship's armada of instruments after World War II, lightships still proved an inevitable target for collision. The vessel normally stationed at the entrance to Ambrose Channel, *WLV-613*, had been taken off station on May 28, 1960, and brought into Staten Island for her annual maintenance. The Ambrose lightship was a vital navigational aid, however, and could not just be removed from her station. The Third Coast Guard District maintained a fleet of two relief lightships for just this situation, and the duties at Ambrose station were picked up by *WAL-505*. The new lightship was easily identifiable by the word "RELIEF" painted along both sides of her red hull in huge white letters.

Dense fog and heavy rain squalls blanketed the New York area on the evening of June 23rd, only a month after the *WAL-505* had taken over Ambrose station. Inclement weather was not enough to halt the precision clockwork of shipping operations in New York Harbor; however, it did slow things down a bit, delaying the arrival of several transatlantic liners, including the *Cristoforo Colombo*, the *Andrea Doria*'s sister ship.

For the most part, however, shipping traffic proceeded unabated. The 10,270-ton freighter *Green Bay* was cleared to leave port by Coast Guard officials that evening, and left on a journey to the Red Sea at 10:45 P.M. It would prove a short voyage.

As the *Green Bay* eased her way down Ambrose Channel toward the open ocean, her captain, Thomas Mazzella, found the lightship's position clearly marked by a bright green blip on his radar screen. He could also hear the lightship's fog signal blaring across the dark sea. Yet somehow he miscalculated its position. About 4:05 A.M., 22-year-old Boatswain's Mate Bobby Pierce, on watch alone in the lightship's pilothouse, heard the booming sound of a freighter's foghorn close by. Looking up he was astounded to see the freighter's lights looming over his ship. Pierce quickly sounded the general alarm, and two minutes later the *Green Bay* crashed into the starboard side of *WAL-505*, tearing a 12-foot gash in her brightly painted red hull.

Awakened by Pierce's alarm, all nine men on board the lightship quickly made their escape in an inflatable rubber raft, the ship's lifeboat having been smashed in the collision. Once launched, the men paddled the raft furiously with their hands to escape the whirlpool of suction they expected when the ship went down. One hour after the collision, the *Green Bay* found the men and picked them up; later they were transferred to a Coast Guard cutter and taken into port. The lightship sank stern first ten minutes after being struck, landing upright on the bottom.

Only 12 hours after the relief ship was sunk, the incompletely repaired Ambrose lightship left port and headed out to resume her station.

GOLIATH SLAYS DAVID: THE MOTORSHIP *PINTA*

In myths and fairy tales it often happens that the "little guy" prevails against tremendous odds and wins a contest of strength over a superior adversary. Real life, however, is usually not so romantic. When two ships of vastly different sizes meet in a collision, it is a safe bet that the bigger vessel will come out the victor. This basic law of survival was proven once again on the evening of May 7, 1963.

On a clear evening just past sundown, two ships came together in an unplanned meeting only seven miles off the New Jersey coast. At 7:59 P.M. the Coast Guard received the following message by radio: "The *City of Perth* struck *Pinta*, registered Rotterdam. This ship and Dutch vessel making water. Require immediate assistance."[1] The *City of Perth* was a 7,547-ton British freighter; the *Pinta* was a 500-ton Dutch diesel-powered motorship. The British ship weighed *15 times* its partner in the collision! The only surprising fact in the accident is that the *Pinta* managed to remain afloat for 48 minutes before taking the inevitable plunge.

Soon after the collision it became obvious to the *Pinta*'s captain, Alie Korpelshoek, that the giant British freighter mortally wounded his ship, and he ordered his 11-man crew to the lifeboats. Leaving the *Pinta* listing to port and dead in the water, the Dutchmen rowed over to the freighter and were taken on board. It was from that vantage point that the crew of the *Pinta* watched as their tiny ship slipped from sight a scant half-hour later. The five helicopters and two cutters the Coast Guard dispatched to the scene proved unneccesary. The *Pinta*'s crew had saved themselves, and their ship was beyond help—one more addition to the fleet of sunken vessels littering the ocean bottom outside New York Harbor.

"Shalom" to the *Stolt Dagali*

In Hebrew, the word "shalom" means peace, and is often used as a greeting, as well as a farewell. In a sense it is perfectly fitting that the ship that cut the Norwegian tanker *Stolt Dagali* in two on November 26, 1964, had been christened with the name *Shalom*. Once again the availability of radar did nothing to prevent the meeting of two ships in the busy shipping channels outside New York Harbor.

The Israeli passenger liner *Shalom*, pride of the Zim Line fleet and only seven months old, had left New York Harbor early on the morning of November 26th bound for the West Indies. On board were 616 passengers on holiday, along with 450 crew whose job it was to make their patrons' stay a pleasant one. After clearing Ambrose lightship just past 1:00 A.M., the *Shalom*'s captain, Avner Freudenberg, retired to his quarters after leaving his standard instructions that he be called if the weather took a turn for the worse. Captain Freudenberg did not rest long, however, for within the hour he was summoned to the bridge as the ship ran into a dense wall of fog.

The 583-foot-long Norwegian tanker *Stolt Dagali* was, rather romantically, named after the beautiful mountain Dagali in eastern Norway; translated, her full name means Pride of Dagali. The tanker had left Philadelphia the previous day bound for Newark with a cargo of solvents and vegetable oils. She had been feeling her way north through heavy fog—a fog her captain, Kristian Bendiksen, later related was so thick that they

just "couldn't see."[2] The Norwegian tanker was manned by a crew of 42 men and one woman, divided between the ship's forward bridge and her stern quarters. It was a division that would soon decide each person's fate.

Nineteen-year-old Aadvar Olsen was fast asleep in his bunk at 2:15 A.M. on board the *Stolt Dagali*. Suddenly there was a crash, and as he snapped awake he found himself swimming in the cold November Atlantic, clad only in his underwear! The *Shalom*, traveling at high speed through the fog had passed *directly through* the tanker's hull, splitting her neatly in two. Captain Bendiksen watched in horror from the *Stolt Dagali*'s bridge as the severed stern of his ship disappeared into the fog; that fog saved him from the nightmare of watching the stern sink beneath the heavy swell, taking almost half the ship's crew with it. The forward two-thirds of the tanker managed to remain afloat, its cargo of oil effectively buoying up the hull. The ship's radio operator quickly sent an SOS signal, which was picked up first in Boston, and then relayed to New York. Six Coast Guard cutters, along with helicopters and aircraft, were immediately dispatched to the scene of the collision.

The *Shalom* had sustained considerable bow damage, but was in no danger of sinking. She stood by to offer assistance, and managed to pick up several of the *Stolt Dagali*'s survivors from the water. As the first streaks of dawn arrived over the horizon, Coast Guard and Navy helicopters appeared on the scene. Lowering a basket by cable, the helicopters evacuated the ten men left on board the *Stolt Dagali*'s bridge, one at a time. It was a scene reminiscent of the days of the United States Life-Saving Service and the use of the breeches buoy, only now deployed from a helicopter instead of fired by a cannon from the beach. Similar rescue efforts were carried out for those survivors found adrift in one of the tanker's lifeboats, while Coast Guard cutters picked up the remainder of the men from the water. Twenty-four survivors were plucked from the cold embrace of the Atlantic that morning; nineteen of their shipmates were not so lucky, however, and thirteen bodies were recovered while another six men were missing.

Throughout the day and that night, cutters and patrol craft searched the frigid waters off the New Jersey coast for the six missing men. The search proved fruitless, however, and was finally called to a halt on the morning of November 27th. Meanwhile, the salvage tug *Cynthia Moran* had managed to get a hawser attached to the still-floating bow section of the *Stolt Dagali*, and was attempting to tow her into New York.

The Norwegian tanker Stolt Dagali *was sliced in two by the liner* Shalom *on the foggy morning of November 26, 1964. The* Stolt Dagali *'s forward section was towed into port, while her stern section sank, taking 19 persons with it. Courtesy of the U.S. Coast Guard.*

A Coast Guard cutter rode alongside, escorting the half-submerged sternless tanker as it fought its way through the rough seas and large swells toward the safety of dry dock. A slick of oil trailed off into the distance as the *Dagali*'s cargo leaked slowly from her damaged tanks. It was not the heavy, black crude that makes headlines after most major oil spills, however, but rather vegetable oils and fats, including a shipment of Philippine coconut oil. The loss of the valuable coconut oil reportedly caused a flurry of buying activity on the London commodities market.

After a difficult tow the remains of the Norwegian tanker were safely deposited in dry dock. She was later purchased by the owners of the *C.T. Gogstad*, a similar tanker that had broken in two after stranding on the coast of Sweden. The *Gogstad*'s stern section had been salvaged, and in another proof that truth is stranger than fiction the two halves of these vessels were welded together to form one ship, christened *Stolt Lady*. The *Shalom* managed to limp into New York under her own power, her gleaming white hull stained brown with oil and her bow a crumpled and twisted mass of steel. She was also repaired and returned to service.

Lawsuits between the vessels' owners later showed that both ships were at fault in the collision. The *Shalom*'s radar set was not working properly at the time, displaying a cluttered and indistinct picture, yet the officer on watch failed to turn on the second radar set. In addition, the *Shalom* had no lookout posted at the time, for he had left the bridge a few minutes earlier to get a cup of coffee. The *Stolt Dagali*'s radar clearly displayed the *Shalom* 11 minutes prior to the collision, but her captain failed to take action. Man's electronic wonders had to be used properly to be effective.

SUNK BY DESIGN: A HANDFUL OF "ARTIFICIAL REEFS"

Ships spend their entire lives fighting to stay afloat, battling the weather, the sea and man's inevitable errors in judgement. Yet on rare but ironic occasions, these same ships are sunk on purpose.

Old and decrepit vessels that have outlived their usefulness are sometimes disposed of at sea and then called artificial reefs. So long as fuel and lubricating oil, or any other substances that might be harmful to the marine environment are removed, this form of disposal is perfectly acceptable. In fact, these vessels do indeed form artificial reef sites and are beneficial to the ocean's ecosystem, providing homes for myriad marine creatures. These reefs also furnish rich new fishing grounds for both commercial and recreational

The Zim Line's Shalom *served as the knife that cut the* Stolt Dagali *in two. While the* Shalom *sustained extensive damage to her bow, she was easily repaired in dry dock. Courtesy of the U.S. Coast Guard.*

fishermen and, more recently, exciting dive sites for weekend scuba enthusiasts.

The idea of purposely sinking ships to form artificial reef sites is actually a fairly recent innovation, although sinking ships on purpose is not. In years past ships were occasionally run onto the beach to collect insurance monies, and some were undoubtedly sunk at sea for the same reason. This was probably rather infrequent due to the inherent danger to the crew. The military, however, has often deliberately sent its old and obsolete vessels to the bottom, usually in dramatic tests of new weapons.

Perhaps the most famous of these deliberate sinkings were the aerial bombardment tests off the Virginia and North Carolina coasts by General "Billy" Mitchell in the early 1920's. A series of World War I naval craft were used as targets to demonstrate their susceptibility to aerial attack. Battleships, such as the German dreadnought *Ostfriesland* and the cruiser *Frankfurt*, along with a number of submarines and destroyers handed over by Germany at the end of the war, were all sunk by aerial bombardment and naval shellfire. Ironically, the German submarines *U-140* and *U-117*, which had so mercilessly preyed on merchant shipping off the U.S. coast during the war, were brought back across the Atlantic to be sunk by her former adversaries.

Before sinking the German warships, the U.S. Navy spent time studying them, particularly the U-boats, which were judged to be far superior to anything the United States possessed at that time. These studies aided the U.S. Navy in building a series of its own large submarines. The first three of these submarines were given the designations *V-1*, *V-2* and *V-3* (at one point these submarines were also designated "B"), and were later renamed the *Barracuda, Bass* and *Bonita.* The large American submarines measured 341 feet in length, much larger than their German counterparts. The *U-117* measured 267 feet long and the *U-140* 302 feet. In practice, the submarines' extreme length resulted in an excessively long diving time and made them unwieldy and difficult to maneuver once submerged. After 13 years of service the *Bass* was put in mothballs, only to be recalled to service during World War II. She made four unsuccessful war patrols in the Pacific before suffering severe damage from a fire in her aft battery compartment. After being repaired she was converted into a submersible cargo carrier similar to Germany's *Deutschland*, but she proved impractical in this mission as well. Obsolete and nearly useless, the *Bass* was designated as a target and used for testing an experimental torpex depth charge dropped by airplane. On March 18, 1945, while the war was still under way, the *Bass* was anchored eight miles south of Block Island and two of the experimental depth charges were dropped on her. The first failed to explode, but the second sent her quickly to the bottom in 160 feet of water. If there were any German U-boats patrolling in the area, this demonstration of American air power would have made quite an impression.

Not all military ships sunk intentionally were done as weapons tests. On April 16, 1961, while being towed from the Boston Reserve Group to Philadelphia, the reserve fleet destroyer USS *Baldwin* parted her towline only four miles south of Block Island. The winds were high and visibility limited due to driving rain and

The submarine USS Bass *was intentionally sunk in the closing months of World War II. Her sinking was a precursor to artificial reef programs that would come years later. Courtesy of the National Archives.*

heavy fog. The *Baldwin* drifted west at nearly two knots, and due to the heavy weather the towing vessel, the Navy tug USS *Keywadin*, was unable to reestablish the tow. Six hours later the *Baldwin* was aground on the rocky beach three miles west of Montauk Point. A veteran of the D-day invasion of Normandy, the now-retired *Baldwin* spent 49 days stranded on the beach before a drawn-out salvage operation patched her battered hull and pulled her free. During the six-week salvage effort, several men were injured and one man was killed when a cable parted and whipped back across the deck of one of the salvage vessels. When the *Baldwin* was finally pulled free of her rocky perch on June 4th, her hull had been damaged so badly that the estimated cost of repairs exceeded her value as a ship. The rocky beach at Montauk had added the USS *Baldwin* to the long list of ships lost off that treacherous spit of land, and the destroyer was towed out to

sea to be sunk. On June 5th, the day before the seventeenth anniversary of D-day when the *Baldwin* had so gallantly served, the destroyer was scuttled in 258 fathoms of water, 73 miles SSE of where she had gone aground.

Despite official Navy documentation that the *Baldwin* was scuttled beyond the edge of the continental shelf, fishermen working out of Montauk have long known of a wreck lying in 260 feet of water that they refer to as the "Baldwin." Often the source of wreck names is obscure and has been lost over the years, and the "Baldwin" is among these. One can't help but wonder, however, if the fishermen knew something more than the Navy records show when they named this wreck. Consider the similarities of her reported depth with that of the naval records—the Navy reports the wreck sunk in 258 *fathoms*, while the fishermen's trawl hang sits in approximately 260 *feet*. Both positions lie on approximately the same compass heading from Montauk, only differing in their distance from the Point. Could it be that the *Baldwin* was actually scuttled much closer to shore than reported? Possibly, but further research favors a different conclusion, namely that the wreck known as the "Baldwin" is actually the hulk of another military vessel, also sunk intentionally.

The navy submarine USS *Spikefish* was a veteran of World War II that went on to set a submarine record: on March 18, 1960, the *Spikefish* became the first U.S. submarine to make 10,000 dives. (According to Keatts and Farr,[3] she was the first submarine in any navy to achieve that many dives.) Three years later, on April 2, 1963, the submarine was decommis-

Discovered by fishermen and identified by recreational divers in 1966, the Bass *has become a popular dive site south of Block Island. The submarine's conning tower rises high above the bottom, making an impressive sight in clear water.*

sioned. Just over one year later on August 4, 1964, the *Spikefish* was sunk as a target, according to U.S. Navy records, somewhere south of Long Island. According to Tim Coleman, writing for the *Fisherman*,[4] the wreck symbol appearing on NOAA chart No. 12300 was reported in "Notice to Mariners" for week 35 of 1964—just after the sinking of the USS *Spikefish*. The plotted position of the "Baldwin" also corresponds with a set of loran A numbers purported to be the sunken *Spikefish*.[5] On June 15, 1995 Jeff Pagano, Pat Rooney, Brian Skerry and the author made a dive on the "Baldwin," confirming that it is indeed a submarine.

More recent sinkings have involved artificial reef programs sponsored by state governments. Ships, both large and small, are occasionally sent to the bottom in designated areas to stimulate fish populations and provide recreational dive sites for scuba divers. The largest of these ships to date was sent to the bottom 16 miles east of Manasquan Inlet, New Jersey on November 21, 1991. The USS *Algol* was a veteran of both World War II and the Korean conflict, when she served as an attack cargo ship carrying supplies for U.S. land forces. Placed in mothballs in 1970, she was later donated to the State of New Jersey for its Shark River Artificial Reef. After being cleansed of all oil, fuel and other potential pollutants, she was subjected to explosive charges placed beneath her hull. She now rests upright in 130 feet of water not far from the sunken stern section of the tanker *Stolt Dagali*.

The Future

In March 1990, the iron ore freighter *Alexandre P.* left Dampier, Australia and disappeared. The only clues ever found were two burned bodies afloat in one of the ship's rafts. In September 1991, the freighter *Algarrobo* left Chile, also carrying a cargo of iron ore; she also vanished, this time without a trace. A similar fate befell the 155,000-ton freighter *Pasithea*, which left Japan in October 1991 and has still not been heard from.[6] Most of us tend to believe that we live in a world far more advanced and risk-free than our forebearers. We generally take it for granted that a ship leaving port today will arrive at its destination tomorrow, and that tragic shipwrecks are a thing of the past. Unfortunately, as the above incidents and many others indicate, this is not the case.

In March 1993, while towing a barge along the New Jersey shore, the tugboat *Thomas Hebert* was suddenly and mysteriously pulled under the moderate seas that were running at the time. The barge was later found anchored by its tow cable to the sunken tug, and all but two men on board went down with their ship. The Coast Guard theorized that the vessel was sunk by a rogue wave, but the seas were relatively calm and this explanation seems more like a set of words needed to fill in the blanks on some official document. Another theory, unproven, is that the tug's tow cable was caught by the sail of a military submarine conducting sub-

The fleet submarine USS Spikefish *was the first U.S. submarine to make 10,000 dives. She was sunk in a weapons test south of Block Island on August 4, 1964. Courtesy of the Submarine Force Library and Museum, Groton, CT.*

Jeff Pagano examines a torpedo loading hatch on the deck of a submarine sitting in 260 feet of water. The wreck lies in the correct position to be that of the USS Spikefish, *but no positive identification has been made.*

During a November gale in 1993, two tugs and a dredging barge were caught off the beach at Westhampton, Long Island. Anchored just offshore, the trio had been working to fill in Little Pike's Inlet, the name given to a breach in the barrier beach created by the terrible nor'easter storm of December 1992. Now, almost one year after the new inlet had been formed, a gale sprang up and broke the dredge free of its mooring, sending it drifting out of control toward the beach. Tied alongside the dredge was the unmanned tug *Volunteer State*; both vessels went aground. A short time later the second tug, *Hoosier State*, capsized in the surf with two men on board. One man was immediately plucked from the rough sea by a Coast Guard helicopter sent aloft when the dredge went aground; the second man was later found drowned in the sunken tug's engine room. While the dredge and both tugs were salvaged, another life had been added to the long list of shipwreck casualties along the treacherous Long Island beaches.

New York was once considered the busiest shipping port in the world. Simple statistics would predict that in an area of such heavy maritime traffic a large number of accidents and calamities would occur. Indeed, over the course of two centuries hundreds upon hundreds, perhaps thousands of ships have been wrecked in the approaches to the port of New York. These shipwrecks have spanned every era in American history, from the discovery of the continent by European explorers to the birth of a new nation; from merchant vessels serving a thriving nation's economy to warships fighting desperate wars for global survival; from small boats smuggling liquor to collisions watched on the glowing screens of modern radar.

Yet shipwrecks are not only a phenomenon of the past. Despite all of man's progress, all of his clever inventions and the accumulation of centuries of seafaring experience, ships continue to go down. It is quite likely that as long as man sends vessels out upon the open ocean, there will be shipwrecks. And given the continued importance of the port of New York, the waters leading into this vast harbor will undoubtedly bear witness to more maritime tragedies in years to come.

merged maneuvers in the area, which pulled the tugboat under. Indeed, unconfirmed reports have it that a U.S. sub put into Norfolk for repairs a few days later with a damaged sail.[7] The real story may never be known.

In June 1993, the tramp steamer *Golden Venture* went aground on the beach near Rockaway, Long Island. The ship's cargo holds were filled with Chinese refugees, lured to America by the prospect of political freedom and economic opportunity. The illegal immigrants had paid large sums of money and endured squalid conditions on board the freighter to pursue their dreams of a better life. Unfortunately for them, their ship was snared by the very trap that has caught so many others over the course of centuries. There were at least seven casualties as refugees tried to reach the beach through the surf; the survivors were taken into custody and faced deportation back to China.

Source Notes

PREFACE

GHOSTS FROM THE PAST

1. Term taken from: Werner, Herbert A. *Iron Coffins.* New York: Bantam Books, 1969.

CHAPTER 1

OAK TIMBERS AND IRON SHOT: THE WOODEN WARSHIP

1. Geibelhaus, Charles. "East River Treasure Ship-Part I," *Long Island Forum,* February 1960, p. 37.
2. King, Irving H. *George Washington's Coast Guard.* Annapolis: Naval Institute Press, 1978, p. 16.
3. Text excerpt of Congressional Act taken from: Naval History Division publication *American Ships of the Line.* Washington: Navy Department, 1969, p. 25.
4. Ibid., p. 5.
5. Excerpt from Naval Constructor Henry Eckfords' list of required timbers for building the USS *Ohio.* Ibid., p. 28.

CHAPTER 2

THE SAILING MERCHANT SHIP: A FORGOTTEN FLEET OF *FLYING DUTCHMEN*

1. Chapelle, Howard I. *The History of American Sailing Ships.* New York: Bonanza Books, 1935, p. 144.
2. Greenhill, Basil. *The Life and Death of the Merchant Sailing Ship.* National Maritime Museum, *The Ship,* vol. 7. London: Her Majesty's Stationary Office, 1980, p. 28.
3. *The New York Times,* 5 December 1881.
4. Ibid., 2 September 1873.
5. Ibid., 16 February 1894.
6. Ibid., 16 July 1896.
7. Ibid., 12 February 1894.
8. Ibid., 2 November 1890.
9. Sheard, Bradley. *Beyond Sportdiving.* Alabama: Menasha Ridge Press, 1992.

CHAPTER 3

THE ASCENDANCY OF THE STEAMSHIP

1. This is actually a simplification of the operating efficiency of a compound engine. The real advantage gained by expanding the steam in stages was a reduction in the temperature drop of the steam during any one expansion. If the steam was expanded completely in one cylinder, excessive cooling of the cylinder walls would occur, causing some condensation of the high pressure steam entering the cylinder on the next cycle. This condensation was lost energy that could otherwise do useful work pushing the piston and developing propulsive power.

2. Rattray, Jeanette Edwards. *The Perils of the Port of New York. New York:* Dodd, Mead & Company, 1983.
3. *The New York Times,* 15 March 1886.
4. Ibid.
5. Ibid., 16 March, 1886.
6. Ibid., 15 March, 1886.
7. Ibid., 16 March, 1886.
8. Laing, Alexander. *American Ships.* New York: American Heritage Press, 1971, p. 219
9. Ibid., p. 222.
10. *The New York Times,* 18 December 1904.
11. Ibid., 20 December 1904.

CHAPTER 4

AGROUND ON THE BEACH!

1. Bennett, Robert F. *Surfboats, Rockets, and Carronades.* Washington, D.C.: United States Government Printing Office, p. v.
2. *East Hampton Star,* 16 December 1927.
3. Ibid., 23 July 1970.
4. Ibid., 15 February 1895.
5. *The New York Times,* 29 December 1904.
6. Ibid., 30 December 1904.

CHAPTER 5

THE WORLD GOES TO WAR: 1914-1918

1. Quoted from a typed summary of the *Mohawk*'s career, evidently taken from her logbook.
2. Navy Department, Office of Naval Records and Library, Historical Section. Publication Number 1: German Submarine Activities on the Atlantic Coast of the United States and Canada. Washington, D.C.: Government Printing Office, 1920, p. 19.
3. United States National Archives, Record Group 45, "Record of Proceedings of a Court of Inquiry Convened on Board the U.S.S. *Maui* by Order of Commander Cruiser and Transport Force to Inquire into the Circumstances Concerning the Loss of the U.S.S. *San Diego,*" 19 July 1918, p. 54.
4. Ibid., p. 88.
5. *The New York Times,* 29 August 1918.
6. United States National Archives, War Diary of the *U-140.*
7. Clark, William Bell. *When the U-boats Came to America.* Boston: Little, Brown, and Company, 1929, pp. 249-250.
8. Grant, Robert M. *U-Boat Intelligence 1914-1918.* Hamden: Archon Books, 1969, p. 156.
9. Sheard, Bradley. *Beyond Sportdiving.* Alabama: Menasha Ridge Press, 1991, for details of the sinking of the *Sommerstad* and the evidence supporting its identity as the "Virginia Wreck."
10. The U.S. Navy later concluded that the *Mirlo* had struck a mine laid by the *U-117.* They were correct in placing

the blame on the *U-117*, but the U-boat's war diary reports that she torpedoed an unidentified tanker in this location.

CHAPTER 6
BETWEEN THE WARS—COLLISIONS & RUMRUNNERS

1. *Boston Daily Globe*, 28 May 1932.
2. *The New York Times*, 29 May 1932.
3. *The Providence Journal*, 28 May 1932.
4. *Boston Daily Globe*, 28 May 1932.
5. *The Providence Journal*, 28 May 1932.
6. Ibid.
7. *The New York Times*, 30 May 1932.
8. Griffiths, Denis. *Power of the Great Liners*. Somerset: Patrick Stephens Limited, 1990, p. 120.

CHAPTER 7
WORLD WAR II: THE U-BOATS RETURN

1. Rossler, Eberhard. *The U-boat: The evolution and technical history of German submarines*. Annapolis: Naval Institute Press, 1981, p. 88.
2. Ibid., p. 103.
3. Shirer, William L. *The Rise and Fall of the Third Reich*. New York: Simon and Schuster, 1959, vol. 1, p. 58.
4. Hughs, Terry and Costello, John. *The Battle of the Atlantic*. New York: The Dial Press/James Wade, 1977, p. 94.
5. *The New York Times*, 15 January 1942.
6. United States National Archives, War Diary of the *U-123*.
7. *The New York Times*, 23 January 1942.
8. Standard Oil Company (New Jersey). *Ships of the Esso Fleet in World War II*. 1946, p. 108.
9. Ibid., p. 110.
10. *The New York Times*, 11 March 1942.
11. United States National Archives, Office of Naval Intelligence, "Summary of Survivors Statements, 1941-1945," Memorandum on the sinking of the SS *Arundo*.
12. *Newsday*, 14 June 1992.
13. Ibid.
14. Botting, Douglass. *The U-Boats*. Alexandria: Time-Life Books—*The Seafarers*, 1979, p. 163.
15. Ibid.
16. Tollaksen, Ensign D.M. "Last Chapter for *U-853*," *U.S. Naval Institute Proceedings*, December 1960, p. 88.

CHAPTER 8
THE ERA OF MODERN NAVIGATION

1. *The New York Times*, 8 May 1963.
2. Ibid., 27 November 1964.
3. Keatts, Henry C. and Farr, George C. *Dive into History: US Submarines*. Houston: Pisces Books, 1991, pp. 140-148.
4. Coleman, Tim. "The 40-Fathom Hang," *The Fisherman*, 9 January 1992.

5. The loran A coordinates for the *Spikefish* were obtained from Henry Keatts.
6. Alvarez, A. "Sinking Fast," *The New York Times*, 17 May 1992.
7. The story of the *Thomas Hebert* was provided to the author by Steve Gatto.

Bibliography

Books

Barry, James P. *Ships of the Great Lakes: 300 Years of Navigation.* Berkeley: Howell-North Books, 1973.

Bennett, Robert F. *Surfboats, Rockets, and Carronades.* Washington, D.C.: Government Printing Office, 1976.

Bonsor, N.R.P. *South Atlantic Seaway.* Jersey Channel Islands: Brookside Publications, 1983.

Braynard, Frank O. *S.S. Savannah, The Elegant Steam Ship.* New York: Dover Publications, Inc., 1963.

Brinnin, John Malcolm. *The Sway of the Grand Saloon.* New York: Delacorte Press, 1971.

Chapelle, Howard I. *The History of the American Sailing Navy.* New York: Bonanza Books, 1949.

_____. *The History of American Sailing Ships.* New York: Bonanza Books, 1935.

Clark, William Bell. *When the U-Boats Came to America.* Boston: Little, Brown, and Company, 1929.

Craig, Robin. *Steam Tramps and Cargo Liners.* National Maritime Museum, The Ship, vol. 7. London: Her Majesty's Stationary Office, 1980.

Dowling, Rev. Edward J. *The Lakers of World War I.* Detroit: The University of Detroit Press, 1967.

Dunbaugh, Edwin L. *Night Boat to New England 1815-1900.* New York: Greenwood Press, 1992.

Estep, H. Cole. *How Wooden Ships are Built.* New York: W.W. Norton & Co., 1918.

Fletcher, Pratt. *The Compact History of the United States Navy.* New York: Hawthorn Books, Inc., 1957.

Gannon, Michael. *Operation Drumbeat.* New York: Harper and Row Publishers, 1990.

Gardiner, Robert, Editor. *The Advent of Steam.* Conway's History of the Ship. Annapolis: Naval Institute Press, 1993.

Gentile, Gary. *Track of the Gray Wolf.* New York: Avon Books, 1989.

_____. *Shipwrecks of New Jersey.* Norwalk: Sea Sports Publications, 1988.

_____. *Shipwrecks of Virginia.* Philadelphia: Gary Gentile Productions, 1992.

Gonzalez, Ellice B. *Storms, Shipwrecks & Surfmen: The Life-Savers of Fire Island.*

Grant, Robert M. *U-Boat Intelligence 1914-1918.* Hamden: Archon Books, 1969.

Greenhill, Basil. *The Life and Death of the Merchant Sailing Ship.* National Maritime Museum, The Ship, vol. 7. London: Her Majesty's Stationary Office, 1980.

_____. *Evolution of the Wooden Ship.* New York: Facts on File, 1988.

Griffiths, Denis. *Power of the Great Liners.* Somerset: Patrick Stephens Limited, 1990.

Halsey, Carolyn D. *The Revolution on Long Island.*

Hough, Richard. *The Great War at Sea 1914-1918.* New York: Oxford University Press, 1986.

Hughs, Terry, and Costello, John. *The Battle of the Atlantic.* New York: The Dial Press/James Wade, 1977.

Keatts, Henry, and Farr, George. *Dive into History: U-boats.* Kings Point: American Merchant Marine Museum Press, 1986.

_____. *Dive into History: US Submarines.* Houston: Pisces Books, 1991.

Keatts, Henry C. *Guide to Shipwreck Diving: New York and New Jersey.* Houston: Pisces Books, 1992.

Lee, Charles E. *The Blue Riband.* London: Sampson Low, Marston & Co., Ltd, date unknown.

Massie, Robert K. *Dreadnought.* New York: Random House, 1991.

McGowan, Alan. *The Century before Steam.* National Maritime Museum, The Ship, vol. 4. London: Her Majesty's Stationary Office, 1980.

Mooney, James L., ed. *Dictionary of American Naval Fighting Ships.* Washington, D.C.: Naval Historical Center, 1981.

Moore, Captain Arthur R. *"A Careless Word...A Needless Sinking".* King's Point, New York: American Merchant Marine Museum, 1983.

Morison, Samuel Eliot. *The Battle of the Atlantic.* Boston: Little, Brown and Company, 1947.

_____. *The Atlantic Battle Won.* Boston: Little, Brown and Company, 1956.

Moscow, Alvin. *Collision Course.* New York: Grosset & Dunlap, 1959.

Naval History Division, Navy Department. *American Ships of the Line.* Washington, D.C.: Government Printing Office, 1969.

Navy Department, Office of Naval Records and Library, Historical Section. <u>Publication Number 1: German Submarine Activities on the Atlantic Coast of the United States and Canada</u>. Washington, D.C.: Government Printing Office, 1920.

Pinckney, Pauline. *American Figureheads and their Carvers.* Port Washington, NY: Kennikat Press, 1969

Rattray, Jeannette Edwards. *The Perils of the Port of New York.* New York: Dodd, Mead & Company, 1973.

Rohwer, Jurgen. *Axis Submarine Successes, 1939-1945.* Annapolis, Maryland: Naval Institute Press, 1983.

Rossler, Eberhard. *The U-boat: The evolution and technical history of German submarines.* Annapolis: Naval Institute Press, 1981.

Rowland, K.T. *Steam at Sea.* New York: Praeger Publishers, 1970.

Schmitt, Frederick P., and Schmid, Donald E. *HMS Culloden.* The Marine Historical Association, Inc., 1961.

Sheard, Bradley. *Beyond Sportdiving.* Birmingham: Menasha Ridge Press, 1991.

Shirer, William L. *The Rise and Fall of the Third Reich.* New York: Simon and Schuster, 1959.

Standard Oil Company (New Jersey). *Ships of the Esso Fleet in World War II.* 1946.

Steoff, Rebecca. *The U.S. Coast Guard.* Broomall, PA: Chelsea House Publishers, 1989.

Willoughby, Malcolm F. *Rum War at Sea.* Washington, D.C.: Government Printing Office, 1964.

ARTICLES

Bell, Mary Conklin. "Wreck of the *John Milton*," *Long Island Forum,* April 1944, p. 67.

Crosby, Richard. "Long Island's Mysterious Tea Wreck," *Skin Diver Magazine,* September 1964, p. 28.

deCamp, Michael A. "The Wreck of the Pinta," *Skin Diver Magazine,* March, 1964, p. 15.

——. "Sinking of the Stolt Dagali," *Skin Diver Magazine,* March, 1965, p. 26.

Geibelhaus, Charles. "East River Treasure Ship-Part I," *Long Island Forum,* February 1960, p. 37.

——. "East River Treasure Ship—Part II," *Long Island Forum,* March 1960, p. 57.

Hausrath, Ralph. "Wreck of the *Louis V. Place*," *Long Island Forum,* February 1978, p. 34.

——. "The Most Heroic Rescue," *Long Island Forum,* January 1966, p. 8.

Horton, H.P. "The Tramp Steamer *Gluckauf*," *Long Island Forum,* May 1959, p. 95.

Huguenin, Dr. Charles A. "Wreck of the *Circassian* in 1876," *Long Island Forum,* August, 1956, p. 143.

Moeran, Edward Henry. "The *Circassian* Tragedy," *Long Island Forum,* September 1942, p. 169.

Roach, Thomas. "Death and Destruction Ride the Wake of a Torpedo Destined for The Ill-Fated *Arundo*," *Skin Diver Magazine,* October, 1974, pp.18-19.

——. "The Secret of the USS *Bass*," *Skin Diver Magazine,* October, 1977, p. 58.

Squires, Harry B. "Wreck of the *Franklin*, 1854," *Long Island Forum,* March 1947, p.45.

Thurston, George. "The *Louis V. Place*," *Long Island Forum,* July 1938, p. 13.

Tuomey, Douglas. "The Death of Margaret Fuller," *Long Island Forum,* December 1960, p. 277.

Wood, Dr. Clarence A, "The Story of a Figurehead," *Long Island Forum,* September 1950, p. 167.

OTHER REFERENCE SOURCES

"Summary of Survivors Statements, 1941-1945," Office of Naval Intelligence, National Archives.

Records of the U.S. National Archives.

Maritime and Naval Museums

Alabama
USS *Alabama* Battleship Memorial Park
2703 Battleship Parkway (US 90)
Mobile, AL 36601
334-433-2703

California
Humbolt Bay Maritime Museum
1410 Second St.
Eureka, CA 95501
707-444-9440

Los Angeles Maritime Museum
Berth 84
Foot of 6th St.
San Pedro, CA 90731
310-548-7618

Maritime Museum of San Diego
The Embarcadero
1306 North Harbor Dr.
San Diego, CA 92101
619-234-9153

RMS Queen Mary
Pier J
P.O. Box 8
Long Beach, CA 90801
562-435-3511

San Francisco Maritime National
   Historical Park
900 Beach St.
San Francisco, CA 94123
415-556-3002

Connecticut
Mystic Seaport Museum
P.O. Box 6000
50 Greenmanville Ave.
Mystic, CT 06355-0990
860-572-0711

Nautilus Memorial Submarine Force
   Library and Museum
Naval Submarine Base New London
P.O. Box 571
Groton, CT 06349-5000
800-343-0079

U.S. Coast Guard Museum
U.S. Coast Guard Academy
Route 32
New London, CT 06320-4195
860-444-8511

Georgia
Ships of the Sea Museum
503 East River St.
Savannah, GA 31401
912-232-1511

Hawaii
Pacific Fleet Submarine Museum
11 Arizona Memorial Dr.
Honolulu, HI 96818
808-423-1341

Illinois
Chicago Marine Society
North Pier Bldg.
435 E. Illinois St.
Chicago, IL 60611
312-421-9096

Chicago Museum of Science and
   Industry
57th St. and Lake Shore Dr.
Chicago, IL 60637
773-684-1414

Indiana
Howard National Steamboat Museum
1101 E. Market St.
Jeffersonville, IN 47130
812-283-3728

U.S. Merchant Marine Museum
1230 Jackson St.
Anderson, IN 46016
765-643-7447

Louisiana
Louisiana Naval War Museum and
   Nautical Center
305 S River Rd.
Baton Rouge, LA 70802
504-342-1942

Maine
Brick Store Museum
117 Main St.
Kennebunk, ME 04043
207-985-4802

Maine Maritime Museum
243 Washington St.
Bath, ME 04530
207-443-1316

Penobscot Marine Museum
Church St.
Searsport, ME 04974-0498
207-548-6634

Maryland
Baltimore Maritime Museum
Pier 4, Pratt St.
Baltimore, MD 21202
301-396-3854

Chesapeake Bay Maritime Museum
Mill St.
St. Michaels, MD 21663
410-745-2916

U.S. Naval Academy
Preble Hall, 118 Maryland Ave.
Annapolis, MD 21402-5034
410-293-2108

Massachusetts
Battleship *Massachusetts*
Battleship Cove
Fall River, MA 02721
508-678-1100

Essex Shipbuilding Museum
Box 277
28 Main St.
Essex, MA 01929
508-768-7541

Hart Nautical Gallery
Bldg. 5, 1st Floor
Massachusetts Institute of Technology
77 Massachusetts Ave.
Cambridge MA 02139

Hull Lifesaving Museum
1117 Nantasket Ave.
Hull, MA 02045
617-925-5433

Marine Museum of Fall River
70 Water St.
Fall River, MA 02722
508-674-3533

Museum of Fine Arts
465 Huntington Ave.
Boston, MA 02115

Peabody Essex Museum
East India Square
Salem, MA 01970-3783
508-745-9500

U.S. Naval Shipbuilding Museum
739 Washington St.
Quincy, MA 02169
617-479-7900

USS *Constitution* Museum
Bldg. 22 Charlestown Navy Yard
Charlestown, MA 02129
617-426-1812

Michigan
Dossin Great Lakes Museum
100 The Strand Belle Isle
Detroit, MI 48207
313-852-4051

Great Lakes Shipwreck Museum
Whitefish Point Rd.
Paradise, MI 49768
906-492-3392

Michigan Maritime Museum
260 Dyckman Ave, At the Bridge
South Haven, MI 49090
616-637-8078

Great Lakes Marine Museum
6199 Murray Rd.
Whitehall, MI 49461
616-894-8265

USS *Silversides* Maritime Museum
1336 Bluff St.
Muskegon, MI 49441
616-755-1230

Minnesota
Marquette County Historical Museum
213 N. Front St.
Marquette, MI 49855
906-226-3571

New Jersey
New Jersey Naval Museum
River and Court Streets
Hackensack, NJ 07602
201-342-3268

Paterson Museum
2 Market St.
Paterson, NJ 07501
201-881-3874

New York
American Merchant Marine Museum
US Merchant Marine Academy
Steamboat Road
King's Point, NY 11024
516-773-5515

Buffalo and Erie County Naval and
Servicemen's Museum
1 Naval Park Cove
Buffalo, NY 14202
716-847-1773

Intrepid Sea-Air-Space Museum
Pier 88, 12th and West 46th
New York NY 10036
212-245-0072

Long Island Maritime Museum
86 West Ave.
West Sayville, NY 11796
516-854-4874

Maritime Industry Museum
6 Pennyfield Ave.
Bronx, NY 10465
718-409-7200

Museum of the City of New York
103rd St. & 5th Ave.
New York, NY 10029
212-534-1672

South Street Seaport Museum
207 Front St.
New York, NY 10038
212-748-8600

Suffolk County Historical Society
300 W Main St.
Riverhead NY 11901-2894
516-727-2881

North Carolina
North Carolina Maritime Museum
315 Front St.
Beaufort, NC 28516
919-728-7317

Ohio
Inland Seas Maritime Museum
480 Main St.
Vermillion, OH 44089
216-967-3467

Oregon
Columbia River Maritime Museum
1792 Marine Dr.
Astoria, OR 97103
503-325-2323

Oregon Maritime Center and Museum
113 SW Front Ave.
Portland, OR 97204
503-224-7724

Pennsylvania
Independence Seaport Museum
Penn's Landing
211 S Columbus Blvd.
Philadelphia, PA 19106-1415
215-925-5439

Rhode Island
Naval War College Museum
Coasters Harbor Island
686 Cushing Rd.
Newport, RI 02841-1207
401-841-4052

South Carolina
Patriots Point Naval and Maritime
    Museum
40 Patriots Point Rd.
Mt. Pleasant, SC 29464
803-884-2727

Texas
Admiral Nimitz State Historical Park
340 East Main St.
Fredericksburg, TX 78624
830-997-4379

Battleship *Texas* State Historical Park
3527 Battleground Rd.
La Porte, TX 77571
281-479-2411

Seawolf Park
P.O. Box 3306
Pelican Island, TX 77552
409-744-5738

Texas Maritime Museum
1202 Navigation Circle
P.O. Box 1836
Rockport, TX 78382
512-729-6644

Texas Seaport Museum
Pier 21
2016 Strand
Galveston, TX 77550
409-763-1877

USS *Lexington* Museum on the Bay
2914 N. Shoreline
Corpus Christi, TX 78402
512-888-4873

Vermont
Lake Champlain Maritime Museum
RR#3 Box 4092
Basin Harbor
Vergennes, VT 05491
802-475-2022

Virginia
The Mariners Museum
100 Museum Dr.
Newport News, VA 23606
757-595-0368

Hampton Roads Naval Museum
One Waterside Dr., Suite 248
Norfolk, VA 23514
757-444-8971

Portsmouth Lightship Museum
London Slip, Water St.
Portsmouth, VA 23704
757-393-8741

Portsmouth Naval Shipyard Museum
2 High St.
Portsmouth, VA 23704
757-393-8591

The Old Coast Guard Station
24th St. and Atlantic Ave.
Virginia Beach, VA 23451
757-422-1587

Washington
Museum of History & Industry
2161 E. Hamlin St.
Seattle, WA 98112
206-324-1125

Puget Sound Maritime Museum
901 Fairview Ave. N.
Seattle, WA 98112
206-624-3028

Washington, D.C.
Naval Memorial Museum
901 M St. SE
Washington, DC 20374-5060
202-433-4882

The Smithsonian Institution
14th St. at Constitution Ave. NW
Washington, DC 20560
202-357-1514

Wisconsin
Manitowoc Maritime Museum
809 S. Eighth St.
Manitowoc, WI 54220
920-684-0218

Canada
Esquimalt Naval and Military Museum
Bldg 20N
Esquimalt Naval Base
Esquimalt, BC, Canada
604-363-4395

HCMS *Haida* Naval Museum
% Ontario Place Corp.
955 Lakeshore Blvd. W
Toronto, ON M6K 3B9 Canada

Le Musee de la mer de Pointe-au-Pere
1034 rue du Phare
Pointe-au-Pere, PQ G5M 1L8 Canada

Maritime Museum of British Columbia
1905 Ogden Ave.
Victoria, BC V8W 1H9 Canada
604-385-4222

Maritime Museum of the Atlantic
1675 Lower Water St.
Halifax, NS B3J 1S3 Canada
902-424-7490

Marine Museum of the Great Lakes
55 Ontario St.
Kingston, ON K7L 1Y2 Canada
613-542-2261

Vancouver Maritime Museum
1905 Ogden Ave.
Vancouver, BC V6J 1A3 Canada
604-257-8300

Index

A **bold** faced page number denotes a picture or diagram caption.